Digital Methods

Digital Methods

Richard Rogers

The MIT Press
Cambridge, Massachusetts
London, England

First MIT Press paperback edition, 2015

© 2013 Massachusetts Institute of Technology

This book was set in Stone Sans and Stone Serif by Toppan Best-set Premedia Limited, Hong Kong.

Library of Congress Cataloging-in-Publication Data

Rogers, Richard, 1965–
Digital methods / Richard Rogers.
   pages   cm
Includes bibliographical references and index.
ISBN 978-0-262-01883-8 (hc), 978-0-262-52824-5 (pb)
1. Internet research. 2. Internet searching. 3. Web search engines. 4. World Wide Web—Research. 5. Social media—Research. 6. Webometrics. 7. Internet—Social aspects.
I. Title.
ZA4228.R64   2013
001.4'202854678—dc23
2012029845

Contents

Introduction: Situating Digital Methods

This is not a methods book, at least in the sense of a set of techniques and heuristics to be lugged like a heavy toolbox across vast areas of inquiry. It is also not the more contemporary exemplar of the instruction manual or list of answers to frequently asked questions, one that would describe how to operate the multipurpose software package by which a number of statistical and network analyses may be performed once the web data set has been collected or delivered separately. Rather, this book presents a methodological outlook for research with the web. As such it is a proposal to reorient the field of Internet-related research by studying and repurposing what I term the methods of the medium, or perhaps more straightforwardly methods embedded in online devices. For example, crawling, scraping, crowd sourcing, and folksonomy, while of different genus and species, are all web techniques for data collection and sorting. PageRank and similar algorithms are means to order and rank. Tag clouds and other common visualizations display relevance and resonance. How may we learn from and reapply these and other online methods? The purpose is not so much to contribute to their fine-tuning and build the better search engine, for that task is best left to computer science and allied fields. Rather, the purpose is to think along with them, and learn how they handle hyperlinks, hits, likes, tags, datestamps, and other natively digital objects. By continually thinking along with the devices and the objects they handle, digital methods, as a research practice, strive to follow the evolving methods of the medium.

Second, digital methods not only think with online devices. They also take stock of the availability and exploitability of digital objects so as to recombine them fruitfully. When studying a web device, building a new tool, or making an interface on top of an existing one, the task is to list the elements at one's disposal, e.g., tweets, retweets, hashtags, usernames, user locations, shortened URLs, @replies, etc. (for Twitter, the microblogging platform). How may the digital objects be combined and recombined in ways that are useful not so much for searching Twitter but rather for social and cultural research questions? Does a particular hashtag, and its set of most retweeted tweets, organize a compelling account of an event, and whose?

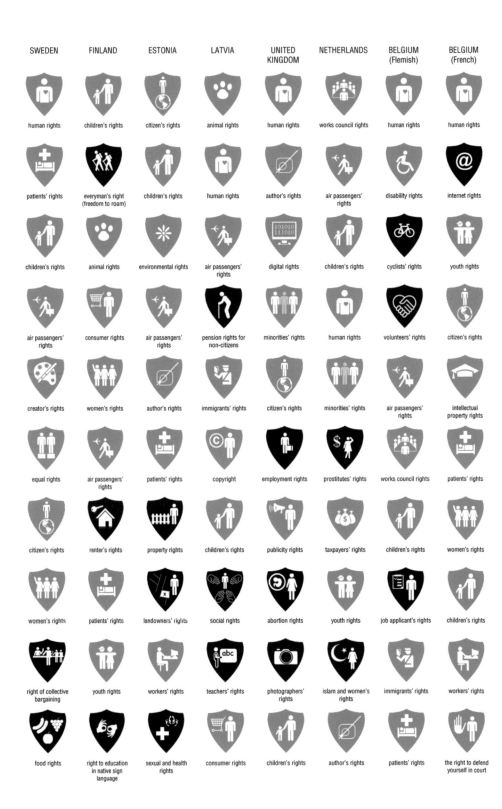

SWEDEN	FINLAND	ESTONIA	LATVIA	UNITED KINGDOM	NETHERLANDS	BELGIUM (Flemish)	BELGIUM (French)
human rights	children's rights	citizen's rights	animal rights	human rights	works council rights	human rights	human rights
patients' rights	everyman's right (freedom to roam)	children's rights	human rights	author's rights	air passengers' rights	disability rights	internet rights
children's rights	animal rights	environmental rights	air passengers' rights	digital rights	children's rights	cyclists' rights	youth rights
air passengers' rights	consumer rights	air passengers' rights	pension rights for non-citizens	minorities' rights	human rights	volunteers' rights	citizen's rights
creator's rights	women's rights	author's rights	immigrants' rights	citizen's rights	minorities' rights	air passengers' rights	intellectual property rights
equal rights	air passengers' rights	patients' rights	copyright	employment rights	prostitutes' rights	works council rights	patients' rights
citizen's rights	renter's rights	property rights	children's rights	publicity rights	taxpayers' rights	children's rights	women's rights
women's rights	patients' rights	landowners' rights	social rights	abortion rights	youth rights	job applicant's rights	children's rights
right of collective bargaining	youth rights	workers' rights	teachers' rights	photographers' rights	islam and women's rights	immigrants' rights	workers' rights
food rights	right to education in native sign language	sexual and health rights	consumer rights	children's rights	author's rights	patients' rights	the right to defend yourself in court

The third principle is to build upon the existing, dominant devices themselves, and with them perform a cultural and societal diagnostics. Digital methods repurpose or build on top of the dominant devices of the medium, and in doing so make derivative works from the results, figuratively and literally. That is, the initial outputs may be the same as or similar to those from online devices, but they are seen or rendered in new light, turning what was once familiar—a page of engine results, a list of tweets in reverse chronological order, a collection of comments, or a set of interests from a social networking profile—into indicators and findings.

Sources are ranked high in engine results pages not only because they are helpful in providing information to the user for the query made. Their ranking also follows extensive link, click-through, freshness, linguistic, textual, and geographical analysis, which may be vetted by qualitative coders checking a small sample of results. Source rankings also carry social significance in an issue or subject area, and certain sources may grow or decline over time, indicating shifting commitment and appeal. Reading Google results, one may see information and even some of the workings and author-ings of Google (including optimized and manipulated results), or one may see societal conditions (see figure 0.1 and chapter 5 on search as research). As I will develop below, this book largely concerns the latter.

One may undertake a similar exegesis for social media sites such as Facebook, and situate digital methods a second time. In this case, I would like to draw into relief not the difference between everyday use of a device and a trained eye pouring over results, as we just did with Google. Rather, I would like to contrast two web *research* outlooks. For example, one's newly made friend has numerous other friends, together with an active news feed as well as a well-groomed profile, comprised of considered interests in movies, music, books, and television programs. Playground, high school, college, and other clique and social formations may be organized on that platform, and there will be measurable levels and potentially new forms of sociality driving changes to them. After all, software is running social life, in part, and that can be reflected upon. If one were to think along with the device and examine the available digital objects to be recombined, however, the researcher's work changes. One may think too with the device makers and the containers they furnished for users to fill in profiles. How to reassemble the objects (friends and profiles) and repurpose the output of the device (friends' profiles and activities) so that it can provide indicators and make findings about (political) culture? One may consider reaggregating the profiles in telling ways. What do the collective interests of the friends of Barack Obama, as against those of the friends of his presidential

Figure 0.1

Rights types: the nationalities of issues. Top ten rights per country, based on a query for [rights], in each of the languages of the local-domain Googles, July 2009. © Digital Methods Initiative, Amsterdam, 2009.

opponents, tell us about the culture wars? Are political leanings aligned with taste and preference divisions, or are the divides far less great when seen through the expression of media preference (broadly defined)? Are social media sites for the study of shared taste?

Put differently, this is a book about Internet research that is not solely about the Internet. In keeping with a general move toward studying web data (as I come to in the conclusion), the book seeks to provide an aim for Internet research that has yet to be made explicit: the development of a methodological outlook and mindset for social research with the web. In other words, it seeks to move Internet research beyond the study of online culture and beyond the study of the users of ICTs only. In the following chapters, digital methods are put forward for working with the tiny particles (hyperlinks) and the large masses (social media). The book in fact could be read as a history of Internet-related research, as it has evolved from hyperlink and individual website analysis and directory-making in the mid to late 1990s (chapters 2 and 3), to critiques of search engines and the blogosphere in the early to mid-2000s (chapters 4 and 5), to the rise of the location-aware as well as the so-called Web 2.0 and social media in the late 2000s (chapters 6, 7, and 8). The chapters reflect upon how each of these is often studied, and how else they might be studied if the principles of digital methods were applied.

Digital methods also strive to provide web research with a *problematic* to work with. The fourth principle of digital methods involves the problem and challenges of employing web data for social research, for it reopens the question of the site of the baseline. Where are the findings to be principally grounded? More specifically, are the findings to be grounded in the online? Or is it necessary to calibrate them or compare them with a traditional (offline) data set or site of study? One can frame this issue by comparing two projects: Google Flu Trends and a map of allrecipe.com users' Thanksgiving recipe queries. These are both digital methods projects, but they work with two different ideas of a baseline.

Google Flu Trends (since 2007/2008) is a classic and teachable case of thinking through the availability of natively digital objects (search engine queries, and the places of those queries), and repurposing engine results for social research (the places of the incidence of flu).[1] The places of queries are employed to pinpoint flu outbreaks on the map. The results are subsequently compared to the data on the locations of flu from the U.S. Centers for Disease Control, and the national or regional equivalents of this agency in the nearly 20 countries where flu queries to Google are monitored. The online findings are thus grounded in the comparison with the agencies' data. This is the traditional manner of grounding, in which the conditions of proof are sought not online in the repurposed methods of the medium but offline, making the web into an anticipatory medium whose trends are later confirmed elsewhere. By contrast, another project may be considered as having grounded its findings in the online, or at least has not grounded them offline. As reported in the *New York Times*, with infographics or data visualizations that are often outputted in digital methods projects, queries at allrecipes.com one day prior to Thanksgiving (the American national feast) were captured and plotted to a geographical map.[2] They show the places of recipe queries, and in doing so a distributed geography of taste or recipe preference across the United States. Whereas for years search engine companies would publish the top queries per month and per year, occasionally categorizing them according to top-level subject matters (e.g., political queries) and giving them trend-spotting, marketing-style project names such as buzz and zeitgeist, the recipe query maps add to the search engine results analysis not only the location of the queries, but also a social research outlook. They display where people seem to like which food. Here the question is whether the researcher would turn next to the offline (telephone surveys, or perhaps supermarket sales data), or continue with online data, grounding the findings further there. Could findings made with search engine queries be grounded through a study of additional web data, e.g., geo-tagged Thanksgiving food photos? Digital methods do not necessarily seek to ground (all) findings in the online, but rather to pose the question of the web's status as potential grounding site.

These first moves and principles espoused by digital methods are in play in this book: Follow the methods of the medium as they evolve, learn from how the dominant devices treat natively digital objects, and think along with those object treatments and devices so as to recombine or build on top of them. Strive to repurpose the methods of the medium for research that is not primarily or solely about online culture. Hyperlinks become means not only to assess the value of a website and assign a ranking to it, as the dominant devices treat them, but also to show the politics of association: the lack of recognition (through the absence of linking) of Armenian nongovernmental organizations by intergovernmental institutions, to take one example of the interpretation of a hyperlink map. Link analysis also may be employed for the purpose of finding related sites and building URL lists. Given an existing list of censored websites in Iran, how may their hyperlinks be analyzed to locate related sites that are not on the list of sites under study? The map shows the results of such dynamic URL sampling, as I term it, and displays the original sites as well as the newly located ones.[3] The newly located related sites, together with the original list, are fetched through proxies in Iran, in order to determine whether each site is blocked. The outcome is a map that shows which sites are blocked and which are accessible, and the pins on the map indicate newly discovered blocked websites (see figure 0.2). Indeed, one ultimately may learn more about the extent of censorship using link analysis (or dynamic URL sampling) to lengthen the URL list beyond the traditional, editorial, list-building approach, as is described in chapter 3 on website analysis.

Archived websites are traditionally used as a solution to the "404 file not found" problem. The Internet Archive's Wayback Machine allows the user to look up and retrieve a page from a website that is down and unreachable, or has been edited. The various historical pages from an archived website also can be so organized and

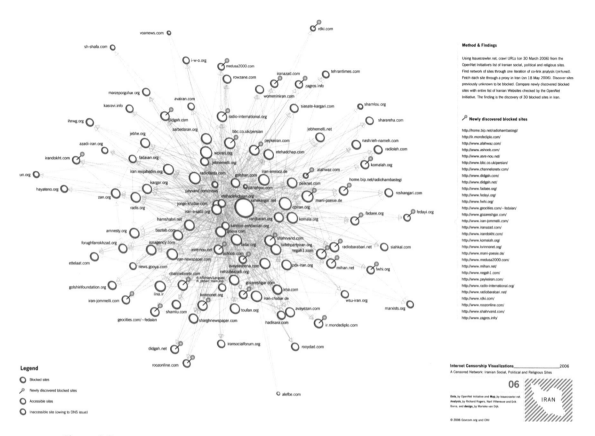

Figure 0.2
Internet censorship discovery technique. Network map of Iranian social, political, and religious websites, showing accessible (blue), blocked (red), and newly discovered blocked websites (red with yellow pins). The outcome of dynamic URL sampling, a hyperlink analysis method with the Issue Crawler, and Internet censorship discovery with the Censorship Explorer tool. Analysis and graphic by Govcom.org, 2006. © Govcom.org Foundation, Amsterdam, 2006.

presented so as to tell histories of the web—such as the rise of the algorithm over the (human) editor, as I come to below. Archived websites also may be compiled, read, and queried to examine changes in tone and sentiment of social groupings, such as the political right wing and its relationship with extremism. Has the right become more extremist over time in its use of specific language? Here one builds a collection of websites from the past to the present, and compares changes in the use of language on them over time.

Search engines author new orders of things in the sense that they rank sources for any topic. Reading and interpreting engine returns as hierarchies of credible sources per subject matter can itself be a form of social research. The relationship between search and research is occasionally lamented in pedagogical discussion, the concern being that search is taking the place of research generally, with students googling instead of making library visits, and employing Wikipedia as a de facto first source rather than others that are not folksonomic but rather expert-vetted.[4] However, engines also can be repurposed for research, with their capacity to index websites and provide means to query each of them singly or thematic sets of them collectively. Of all the (leading) websites in the area of climate change, which ones mention the climate change skeptics, and with what frequency and fervor? Are the skeptics becoming more prevalent in the leading sources on climate change? Here the web becomes a site of research, expanding the source types, for example, beyond the scientific (and their metasource, ISI Web of Science) and the news (or Lexus Nexus). Larger questions arise about using the web as site of research. Are engines demarcating source sets and indexing individual sources with the same thought and rigor as their traditional research counterparts? How solid is the demaraction of sources, and the web findings that result from them? Under which conditions may they stand beside those yielded by the scientometric or press attention research techniques? The comparison of digital methods with those of more traditional techniques extends beyond media research. Can search engine log data compete in research outcomes with polls, and social media preferences with surveys?[5]

If this book may be read as a history of Internet-related research, it also grows from the Digital Methods Initiative, a project I launched in 2007 as a research program at the University of Amsterdam, a wiki (digitalmethods.net), and a Summer School. The Digital Methods Initiative also received a grant from the Mondriaan Foundation in its *interregeling* program, which is for projects that do not fit into any category. It is the "other" in the form fields (and since has been discontinued). The first digital methods technique taught at the then small and informal Summer School I called "source distance." How far from the top are stories and sources in media? A story can be at the top of the news, a leading story. It can be front-page news in a newspaper. How to construe the top of the web? The exemplary case study concerned climate change skeptics. At the time, BBC news recently had announced the cancellation of Planet Relief, an awareness-raising event modeled on Live 8 (2006) and Live Earth (2007). The reasoning behind the cancellation was that the BBC should not be construed as taking sides, and that Planet Relief would not give the skeptics' views their journalistic due. The environmental activist quoted in a news story about the cancellation of the show put it this way:

The only reason why this became an issue is that there is a small but vociferous group of climate "sceptics" lobbying against taking action, so the BBC is behaving like a coward and refusing to take a more consistent stance.[6]

In the case of the BBC cancellation story and other news about climate change, the skeptics were increasingly at the top of the news. The question posed to the Digital

Methods Summer School participants read: Are the skeptics at the top of the web, too? "Source distance" would measure the distance between the top of the web and the skeptic-friendly sources, according to the dominant web device, Google, as I explain in more detail in chapter 5. In our research procedure, one queries Google for ["climate change"] and saves the results; subsequently one queries each of the results for climate change skeptics, noting where in the ranked list of sources they are mentioned. Distance from the top is thereby measured.[7]

Source distance subsequently became a technique for more than the analysis of the "web sphere" (a term that had been coined by web archive researchers, and which colleagues and I appropriated for comparative media analysis, or in fact the web version thereof). As a starting point, we showed how media analysis across source types such as newspapers, news magazines, and TV news has been done in the past and introduced such a practice for the web, comparing the dominant spheres online at the time: web sphere, blogosphere, and news sphere. Spheres are construed as engine-demarcated spaces. Each sphere has a dominant engine (largely Google, though at the time Technorati was a leading engine for the blogosphere), and each engine has a different, general logic for ranking sources per sphere. The rankings for the web sphere differ from that of the blogosphere and for that of the news sphere. Thus the spheres invite comparison. Given a subject matter or story, which sources are at the top of the respective spheres? "Cross-spherical analysis" is comparative source distance research across the web sphere, the blogosphere, and the news sphere. (We later added other spheres, too.)

Source distance lends itself particularly well to an analysis of the blogosphere, for the means by which it enables both critique as well as empirical analysis of the "sphere." For some, the notion of the "sphere" in blogosphere invites thought about the public sphere. The equality of voices, the egalitarian ideal, also is in evidence in the geometrical shape of the sphere, where sources are equidistant from the core. Indeed, the sphere in blogosphere initially would challenge the hierarchy of the ranked lists (and engine results) that once ordered the web, prior to the growth of the blogosphere. With its new shape, the blogosphere would eschew that web hierarchy of sources (even if in practice there was continual reference to A-list bloggers, using language from the entertainment news and celebrity culture). If all blogs were equidistant from a core, then in principle each blog could be knowable by all.

These info-political geometries and spaces (ranked lists, networks, spheres, dark web) are the subject of chapter 2 on hyperlinks and the politics of web space. This chapter was originally written for *The Handbook of Internet Politics* (2007), and other versions have appeared in the edited volumes *Nouvelles technologies cognitives et épistémologie* (2007) and *Digital Cognitive Technologies: Epistemology and Knowledge Society* (2010), both edited by Claire Brossard and Bernard Reber. A slightly longer version appeared in *Theory, Culture and Society* (2012), in the special issue on the topological approach to cultural dynamics, edited by Celia Lury.

My critique of search engines as "inculpable," the subject of chapter 4, is in fact a reaction to the means by which the personalization of engine results would affect source distance research. In the study of what I term web epistemology, the new hierarchies of sources, and credibility, outputted by engines are of interest. If no two individuals receive the same results for the same query (since December 2009), then it becomes inappropriate to "blame" search engines for placing the climate change skeptics (to return to them) at the top of the web when one queries climate change.[8] With personalization, search engine results are coauthored by the engine and the user. That is, the results you receive are partly of your own making, based on your search history, location, and other signals, as Google calls the data points it has collected. The question then becomes whether one can train one search engine (account) to be skeptic-friendly, placing sources mentioning skeptics at the top of engine returns for the query ["climate change"], and another search engine (account) to be skeptic-unfriendly, placing sources mentioning skeptics at the bottom. Similarly, one could imagine the desire to train a search engine account to be of one political persuasion, and a second of another. This kind of work, undertaken by colleagues, opens up the study of the impact of personalization on engine returns, an important web-epistemological question.[9] The "inculpable engine" piece was published in *Deep Search: The Politics of Search beyond Google* (2010), along with the German version, *Deep Search: Politik des Suchens jenseits von Google*, edited by Konrad Becker and Felix Stalder. It also is a contribution that I wrote particularly for Googlization scholars, especially Siva Vaidhyanathan, in an effort to shape a research agenda.[10]

Digital Methods Summer Schools (2007–) and Govcom.org workshops (1998–) provide much of the material in this book, including the contributions I would like to make to the study of the website and to the study of social media. Websites are predominantly blue, as we found at the Recalling RFID workshop organized at de Balie, Amsterdam, in 2007 (see figure 0.3). Apart from color analysis and usability, a website may be studied for its genealogy, (template) anatomy, features, and other points of departure I list in chapter 3. One device that organizes websites as objects of study is the Wayback Machine of the Internet Archive. Studies continually lament the lack of its use as well as that of national web archives by scholars and other researchers, apart from legal teams seeking evidence or legal departments looking up their own company's websites and asking for them to be removed, or having *user-agent: ia_ archiver Disallow: /* inserted in the site's robots.txt file, which not only excludes the Internet Archive's crawlers but also wipes the history of the site from the Archive. How else to study the website as archived object? At the 2008 Digital Methods Summer School (which also was the Govcom.org 10-year jubilee event), I sought to apply digital methods principles by following the dominant device and repurposing it for research. At the Wayback Machine one enters a URL that outputs the pages archived. Fundamentally, it organizes the history of the web into single-site or single-page histories. It has an in-built historiography in the biographical tradition. In considering how to repurpose its output, colleagues and I captured the historical pages of a URL (Google.com's, during what was its tenth anniversary, too). We compiled the unique pages (the ones with an * next to them in the Wayback Machine's results page), loaded them in a slide show, and played them back in the style of time-lapse photography, or screencast documentary, with a voiceover track telling the history of Google from the changes to its interface from 1998 to 2007, a project we called *Google and the Politics of Tabs*. (The Internet Archive is often six months behind or longer in listing archived website content.) The more ambitious project was put forward for the 2009 Digital Methods Summer School. How to move beyond single-site histories? The unattainable goal that we set was to conjure a past state of the web so as to enable the study of a period, instead of only a site biography such as we undertook with the Google movie. Apart from site biographies, there are also event histories as organized by many of the special website collections to date, such as the September 11, 2001, collection as well as those on natural disasters and elections, as I will discuss. In keeping with what one would call a more general new media platform outlook (make not a tool, but a toolmaker), and in keeping with precisely that practice in contemporary web archiving (the archive-IT project), colleagues and I put forward a technique to create a collection of already archived websites for the study of web history, or history with the web. What is left of the early blogosphere was determined as well as captured so as to perform what I believe is one of the first historical hyperlink analyses, or mappings. In any case, early blogs that are not archived come to life on the hyperlink map, showing not only their presence and positioning through the links they received at the time (August 2000), but also a past state of (part of) the web, including the relative sphereness of the blogosphere. The technique of conjuring past states of the web has been applied subsequently to the Dutch blogosphere as well as the Palestinian web, and is thus a digital method (like source distance and others) that has stuck.

The continuing relevance of the work at early Digital Methods Summer Schools (2007, 2008, and 2009) became clear not only for the methods that have endured, such as source distance (discussed in chapter 5) and screencast documentaries as well as historical link analysis from pages in web archives (chapter 3). Certain fledgling projects from the early days also later matured, such as our efforts to demarcate and diagnose the condition of the Iraqi web, in the summer of 2007, some five years into the Iraq War, when blogging voices from the ground (Salam Pax, the Baghdad Blogger) and U.S. senators on fact-finding trips through a Baghdad market (filmed with a handheld camera) each strove to provide authentic accounts of the conditions there. Could we add to those accounts of the situation in Iraq by analyzing the health of its web? In making a collection of Iraqi websites, we ultimately found a broken web, with university sites ill maintained or down, for example. One of the few lively

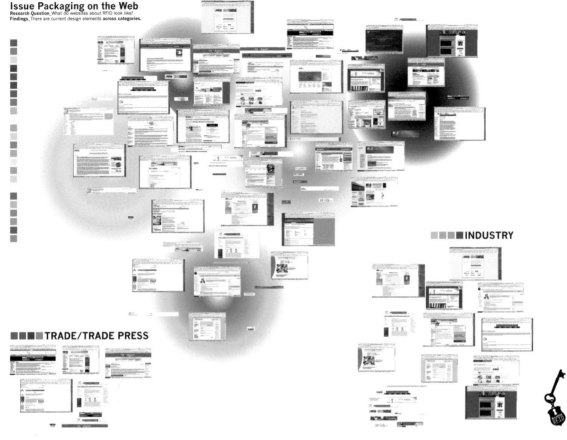

Figure 0.3
Color study of websites in the RFID issue space, recalling RFID workshop, Amsterdam, 2009.
Graphic by Studio Léon&Loes, Rotterdam. © Studio Léon&Loes, 2009.

websites was the Iraqi Ministry of Oil's, which was the only one in our collection that carried an advertisement! During the project, we put forward an approach to the study of a national web that rested on a series of metrics for diagnosing its health, such as the responsiveness and freshness of national web pages, that are applied in chapter 6. The case study is Iran, where in 2011 we demarcated a national web (over 10,000 unique hosts) by relying on "device cultures" dominant for Iranians, i.e., engines and platforms that recursively collect data from users and recommend URLs back to them. Studying Iran, however, introduced the further complication that many of its websites are censored by the state. In the piece of research undertaken for the Iran Media Program (Center for Global Communication Studies, Annenberg

School for Communication, University of Pennsylvania), Esther Weltevrede, Sabine Niederer, Erik Borra, and I found a censored yet lively Iranian web, with bloggers still blogging despite their sites' being blocked. We also put forward a set of metrics for studying the health of a national web, in the style of a web index. A shortened version of the study has appeared in the *Blackwell Companion to New Media Dynamics* edited by John Hartley, Jean Burgess, and Axel Bruns.

The thoughts developed for the study of social media, and the term "postdemographics," the subject of chapter 7, came together at "Space for People: Suggested Fields," a workshop supported by the Netherlands Media Art Institute and Montevideo/Time Based Arts, and at the "Walled Garden" event organized by the Virtual Platform, both in Amsterdam in 2008. The outcomes were media art software projects, Elfriendo.com and Leakygarden.net, though only the former was the subject of coverage by an Amsterdam media arts magazine (for youth).[11] Importantly, both projects had as their points of departure to think along with online devices and build atop them for the purposes of research into social media, and specifically online profiles. Elfriendo, with its slogan "taking the work out of social networking," would create an entire personal profile from scratch on the basis of inputting a single interest. There were two other services provided at Elfriendo.com: it would check the compatibility of two profiles, and provide a profile "makeover." Built on top of Myspace, and more specifically Myspace's interest search (which was subsequently discontinued), the software would scrape the (top) profiles of those with a particular general interest or favorite music, movies, television shows, books, and heroes.[12] It would aggregate them, thereby creating a new profile or a profile makeover (one's fields freshened up, if you will). It also would compare two profiles for compatibility, providing a matching percentage. Significantly, it would compare for compatibility those sets of profiles with particular interests. What is the aggregate profile for those interested in Barack Obama, and for those interested in John McCain, Obama's opponent in the 2008 U.S. presidential election? Are they compatible? To what degree do individuals interested in Obama listen to the same music, watch the same movies and television programs, read the same books, and have the same heroes as those interested in other candidates? "Postdemographics" as a term is an invitation to study societally or culturally significant profiles in the aggregate and inquire into the relationships between them. It is also an invitation to ask about what is shared. Is Islam compatible with Christianity, in the sense that those listing one or the other as interest have other media favorites in common? The chapter on social media was published as "Post-demographic Machines" in the *Walled Garden* volume (2009), edited by Annet Dekker and Annette Wolfsberger, and an expanded version appeared as "Post-demografisch onderzoek: voorbij het doelgroepdenken" (Postdemographic research: Beyond target group thinking) in the special issue of *De Gids* (2010) exploring the web's rewriting of the Dutch literary canon, edited by Noortje Marres.

This Painting Is Not Available in Your Country, an artwork by Paul Mutant (2010), summarizes the idea of the end of the virtual, the subject of chapter 1. The chapter is the *oratie* or speech I gave on the occasion of the inauguration of the professorship in new media and digital culture at the University of Amsterdam. It has been published as "The End of the Virtual: Digital Methods" (2009) by Amsterdam University Press, and in shortened form in German in the *Zeitschrift für Medienwissenschaft* (2011). Both in the "End of the Virtual" and in the "Politics of Web Space" (now chapter 2), I strive to point out the significance of the advent of IP-to-geo technology as the revenge of geography on cyberspace. The more dramatic formulation is the "death of cyberspace," by which is meant that the web is increasingly less placeless—if it ever was, considering the close relationship between virtual community and real place discussed in the literature of the early to mid-1990s, and how the local appropriates the Internet to suit its own purposes, as ethnographers found in visiting cybercafés in Trinidad and Tobago in the 1990s. That is, geolocation technology locates the user and loads tailored content (or blocks it) accordingly in the user's browser. This technology was implemented widely as a result of the lawsuit brought against Yahoo! in France in 2000 by antidefamation nongovernmental organizations, and has been implemented most readily for advertising as well as intellectual property contexts, such as for streaming television programs, including the 2008 Olympic Games where many, it seemed from personal observation, noticeably experienced its effects. Locative media was normal. The local-domain Googles (e.g., Google.fr) are also cases in point in geolocation effects, as the Google that loads by default is the one associated with the user's location. On most local-domain Googles, there is a link to "Google.com in English," and there is also a separate URL (Google.com/ncr) offered for "no country redirect," which suppresses the autodetection of one's location. Placelessness, once the experience and rhetoric of cyberspace, nowadays is a workaround URL.

Chapter 8, on Wikipedia as cultural reference, is a collaboration with Emina Sendijarevic, who during the 2010–2011 Digital Methods course at the University of Amsterdam dissected the articles on the fall of Srebrenica, the Srebrenica massacre, and the Srebrenica genocide from the Dutch-, Serbian-, and Bosnian-language Wikipedias, respectively (and others, too). With exceptions (e.g., the Dutch article), the articles originated from a translation of the corresponding English-language one; over the course of six years of edits, they then developed distinctive storylines and viewpoints, which we initially described as national rather than neutral points of view, as the Wikipedia principle (NPOV) is called. In the analysis, we are interested in whether we could step out of the frame of Wikipedia as encyclopedia and move beyond the accuracy debate. We propose the comparative study of Wikipedia articles across language versions as cultural, rather than as standard or universal reference, which is in keeping with the digital methods principle of employing the web to study cultural change, preference, and commitment. Directly after nearly the same version of the article was

Figure 0.4
This Painting Is Not Available in Your Country by Paul Mutant, 2010. © Paul Mutant, 2010. Reproduced with permission.

posted on the Bosnian, Croatian, and Serbian Wikipedias in 2005, a Serbian user put up the template disputing its neutral point of view, while Bosnian and Croatian users praised its quality and ultimately made the Bosnian a featured article, a badge of merit given to entries of particular note. After five years of editing, the Dutch and the Serbian articles have lower victim counts than the Bosnian (and the others we analyzed), throwing into relief rather distinctive sources (and outlooks) on the events. While Srebrenica is a special case, the approach to studying the "same" article across different Wikipedia language versions is generalizable; time will tell if that method sticks.

"After Cyberspace: Big Data, Small Data," the final chapter, situates digital methods one last time in the so-called computational turn in the social sciences and digital humanities, and seeks to make distinctions between a series of contemporary approaches to the study of digital data and the one put forward here. At the outset of the final chapter, as in the opening, I return to the difference between the natively digital and the digitized, both for data and for method. Portions of the chapter were presented at the MiT7 conference on Unstable Platforms in 2011, and also borrow thoughts I wrote up in the context of two projects funded by the European

Commission: A Topological Approach to Cultural Dynamics (ATACD), the 6th Framework project mentioned above, and Mapping Controversies on Science for Politics (Macospol), the 7th Framework project led by Bruno Latour at Sciences Po, Paris. The Macospol project also had as one of its products the transformation of the Google Scraper (the tool used for source distance research) into the Lippmannian Device (the tool used for partisanship and issue commitment analysis). The Digital Methods group, Amsterdam, built the Macospol controversy mapping platform at mappingcontroversies.net.

The distinction between the natively digital and the digitized is made as a positioning move.[13] Many of the methodological approaches to the study of new or digital media work with digitized data, such as "cultural analytics" as well as "culturomics," as I relate in the concluding chapter. The one seeks patterns across complete sets of paintings by a single artist or the covers of a tone-setting magazine, while the other studies changes in word use over time by querying books scanned by Google (in the Google Books project). In other words, for these and other approaches, digital media means the study of the digitized and the scanned, where data access and special query privileges are often needed. Here, by contrast, I put forward an approach to make use of the forms and materials of specific digital media (such as the blog post and the Wikipedia edit), rather than principally those that have been digitized and scanned and uploaded to a digital medium (such as scanned photographs from World War II mounted on a website, as discussed in chapter 3 in an example of a web archivist's selection of a valuable website to be archived). The work in this book on the website as archived object was written in the spring of 2011, while I was Annenberg Fellow at the Annenberg School for Communication, University of Pennsylvania. I would like to thank Joseph Cappella, Joseph Turow, and Michael Delli Carpini for bringing me to Philadelphia. Klaus Krippendorff inspired a digital methods version of web content analysis, in the Wikipedia study introduced above.

Special access is also required for the study of certain natively digital objects such as engine query logs, leading to the discussion of the tension between employing the APIs offered by the companies and scraping data. There is a requirement of ethical review often accompanying proposals to scrape online data, including profiles.[14] In part, it has been inherited from the disappointment surrounding the release of allegedly anonymized AOL user search histories in 2006, following which journalists were able to "de-anonymize," or identify, one of the search engine users, an older lady in Georgia. The AOL data were released for scientists to use in improving (personalized) search. I contrast the detective's or voyeur's outlook that comes along with individually numbered search engine users and lists of their queries—the data formats provided—with another outlook, more in tune with social research needs. Not the individuals but the places of substantive queries are the data of choice for the research outlook I wish to describe as digital methods.

I would like to acknowledge the work of the Digital Methods Initiative (DMI), Amsterdam: Anat Ben-David, Erik Borra, Marieke van Dijk, Anne Helmond, Koen Martens, Sabine Niederer, Michael Stevenson, and Esther Weltevrede. Each project should bear most or all of their names, if they do not already (in print or on the web). Thanks are also extended to Noortje Marres, whose questions are not only incisive but also the source of our FAQs at digitalmethods.net. The Digital Methods Initiative and Summer School have had waves of dedicated researchers. Marijn de Vries Hoogerwerff, Rosa Menkman, Bram Nijhof, and Laura van der Vlies were present in the early years, contributing to multiple projects, including the 2008 Summer School, which was also the Govcom.org Foundation's Jubilee. Govcom.org, the group of researchers, programmers, and designers first formed at the Jan van Eyck Academy in Maastricht in the late 1990s, celebrated its tenth anniversary in 2008, with special guests including Greg Elmer and Warren Sack. Alexander Galloway's presence there led to the *IP Browser*, exhibited at the Impakt Festival Utrecht (2009), Arts Santa Monica, Barcelona (2009–2010), and Transmediale Berlin (2011). *For the ppl of Iran: #iranelection RT*, a product of the 2009 Summer School and exhibited at the same events in Barcelona and Berlin, was selected with the *IP Browser* by the Netherlands Media Art Institute for distribution in their 2010 catalog. Josep Perelló and Pau Alsina curated the exhibition "Social Atoms and Electronic Lives" at Arts Santa Monica in Barcelona, with assistance from Irma Vilà. The other 2008 Summer School production, *Google and the Politics of Tabs*, the screencast documentary, was produced by Theun Hendrikx and Menno Endt of Crooked Line, Amsterdam. I first told the story of the demise of the online librarian at the tenth-anniversary meeting of *Informatieprofessional* magazine, in spring of 2007, and later worked along with DMI researchers and Kim de Groot, who designed the accompanying information graphic, *The Demise of the Directory: Web Librarian Work Removed in Google*. The Issue Dramaturg, the software that shows the rankings of sources for Google queries over time, also discussed in the "inculpable engine" chapter, is a 2007 project that extends back to work on understanding the web as a hyperlink economy (including an article I published in *Science as Culture* in 2002 and a set of information graphics made in 2005 with work by Dragana Antic, then a student at the Piet Zwart Institute, Rotterdam). The Issue Dramaturg seeks to put on display the drama of search engine space—the precipitous rise and prodigious fall of an organization or company in engine returns for particular queries (or in general PageRank terms). As I presented the project in September 2007 at the Impakt Festival Utrecht (for which it was commissioned), the Issue Dramaturg captured drama. The site 911truth.org had held its top 5 ranking for the query [9/11] until it suddenly dropped to result 200, then fell off the charts in the 1,000 results served on 18 September 2007. The larger project of saving search engine results for the query [9/11] also drew interest from the 9/11 Memorial Museum in New York City.

"We look at Google results and see society, instead of Google" is the lead-in to an article reporting on employing the results of queries in local-domain Googles as indicators of hierarchies of national concerns. Applied to types of rights (such as human rights, children's rights, air passenger rights, and, as is popular in Italy, the right to oblivion), the short study was published in *Global Information Society Watch* [*GISWatch*] *2009* by the Association for Progressive Communication (APC) and Hivos, the Humanist Institute for Cooperation with Developing Countries (a Dutch development agency). The accompanying info-graphic, *Rights Types: The Nationalities of Issues* (reproduced here as figure 5.4), which appears over several pages in the *GISWatch* book, was designed together with Vera Bekema and relies on the search and language skills of Liliana Bounegru, Andrea Fiore, Simon Marschall, and Elena Tiis (and their friends and colleagues with diverse language skills). It is also listed in the Netherlands Media Art Institute catalogue "Computer- and Internet-Based Art in Distribution 2010," though to date it has not been exhibited (to my knowledge).

This Painting Is Not Available in Your Country, the image of Paul Mutant's 2010 artwork, appears courtesy of this Budapest-based artist. The *Cyberspace* image in chapter 2 is reproduced with permission from the DiploFoundation, Malta. John December kindly granted permission for the reprinting of his *CyberMap Landmarks* of 1994 (in chapter 2). The collection of homespun and professional web awards from the 1990s is the author's own, and was made into an artwork by Anja Lutz; it is also the back cover of the *Preferred Placement* book, a volume I edited, published by the Jan van Eyck Academy in 2000. Jude Buffum graciously supplied his 2008 artwork *Stopping Google* (chapter 4). Hendrik-Jan Grievink kindly allowed republication of a work from his set of ghostly website portraits (to borrow a phrase from an earlier set of templates by sumoto.iki), *Template Culture: Form Follows Format* of 2009 (chapter 3).

Finally, digital methods evolve with the medium and thus are best kept online, where they are continually edited, with feedback from those attending the research seminar course of the same name at the University of Amsterdam, and the Digital Methods Summer School and Winter School.

1   The End of the Virtual: Digital Methods

An ontological distinction may be made between the natively digital and the digitized, that is, between the objects, content, devices, and environments that are "born" in the new medium and those that have "migrated" to it. Such a distinction opens up the question of method for Internet-related research. Should the current methods of study change, slightly or wholesale, given a focus on objects as well as the contents that are "of the medium"? Such a question engages "virtual methods" that import standard methods from the social sciences and the humanities into the medium. That is, the distinction between the natively digital and the digitized also could apply to current research methods. What kind of research may be performed with methods that have been digitized (such as online surveys and directories) vis-à-vis those that are natively digital (such as recommendation systems and folksonomy)?

In order to begin to answer that question, I would like to propose that web research be put to new uses, given an emphasis on the study of natively digital objects and the methods that routinely make use of them. That is, I will strive to shift the attention in new media and digital culture generally and web research more specifically away from the opportunities afforded by transforming ink into bits, and instead inquire into how Internet research may move beyond the study of online culture only. How to capture and analyze hyperlinks, tags, search engine results, archived websites, social networking sites' profiles, Wikipedia edits, and other digital objects? How may one learn from how online devices (e.g., engines and recommendation systems) make use of the digital objects, and, crucially, how may such uses be repurposed for social and cultural research? Ultimately, I propose a research practice that learns from the methods of online devices, repurposes them, and seeks to ground claims about cultural change and societal conditions in web data, introducing the term "online groundedness." The overall aim is to rework methods for Internet-related research, developing a novel strand of study, digital methods.

To date, the methods employed have served the purpose of critiquing the persistent idea of the Internet as a virtual realm apart. Such thinking arose from the discourse surrounding virtual reality in the late 1980s and early 1990s, and the Internet came to stand for a virtual realm, with opportunities for a redefinition of consciousness, identity, corporality, community, citizenry, and politics.[1] Indeed, in 1999 in one of the first efforts to synthesize Internet research, the communications scholar Steve Jones invited researchers to move beyond the perspective of the Internet as a realm apart, and opened the discussion of method.[2] How would social scientists study the Internet, if they were not to rely on the approaches associated with it to date: human-computer interaction, social psychology, and cybercultural studies?[3] In their ground-breaking work on Internet use in Trinidad and Tobago, the ethnographers Daniel Miller and Don Slater challenged the idea of cyberspace as a realm apart where all "inhabiting" it experienced its identity-transforming affordances, no matter their location.[4] Slater and Miller grounded the Internet, arguing that Trinis appropriated the medium, making it fit their own cultural practices. While a case study, the overall thrust of the research was its potential for generalizability. If Trinis were using the Internet to stage Trini culture, the expectation was that other cultures were doing the same.

The important Virtual Society? program (1997–2002) marked another turning point in Internet research, with its debunking of the transformative capacities of cyberspace through multiple empirical studies about Internet users. The program ultimately formulated five "rules of virtuality."[5] In what is now the classic digital divide critique, researchers argued that the use of new media is based on one's situation (access issues), and that the fears and risks are unequally divided (skills issues). With respect to the relationship between the real and the virtual, virtual interactions supplement rather than substitute for the "real," and stimulate more real interaction, as opposed to isolation and desolation. Finally, the research found that identities are grounded in both the online as well as the offline. Significantly, the program settled on approaches that have been characterized as virtual methods, with an instrumentarium for studying users. Surveys, interviews, observation, and participant-observation became the preferred methods of inquiry. In the humanities, subsequent user studies—concentrating on the amateur, the fan, and the "produser"—also have been grappling with the real/virtual divide, seeking to demonstrate and critique the reputational status of online culture.[6] The argument put forward in this book is that virtual methods and user studies in the social sciences and the humanities have shifted the attention away from the *data* of the medium, and from the opportunities for study of far more than online culture.

How may one rethink user studies with data that are (routinely) collected by software? User studies to date have relied on accounts that privilege observation, interviews, and surveys, owing, in one reading, to the difference in armatures between social scientific and humanities computing, on the one hand, and the large commercial companies, with their remarkable data collection achievements, on the other. In a sense, Google, Amazon, and many other dominant web devices are already conducting user studies, however little the term is used. User inputs (preferences, search history, purchase history, location) are captured and analyzed so as to tailor results. Taking a lead from such work, there are increasingly calls for a methodological turn in Internet research, at least in the sense of data collection. With "cultural analytics," named after Google Analytics, the proposal is to build massive collection, storage, and analytical facilities for digital humanities.[7] One manner to describe the methodological turn is its marked departure from the reliance on (negotiated) access to commercial data sets, e.g., Linden Lab's set of the activities of millions of users in Second Life or Sony's for Everquest, however valuable the findings have been.[8] Cultural analytics would like to take on the mantle of "big science."[9] "Visualizations should be designed to take full advantage of the largest gigapixel wall-size displays available today."[10]

In a sense the research programs are an answer to the question, What would Google do? The research programs could be situated in the larger context of the extent and effects of "googlization."[11] To date the googlization critique, which originated in the reaction to the search engine company's entrance into the library (the Google Books project), has examined the growing "creep" of Google, its business model as well as its aesthetics, across information and knowledge industries.[12] Especially library science scholars concern themselves with the changing locus of access to information and knowledge (from public shelves and stacks to commercial servers). "Google effects" are media effects. They may be couched in terms of the supplanting of surfing and browsing by search. They may be studied in terms of the demise of the expert editor, and the rise of the back-end algorithm, themes to which I return. Here, however, the point is that they also may be studied in terms of models for research—ones that seek to replicate the scale of data collection as well as analysis.

The proposal I am putting forward is more modest, yet still in keeping with what are termed approaches to user studies that are registrational. Online devices and software installed on the computer (e.g., browsers) capture users' everyday use through what is termed "registrational interactivity."[13] Browser histories would become a means to study use. The larger contention is that data collection, in the methodological turn described above, could benefit from thinking about how computing may have techniques which can be repurposed for research. Thus the proposal is to consider first and foremost the availability of computing *techniques*.

I would like to help define a new era in Internet research, one that no longer concerns itself with the divide between the real and the virtual. It concerns a shift in the kinds of questions put to the study of the Internet. The Internet is employed as a site of research for far more than *just* online culture. The issue no longer is how much of society and culture is online, but rather how to diagnose cultural change and societal conditions by means of the Internet. The conceptual point of departure is the recognition that the Internet is not only an object of study but also a source. Knowledge claims may be made on the basis of data collected and analyzed by devices such as

Table 1.1
U.S.-Based Flu-Related Queries, the Geolocation Results of Which Correlate with Surveillance Data from the Centers for Disease Control, 2011

treatment for flu
how to treat the flu
treat flu
cure flu
cold or flu
treat the flu
how to treat flu
dangerous fever
remedies for flu
influenza type a
human temperature
flu medicine
symptoms of flu
is flu contagious
flu and fever
length of flu
flu or cold
flu duration
cure the flu
duration of flu
when is the flu contagious
how long is flu contagious
medication for flu
flu contagious
thermoscan
flu vs cold
remedies for the flu
fever and flu
is it the flu
flu fever

Source: Google Correlate results for Influenza-like Illness (CDC), http://correlate.googlelabs.com/, May 26, 2011.

search engines. One of the more remarkable examples is Google Flu Trends, a non-commercial (Google.org) project launched in 2008, which anticipates local outbreaks of influenza by counting search engine queries for flu, flu symptoms, and related terms, and "geolocates" the places where the queries have been made. It thereby complements and challenges existing methods of data collection (hospitalization, outpatient, and laboratories reports) and reopens the discussion of the web as antici-patory medium, closer to the ground than one expects.[14]

Where did the "grounded web," and its associated geolocative research practice, originate? The "end of cyberspace" as a placeless space (in the terms of Manuel Cas-tells) may be located in the technical outcomes of the famous Yahoo! lawsuit brought by two nongovernmental organizations in France in 2000.[15] At the time French web users were able to access the Nazi memorabilia pages on Yahoo.com in the United States, and two French nongovernmental organizations desired that the pages be inaccessible—in France. Following the lawsuit, IP-to-geo (address location) technology was furthered specifically to channel content nationally; when one types google.com into a browser in France, now google.fr is returned by default. This "grounding" of the web has been implemented by major content-organizing projects such as YouTube; online television is served geographically, too.

Diagnostic work whereby claims about societal conditions are made on the basis of captured Internet practices leads to new theoretical notions. For the third period of Internet research, the digital methods program introduces the term *online grounded-ness* to conceptualize research that follows the medium, captures its dynamics, and makes grounded claims about cultural and societal change. Indeed, the broader theo-retical goal of digital methods is to think through anew the relationship between the web and the ground. Like the ethnographers who came before them for the U.K. Virtual Society? program, one needed to visit the ground in order to study the web. Here the research program complicates the order in which one's findings are grounded.[16] For example, journalism has methodological needs now that the Internet has become a significant metasource, where the question normally concerns the trustworthiness of a source. Snowballing from source to source was once a social network approach to information-checking, to speak in terms of method. Who else should I speak to? That is the question at the conclusion of the interview, if trust has been built. The relation-ship between "Who I should speak to" and "Who else do you link to" is asymmetrical for journalism, but the latter is the question asked by search engines when recom-mending information. How to think through the difference between source recom-mendations from verbal and online links? Is search the beginning of the quest for information that ends with some grounded interview reality beyond the net, whereby we maintain the divide between some real and some virtual? Or is that too simplistic? Our ideal source set divide (real and virtual, grounded or googled) raises the question of what is next. What do we "look up" upon conclusion of the interview to check the reality? The Internet may not be changing the hierarchy of sources for some (e.g., the restrictions on citing Wikipedia in certain educational settings), but it may well be changing the order of checking, and the relationship of the web to the ground.

I developed the notion of online groundedness after reading a study performed by the Dutch newspaper *NRC Handelsblad*. The paper's investigation into right-wing as well as hate groups in the Netherlands inquired into whether the language used was becoming more extremist over time, perhaps indicating a "hardening" of right-wing and hate culture more generally. Significantly, the investigators elected to use the Internet Archive rather than an embedded researcher (going native), an expert survey, or the pamphlets, flyers, and other ephemera at the Social History Institute.[17] They located and analyzed the changes in tone over time on right-wing as well as extremist sites, finding that right-wing sites were increasingly employing more extremist language. Thus the findings made about culture were grounded through an analysis of websites. Most significantly, the online became the baseline against which one might judge the extent of a perceived societal condition.

Follow the Medium: The Digital Methods Approach to Research

Why follow the medium? A starting point is the recognition that Internet research is often faced with unstable objects of study. The instability is often discussed in terms of the ephemerality of websites and other digital media and the complexities associated with *fixing* them, to borrow a term from photography. How to make them permanent so that they can be studied with care? Web archiving is continually faced with the dilemma of capturing websites on the one hand, and maintaining their liveliness on the other. In one approach, vintage hardware and software are maintained so as to keep the media "undead." In another, also practiced in game studies environments, the ephemerality issue is addressed through simulation/emulation, which keeps the nostalgic software, such as Atari games, running on current hardware. The ephemerality issue, however, is much larger than the issues of preservation. The Internet researcher is often overtaken by events of the medium, such as software updates that abruptly disrupt and sometimes even "scoop" one's research.

As a research practice, following the medium, as opposed to striving to fix it, may also be discussed using a term borrowed from journalism and the sociology of science: "scooping." Being the first to publish is to "get the scoop." "Being scooped" refers to someone else publishing the findings first. The sociologist of science Michael Lynch has applied this term to the situation in which one's research subjects come to the same or similar conclusions as the researchers, and go on record with their findings first. The result is that the "[research subjects] reconfigure the field in which we previously thought our study would have been situated."[18] In Internet research, "being scooped" is common. Industry analysts, watchdogs, and bloggers routinely coin terms (e.g., googlization) and come to conclusions that shape ongoing academic work. I would like to argue, however, that scooping is also done by the objects, which are continually reconfigured. For example, Facebook, the social networking site, has been considered a case of a "walled garden," a relatively closed community system, where by default only "friends" can view information and activities of other friends. The "walled garden" is a series of concentric circles: a user must have an account to gain access, must friend people to view their profiles, and must change privacy default settings to let friends of friends view one's own profile. Maximum exposure means opening profiles to friends of friends. In March of 2009, Facebook changed a setting; users may now make their profile open to all other users with accounts, as opposed to just friends, or friends of friends, in its previous configuration.[19] Which types of research would be "scooped" by Facebook's flipping of a switch? Which would benefit? Facebook serves as one notable example of the sudden reconfiguration of a research object, which is common to the medium.

More theoretically, following the medium is a particular form of medium-specific research. Medium specificity is not only how one subdivides disciplinary commitments in media studies according to the primary objects of study: film, radio, television, etc. It also refers to media's ontological distinctiveness, though the means by which the ontologies are built differ. To the literary scholar and media theorist Marshall McLuhan, media are specific in how they engage the senses.[20] Depth, resolution, and other aesthetic properties have effects on how actively or passively one processes media. One is filled by media, or one fills them in. To the cultural theorist Raymond Williams, medium specificity lies elsewhere. Media are specific in the forms they assume—forms that are shaped by the dominant actors to serve interests.[21] For example, the creation of "flow," the term for how television sequences programming so as to keep viewers watching, serves viewer ratings and advertising. Thus, to Williams, media are not distinctive from one another a priori but can be made so. To Katherine Hayles, media have characteristics in their materiality; book specifies, while text does not.[22] Her proposal for "media-specific analysis" is a comparative media studies program, which takes materially instantiated characteristics of media (e.g., hypertext in digital media) and enquires into their (simulated) presence in other media (e.g., print). One could take other media traits and study them across media. For example, as Alexander Galloway has argued, flow is present not only in radio and television but also on the web, where dead links disrupt surfing.[23]

Hayles's point of departure may be seen in Mathew Fuller's work on Microsoft Word and Adobe Photoshop, which studies how particular software constrains or enables text.[24] To Fuller a Microsoft document or a Photoshop image are specific outputs of software, distinctive from some document or some image. An accompanying research program would study the effects of (software) features, as Lev Manovich also points to in his work on the specificity of computer media. With these media Manovich's ontology moves beyond the outputs of media (Hayles's hypertextual print, Fuller's Word document and Photoshop image) and puts forward the term "metamedia."[25] Computer media are metamedia in that they incorporate prior media forms, which is in keeping with the remediation thesis put forward by Jay David Bolter and Richard Grusin.[26] But, to Manovich, computer media not only refashion the outputs of other media; they also embed their forms of *production*.

The medium specificity put forward here lies not so much in McLuhan's sense engagement, Williams's socially shaped forms, Hayles's materiality, or other theorists' properties and features, whether they are outputs (cultural forms) or inputs (forms of production). Rather the medium specificity I put forward is one of method, both in the sense of preferred means of studying particular media (audience research with diary-keeping in TV studies, for example) and in the sense of methods of the medium. Previously I described such work for the web as "web epistemology."[27] On the web, information, knowledge, and sociality are organized by recommender systems—algorithms and scripts that prepare and serve up orders of URLs, media files, friends, etc. In a sense, Manovich has shifted the discussion in this direction, both with his focus on forms of production (method in a craft sense) as well as with the methodological turn associated with the cultural analytics initiative, but largely for digitized as opposed to natively digital content. I would like to take this turn further, and propose that the underinterrogated methods of the web also are worthy of study, both in and of themselves as well as in the effects of their spread to other media (e.g., TV shows recommended to Tivo users on the basis of their profiles).

The initial work in the area of web epistemology was in the context of the politics of search engines.[28] It sought to consider the means by which sources are adjudicated by search engines. Why, in March of 2003, were the U.S. White House, the Central Intelligence Agency, the Federal Bureau of Investigation, the right-of-center Heritage Foundation, and leading news organizations such as CNN the top returns for the query [terrorism]? In a sense the answer lies in how hyperlinks are handled. Hyperlinks, however, are but one digital object, to which may be added the thread, tag, PageRank, Wikipedia edit, robots.txt, post, comment, trackback, pingback, IP address, URL, whois, timestamp, permalink, social bookmark, and profile. In no particular order, the list goes on. The proposal is to study how these objects are handled, specifically, in the medium, and learn from medium method.

In the following, I would like to introduce a series of medium objects, formats, devices, as well as platforms, first touching briefly on how they are often studied with digitized methods and conceptual points of departure from without the medium. Subsequently, I would like to discuss the difference it would make to research if one were to follow the medium—by learning from and reapplying how digital objects (such as hyperlinks) are treated by devices, how websites are archived, how search engines order information, and how geo-IP location technology serves content nationally or linguistically. What kinds of research can be performed through hyper-link analysis, repurposing insights from dominant algorithms? How to work with the Internet Archive for social research? Why capture histories of websites? How may search engine results be studied so as to display changing hierarchies of credibility, and the differences in source reliance between the web sphere, the news sphere, and the blogosphere? Can geo-IP address location technology be reworked so as to profile countries and cultures? How may the study of social networking sites reveal cultural tastes and preferences? How are software robots changing how quality content is maintained on Wikipedia? What would a research bot do?

Thus, from the micro to the macro, I treat the hyperlink, website, search engine, spheres, and the web (or webs, including national ones). I finally turn to platforms—social media sites as well as Wikipedia—and seek to learn from these profiling and bot cultures (respectively) and rethink how to deploy them analytically. The overall purpose of following the medium is to reorient Internet research to consider the Internet as a source of data, method, and technique.

The Link

There are at least two dominant approaches to studying hyperlinks: hypertext literary theory and social network theory, including small world and path theory.[29] To literary theorists of hypertext, sets of hyperlinks form a multitude of distinct pathways through text. The surfer, or clicking text navigator, may be said to author a story by choosing routes (multiple clicks) through the text.[30] Thus the new means of authorship as well as the story told through link navigation are of interest. For small world theorists, the links that form paths show distance between actors. Social network analysts use pathway thought, and zoom in on how the ties, unidirectional or bidirectional, posi-tion actors.[31] A special vocabulary has been developed to characterize an actor's posi-tion, especially an actor's centrality, within a network. For example, an actor is "highly between" if there is a high probability that other actors must pass through him to reach each other.

How do search engines treat links? Theirs arguably is a scientometric (and associa-tional sociology) approach. As with social network analysis, the interest is in actor positioning, but not necessarily in terms of distance from one another or the means by which an actor may be reached through networking. Rather, ties are reputational indicators, and may be said to define actor standing. Additionally, the approach does not assume that the ties between actors are friendly or otherwise have utility, in the sense of providing empowering pathways or clues for successful networking.

Here I would like to follow how engines treat links as markers of impact and reputation. How may an actor's reputation be characterized by the types of hyper-links given and received? Actors can be profiled not only through the quantity of links received and the quantity received from others which themselves have received many links, in the basic search engine algorithm. Actors may also be profiled by examining which links they give and receive in particular.[32] In previous research colleagues and I found linking tendencies among domain types, i.e., governments tend to link to other governmental sites only, nongovernmental sites tend to link to a variety of sites, occasionally including critics. Corporate websites tend not to link, with the exception of collectives of them—industry trade sites and industry "front groups" do link. Academic and educational sites typically link to partners and initiatives they have created. Taken together, these linking proclivities of organization types show an everyday "politics of association."[33] When characterizing an actor according to inlinks and outlinks, one notices whether there is some divergence from the norms, and more generally whether particular links that are received may be telling for an actor's reputation. A nongovernmental organization receiving a link from a governmental site could be construed as a reputation booster, for example.[34]

Apart from capturing the micropolitics of hyperlinks, analysis of links also may be put to use in more sophisticated sampling work. Here the distinction between digitized and natively digital method stands out in greater relief. The Open Net Initiative at the University of Toronto conducts Internet censorship research by building lists of websites (from online directories such as the Open Directory Project and Yahoo) and then checking whether the sites are blocked in a variety of countries. It is important work that sheds light on the scope as well as technical infrastructure of state Internet censorship practices worldwide.[35] In the analytical practice, sites are grouped by category: famous bloggers, government sites, human rights sites, humor, women's rights, etc.; there are approximately 40 categories. Thus censorship patterns may be researched by site type across countries.

The entire list of websites checked per country (some 3,000) is a sample, covering of course only the smallest fraction of all websites as well as those of a particular subject category. How would one sample websites in a method that follows the medium, learning from how search engines work (link analysis) and repurposing it for social research? Colleagues and I contributed to the Open Net Initiative work by employing a method that crawls all the websites in a particular category, captures the hyperlinks from the sites, and determines additional key sites (by colink analysis) that are not on the lists. I dubbed the method "dynamic URL sampling," in an effort to highlight the difference between manual URL list compilation and more automated techniques of finding significant URLs. Once the new sites are found, they are checked for connection stats (through proxies initially, and later perhaps from machines located in the countries in question) in order to determine whether they are blocked. In the research project on "social, political, and religious" websites in Iran, researchers and I crawled all the sites in that ONI category, and through hyperlink analysis found some 30 previously unknown blocked sites. Significantly, the research was also a page-level analysis (as opposed to host only), with one notable finding being that Iran was not blocking the BBC news front page (as ONI had found) but only its Persian-language page. The difference between the two methods of gathering lists of websites for analysis—manual directory-style work and dynamic URL sampling—shows the contribution of medium-specific method (see figure 0.2).

The Website

Until now, investigations into websites have been dominated by user and "eyeball studies," where attempts at a navigation poetics are met with such sobering ideas as "don't make me think."[36] Many of the methods for studying websites are located over the shoulder: one observes navigation or the use of a search engine and later conducts interviews with the subjects. In what one may term classic registrational approaches, a popular technique is eye tracking. Sites load and eyes move to the upper left of the screen, otherwise known as the golden triangle of search. The resulting heat maps provide site redesign cues, and a sense of the value of different sections of the page for advertising purposes. Another dominant strand of website studies lies in feature analysis, where sites are compared and contrasted on the basis of levels of interactivity, capacities for user feedback, etc.[37] The questions concern whether a particular package of features results in more users and more attention. In this tradition, websites are often archived for further study. Thus, much of the work lies in the archiving of sites prior to the analysis. One of the crucial tasks ahead is further reflection on the means by which websites are captured and stored, so as to make available the data on which findings are based. Thus the digital methods research program engages specifically with the website as archived object, made accessible, most readily, through the Internet Archive's Wayback Machine.

Which types of research approach are favored by the current organization of websites by the Internet Archive? With the Wayback Machine, one can study the evolution of a single page (or multiple pages) over time, for example by reading or collecting snapshots from the dates that a page has been indexed. How can such an arrangement of historical sites be put to use? Previously I mentioned the investigative reporting work done by the *NRC Handelsblad* in their analysis of the rise of extremist language in the Netherlands. The journalists read some hundred websites from the Internet Archive, some dating back a decade. It is work that should be built upon, methodologically as well as technically. One could scrape the pages of the right-wing and extremist sites from the Internet Archive, place the text (and images) in a database, and systematically query it for the presence of particular keywords over time. As the *NRC Handelsblad* did, one could determine changes in societal conditions through archived website analysis of particular sets of sites.

How else to perform research with the Internet Archive? The digital methods program has developed means to capture the history of sites by taking snapshots and assembling them into a movie, in the style of time-lapse photography.[38] As a demonstration of how to use the Internet Archive for capturing such evolutionary histories, colleagues and I took snapshots of the front pages of Google from 1998 up to the end of 2007. The analysis concerned the subtle changes made to the interface, in particular the tabs. We found that the directory project, the organization of the web by topic undertaken by human editors, has been in decline. Are the histories of search engines, captured from their interface evolutions, indicating changes in how information and knowledge are ordered more generally? A comparative media studies approach would be useful, with one of the more poignant cases being the online newspaper. With the *New York Times* online, for example, articles are still placed on the front page and in sections, but are also listed by "most emailed" and "most blogged," providing a medium-specific recommender system for navigating the news. The impact of recommender systems—the dominant means on the web by which information and knowledge are ordered—may also be studied through user expectations. Are users increasingly expecting weblike orderings at archives, libraries, tourist information centers, and other sites of knowledge and information queries?

The Search Engines and the Spheres

The study of search engines was jolted by the now infamous AOL search engine data release in 2006, in which 650,000 users' searches over three months were put online, with frightening and often salacious press accounts about the level of intimate detail revealed about searchers, even if their histories were anonymized (no names) and decoupled from geography (no IP address). One may interpret the findings from the AOL case as a shift in how one considers online presence, if that remains the proper term. If a person is googled, his or her self-authored presence often appears at or toward the top of the returns, while what others have written about the person appears lower down in the rankings. However, with search engine queries stored, a third set of traces could come to define an individual or a databody: one's search history. It opens up policy questions: How long may an engine company keep search histories? Thus search engines are being studied in the legal arena, especially in terms of how data retention laws may be applied to search.

Another strand in search engine studies, summed up in the term "googlization," is a political-economy-style critique that considers how Google's free-service-for-profile model may be spreading across industries and (software) cultures. Below I discuss the critique and propose research that treats both front-end and back-end googlization. Front-end googlization would include the study of the information politics of the interface. Back-end googlization concerns the rise of the algorithm that recommends sources hierarchically, both on the basis of what all have clicked or read ("most emailed") as well as on the basis of an individual's reading history ("recommended for you," as the *New York Times* online puts it). The significance of studying the new information hierarchies of search engines also should be viewed in light of user studies. A small percentage of users set preferences to more than 10 results per page; typically they do not look past the first page of results; and they increasingly click the results appearing toward the top.[39] Thus the power of a search engine lies in the combination of its ranking practices (source inclusion in the top results) together with the users' apparent "respect" for the orderings (not looking further). Google's model also relies on registrational interactivity, in which a user's preferences as well as history are registered, stored, and employed, increasingly, to serve tailored results. Whereas queries once would return the same information for all users at any given time, now the results are dynamically generated based on one's registered preferences, history, and location.

The different orders of sources and things served by engines are understudied, largely because they are not stored and made available for research, apart from the AOL data release or other negotiated agreements with search engine companies. Google once made available an API (application programming interface) that allowed for data collection; a limited number of queries could be made per day, and the results repurposed. Researchers relying on the API were scooped by Google when it discontinued or "deprecated" the service in late 2006. With its reintroduction in a different form in 2009, Google emphasized, however, that automated queries and the permanent storage of results are against the terms of service. How to study search engine results under such conditions? Colleagues and I scrape Google, and put up a notice appreciating Google's forbearance.[40]

What may be found in Google's search engine results? As I have remarked, search engines, a crucial point of entry to the web, are epistemological machines in the sense that they crawl, index, cache, and ultimately order content. Previously I described the web, and particularly a search-engine-based web, as a potential collision space for alternative accounts of reality.[41] The phrasing built on the work of the sociologist C. Wright Mills, who characterized the purpose of social research as "no less than to present conflicting definitions of reality itself."[42] Are engines placing alternative accounts of reality side by side, or do the results align with the official and the mainstream? Storing and analyzing search engine results could answer such questions. It is important to point out that top engine placements are highly sought after; organizations make use of search engine optimization techniques so as to boost their sites' visibility. There are white hat and black hat techniques for this, that is, those accepted by engines and others that prompt engines to delist websites from results until they comply again with engine etiquette.

In the Issue Dramaturg project, discussed in chapter 4, colleagues and I have stored Google search engine results for the query [9/11], as well as other keywords, enquiring into source hierarchies. Which sources are privileged? Which are "winning" the competition to be the top sources returned for particular queries? Another purpose has been to chart particular sources, in the approach to engine studies that I have termed "source distance." For the query [9/11], how far from the top of the engine returns are such significant actors in 9/11 accounts as the New York City government and the *New York Times*? Are such sources prominent, or do they appear side by side with sources that challenge more official and familiar views? Thus, apart from the New York City government and the *New York Times* another actor that we have monitored is the 9/11 truth movement (911truth.org). For months between March and September 2007, the 9/11 truth movement's site appeared in the top five results for the query [9/11], while the city government and the *Times* were well below result fifty. In mid-September 2007, around the anniversary of the event, there was drama. 911truth.org fell precipitously to result two hundred, and subsequently out of the top one thousand, that is, the maximum number of results served by Google. I believe it is one of the first fully documented cases of the apparent removal of a website in Google—from a top-five placement for six months to a sub-one thousand ranking. The case leads to questions of search engine result stability and volatility, and opens up an area of study.

However dominant it may be, there are other search engines besides Google's. What is less appreciated, perhaps, is that there are other dominant engines for particular sections or spheres of the web. For the blogosphere, there is Technorati (and Google Blog Search), for the news sphere Google News, and for the tagosphere or social bookmarking space Delicious. Indeed, thinking of the web in terms of spheres refers initially to the name of one of the most well-known, the blogosphere, as well as to scholarship that seeks to define another, the "web sphere."[43] The "sphere" in "blogosphere" refers in spirit to the public sphere; it also may suggest the geometrical form, in which all points on the surface are the same distance from the center or core. One could think of such an equidistance as an egalitarian ideal, in which every blog, or even every source of information, is knowable by the core and vice versa. It has been found, however, that certain sources are central on the web. They receive the vast majority of links as well as hits. Following such principles as that the rich get richer (aka Matthew effect and power law distributions), the sites already receiving attention tend to garner more. The distance between the center and other nodes may only grow, with the idealized sphere being a fiction, however much a useful one. I would like to put forward an approach that takes up the question of distance from core to periphery, and operationalizes it as the measure of differences in rankings between sources per sphere. Spherical analysis is a digital method for measuring and learning from the distance between sources in different spheres on the web.

Conceptually, a sphere is considered to be a device-demarcated source set, i.e., the pure PageRank of all sources on the web (most influential sites by inlink count), or indeed analogous PageRanks of all sources calculated by the dominant engines per sphere, i.e., Technorati, Google News, and Delicious. Thus, to study a sphere, I propose first to allow the engines to demarcate it. In sphere analysis one considers which sources are most influential, not only overall but per query. Cross-spherical analysis compares the sources returned by each sphere for the same query. It can therefore be seen as comparative ranking research. Most importantly, with cross-spherical analysis, one may think through the consequences of each engine's treatment of links, freshness, tags, etc. Do particular sources tend to be in the core of one sphere and not in others? What do comparisons between sources, and source distances, across the spheres tell us about the quality of the new media? What do they tell us about current informational commitments in particular cultures?

In a preliminary analysis, colleagues and I studied which animals are most associated with climate change on the (English-language) web, in the news and in the blogosphere. We found that the web sphere had the most diverse set of animals associated with climate change. The news sphere favored the polar bear, and the blogosphere amplified, or made more prominent, the selection in the news sphere. Here we cautiously concluded that the web sphere may be less prone to the creation of media icons than the news sphere, which has implications for studies of media that take as their point of departure a publicity culture. The blogosphere, moreover, appeared parasitic on the news as opposed to an alternative to it.

The Webs

As mentioned above, Internet research has been haunted by the virtual/real divide. One of the reasons for such a divide pertains to the technical arrangements of the Internet and how they became associated with a virtual realm, cyberspace. Indeed, there was meant to be something distinctive about cyberspace, technologically.[44] The protocols and principles, particularly packet switching and the end-to-end principle, initially filled in the notion of cyberspace as a realm free from physical constraints. The Internet's technical indifference to the geographical location of its users spawned ideas of placelessness; in its architecture, it also supposedly made for a space untethered from the nation-states, and their divergent ways of treating flows of information.[45] One recalls the famous comment attributed to John Gilmore, cofounder with John Perry Barlow of the Electronic Frontier Foundation: "The Internet treats censorship as a malfunction, and routes around it."[46] Geography, however, was built into cyberspace from the beginning, if one considers the locations of the original thirteen root servers, the unequal distributions of traffic flows per country, as well as the allotment of IP addresses in ranges, which later enabled the application of geo-IP address location technology to serve advertising and copyright needs. Geo-IP technology as well as other technical means that locate (aka locative technology) also may be put to use for research that takes the Internet as a site of study, and inquires into what may be learned about societal conditions across countries. In the digital methods research program, colleagues and I have dubbed such work national web studies.

Above, I discussed the research by the British ethnographers who grounded cyberspace through empirical work on how Caribbean Internet users appropriated the medium to fit their own cultural practices. This is, of course, an example of national web studies, though using observational methods (from outside of the medium). To study the web nationally, one also may inquire into the data that are routinely collected, for example by large enterprises such as Alexa's top sites by country (according to traffic). Which sites are visited most frequently per country, and what does site visitation say about a country's informational culture? Alexa pioneered registrational data collection with its toolbar, which users would install in their browsers. The toolbar provided statistics about the website one had loaded in the browser, such as its freshness. All the websites that the user loaded, or surfed, also would be logged, and the logged URLs would be compared with the URLs already in the Alexa database. Those URLs not in the database would be crawled, and fetched. Thus was born the Internet Archive.

The Internet Archive (1996–) was developed during the period of Internet history that one might term cyberspace. (I develop further periodizations of Internet history in the next chapter.) To illustrate the difference in design and thought between the Internet Archive and the national web archives that are sprouting up in many countries, it may be pointed out that the Internet Archive was built for surfing—an Internet usage type that arguably has given way to search.[47] At the Wayback Machine of the Internet Archive, one can type in a single URL, view available pages, and browse them. If one reaches an external link, the Internet Archive looks up the page closest in date to the site one is exiting and loads it. If no site exists in the Internet Archive, it connects to the live website. It is the continuity of flow, from website to website, that is preserved.[48] National web archives, on the other hand, have ceased to think of the web in terms of cyberspace. Instead their respective purposes are to preserve national webs. For the purposes of contributing method to Internet research, the initial question is, How would one demarcate a national web?

At the National Library in the Netherlands, for example, the approach is similar to that of the Internet censorship researchers discussed above. It is a digitized method, that is, a directory model, in which an expert chooses significant sites based on editorial criteria. These sites are continually archived with technology originally developed in the Internet Archive project. At the time of writing, approximately 998 national websites are archived in the Netherlands—a far cry from what is saved at the Internet

Archive. In accounting for the difference in approaches and outcomes of the two projects, I would like to observe that the end of the virtual, and the end of cyberspace, have not been kind to web archiving; the return of the nation-state and the application of certain policy regimes (especially copyright) have slowed efforts dramatically. Would digital methods aid in redressing the situation? I would like to invite national web archivists to consider a registrational approach, e.g., the Alexa model adapted for a national context. The results may be salutary.

Social Media Sites and Postdemographics

Social networking sites such as the Dutch Hyves and its American predecessor Facebook are platforms popular for the opportunities they provide for social and cultural research. Until now, leading research has focused on how users present themselves and manage their identities and privacy, and how online friendship is related to being friends for real.[49] Larger-scale work, with big data sets, compares online networks to offline, or otherwise preexisting, social networks. Another approach, which originates in computer and information science, seeks to put to use the enormous amounts of data that people have put up online in their so-called profiles. The personal information in each profile contains traditional demographic information such as gender, age, and location, but also "postdemographic" information such as interests, taste in music, favorite books, and television programs. Thus social network sites offer new opportunities for research, and perhaps especially for research into publics. While public opinion research has been associated for some time with surveys as well as television viewership ratings and shares, could the information contained in profiles on social networking sites provide different sorts of insights into the composition and characteristics of publics? The question concerns which forms of analysis may be performed, also ethically, a subject discussed in the concluding chapter. Here I have chosen an experimental approach, situated more in an arts-based tradition, so as to create aggregated profiles and compare them, such as the interests and (media) tastes of the friends of President Barack Obama and Senator John McCain. Do Obama's and McCain's "friends" watch the same television shows, read the same books, and have similar general interests? Thus to gender, age, location, and other demographic information, one may add media and other interests, thereby describing publics in ways that may show similarity when division is expected, for example. I also explore profiling web usernames, that is, the aliases people choose alongside their real names for making online accounts and subscriptions to services. Typically a person has two web names, his or her own and his or her alias. Which combinations of services does a username (and aggregates of usernames) use? Here one is in the realm of research into related matters, which web methods often use to recommend products, services, information, and friends, but which may be repurposed. Colleagues and I have developed tools that sit atop social networking sites (such as MySpace) and social-media-related tools (such as User Name Check) to show how one may repurpose the outputs of queries. Elfriendo.com is built on top of MySpace, and creates aggregated profiles on the basis of a set of MySpace friends. Leakygarden.net creates a list of web services to which a username or alias has subscribed, thereby creating a metaprofile of a user. The two tools strive to show compositions of publics according to preferences (as opposed to demographics), thereby opening up a line of inquiry called postdemographics.

Wikipedia and Networked Content

To date, the approaches to the study of Wikipedia have followed from certain qualities of the online encyclopedia, all of which appear counterintuitive at first glance. One of these is that Wikipedia is authored by so-called amateurs, yet is surprisingly encyclopedia-like, not only in form but in accuracy.[50] The major debate concerning the quality of Wikipedia vis-à-vis *Encyclopaedia Britannica* has raised questions relevant to digital methods, in that the web-enabled collective editing model has challenged the digitized work of a set of experts. However, research has found that there is only a tiny ratio of editors to users in Web 2.0 platforms, including Wikipedia, illustrating what is known as the myth of user-generated content.[51] Wikipedia cofounder Jimmy Wales has often remarked that the dedicated community is indeed relatively small, at just over 500 members. Thus the small cadre of Wikipedia editors could be considered a new elite; one research exercise thus consists in relativizing the alleged differences between amateurs and experts, such as through a study of the demographics of Wikipedians.[52] Another counterintuitive aspect of Wikipedia is that the editors are unpaid yet committed and highly vigilant. The vigilance of the crowd, as it is termed, is something of a mythical feature of a quality-producing web, until one considers how vigilance is performed. Who is making the edits? One approach to the question lies in the Wikiscanner project (2007–), developed by Virgil Griffith studying at the California Institute of Technology. The Wikiscanner outs anonymous editors by looking up the IP address of the editor and checking it against a database with IP address locations (IP-to-geo technology). Wikipedia quality is ensured, to Griffith, by scandalizing editors who make self-serving changes, such as a member of the Dutch royal family who embellished an entry and made the front page of the newspaper after a journalist used the tool.

How else are vandals kept at bay on Wikipedia, including those experimenters and researchers making erroneous changes to an entry, or creating a new fictional one, in order to keep open the debate about quality?[53] Colleagues and I have contributed to work about the quality of Wikipedia by introducing the terms "networked content" and the "technicity of content." The former refers to content held together by human authors and nonhuman tenders, including bots and alert software that revert edits or notify Wikipedians of changes made. The latter focuses on the bots, arguably left out of most Wikipedia analysis, at least the studies concentrating in particular on the vigilance of the crowd. Indeed, looking at the statistics available on Wikipedia on the number of edits per Wikipedian user, it is remarkable to note that the bots are by far the top users. The implication, which has been researched in the digital methods program, is that the bots and the alert software are the significant agents of vigilance.[54]

As the Wikiscanner project and the bots statistics remind us, Wikipedia is a compendium of network activities and events, each logged and made available as large data sets. Wikipedia also has in-built reflection or reflexivity, as it shows the process by which an entry has come into being, something missing from encyclopedias and most other *finished* work more generally. One could study the process by which an entry matures; the materials are largely the revision history of an entry, but also its discussion page, perhaps its dispute history, its lockdowns and reopenings. Another approach to utilizing the data of Wikipedia would rely on the edit logs of one or more entries, and repurpose the Wikiscanner's technical insights by looking up where they have been made. "The places of edits" show subject matter concerns and expertise by organization and by country.

The End of the Virtual: Grounding Claims Online

My aim is to set into motion a transformation in how and why one performs research with the Internet. The first step is to move the discussion away from the limitations of the virtual (how much culture and society are online) to the limitations of current method (how to study culture and society, and ground findings with the Internet).

I would like to conclude with a brief discussion of these limitations in Internet research as well as a proposal for renewal. I would point out first that the end of cyberspace and its placelessness, the end of the virtual as a realm apart, is lamentable—for particular research approaches and projects. In a sense the real/virtual divide served specific research practices.[55] Previously I mentioned that Internet archiving thrived in cyberspace, and more recently it suffers without it. Where cyberspace once enabled the idea of massive website archiving, the grounded web and the national webs are shrinking the collections.

Indeed, I would argue that one may learn from the methods employed in the medium, moving the discussion of medium-specific theory from ontology (properties and features) to epistemology (method). The Internet, and the web more specifically, have their ontological objects, such as the link and the tag. Web epistemology, among other things, is the study of how these natively digital objects are handled by devices.

The insights from such a study lead to important methodological distinctions, as well as insights about the purpose of Internet research. Where the methodological distinction is concerned, one may view current Internet methods as either those that follow the medium (and the dominant techniques employed in authoring and ordering information, knowledge, and sociality) or those that remediate or digitize existing method. The difference in method may have significant outcomes. One reason for the fallowing of the web archiving efforts may lie in the choice of a digitized method (editorial selection) over a digital one (registrational data collection), such as that employed in the original Internet Archive project, where sites surfed by users were recorded. Indeed, I have employed the term "digital methods" so that researchers may consider the value and the outcomes of one approach over another. As a case in point, the choice of dynamic URL sampling rather than the editorial model could be beneficial to Internet censorship research, as I discussed.

Third, and finally, I would argue that the Internet is a site of research for far more than online culture and its users. With the end of the virtual/real divide, however useful, the Internet may be rethought as a source of data about society and culture. Collecting it and analyzing it for social and cultural research requires not only a new outlook about the Internet but new methods, too, to ground the findings. Grounding claims in the online is a major shift in the purpose of Internet research, in the sense that one is not so much researching the Internet, and its users, as studying culture and society *with the Internet*.

2 The Link and the Politics of Web Space

This chapter concerns efforts to see politics in web space. Here I briefly periodize understandings of web space, and the distinctive types of politics associated with their mappings, broadly conceived. In the web-as-hyperspace period, when random site generators invited surfers to jump from site to site, mapping was performed for sites' backlinks. It tethered websites to one another, showing distinctive "politics of association" from the linking behaviors of government, nongovernmental organizations, and corporations. In the web-as-public-sphere or neopluralist period, circle maps served as virtual roundtables. What if the web were to decide who should be at the table? As ideas about the web shifted from new public spheres to a set of social networks, the cluster maps displayed "issue spaces," clusters of actors engaged in the same issue area, but now either central or marginal. Finally, in what I dub the revenge of geography, in the current locative period, maps show the distributed geography of engagement. Networking actors are temporarily "based" and traveling physically from event to event; do they remember what is happening on the ground? This chapter treats the shift in focus away from the "metaphysics" of *software-enabled* spaces (the "virtual" spheres) and critiques of the new "grounds" (mobile network) toward the return of classic questions now that cyberspace has been grounded.

The Death of Cyberspace

The symbolic end of cyberspace may be located in the lawsuit against Yahoo! in May 2000, brought before the Tribunal de Grande Instance de Paris by two French nongovernmental organizations, the French Union of Jewish Students and the League Against Racism and Anti-Semitism. The suit ultimately led to the ruling in November 2000 that called for software to block Yahoo!'s Nazi memorabilia pages from web users located in France.[1] Web software now routinely knows a user's geographical location, and acts upon the knowledge. You are reminded of the geographical awareness of the web when in France you type into the browser "google.com" and are redirected to google.fr. While it may be viewed as a practical and commercial effort to connect users with languages and local advertisements, the search engine's IP-to-geolocation handling also may be described as the software-enabled demise of cyberspace as placeless space. With location-aware web devices (e.g., search engines), cyberspace becomes less an experience in displacement than one of re-placement—you are sent home by default.

The announcement of the death of cyberspace through the revenge of geography, which virtual ethnographers also have sounded, has consequences for any theorizing of the history of web space.[2] The web's location awareness could be described as a redrawing not only of space online but of its cybergeographic study.[3] The online "realm," once routinely thought of and mapped as placeless, now foregrounds location, spelling an end, in a sense, to cybergeography as topological approach to online shape- and space-making, as I argue. In the following I periodize or at least distinguish chronologically between a number of overlapping conceptions of space online over the past 15 to 20 years. Prior to the grounding of the web for the search engine user according to a geography of location, or what one may call the current locative period, the Internet offered shapes, or space arrangements, that were not based on the coordinates of a locality. From hyperspace in the early 1990s to spheres in the early 2000s and later to networks, these space arrangements, or topologies, draw upon diverse sources for their conception as well as the work they do. The hyperspace button in an Atari game, Habermas's public sphere theory, and social network analysis have served to conceive of space, navigate it, as well as map it, however disparately. Indeed, as has been pointed out, the mapping of the web for the user is perhaps less concerned with the territory (however cyber-) than with navigation.[4] Consider the names of the browsers from the 1990s and early 2000s: Netscape Navigator, Microsoft's Internet Explorer, and Apple's Safari, all inviting navigation of the sea, space, or jungle of information. More recently, in keeping with the demise of cyberspace, these cybergeographical devices have given way to browsers (or browser names) less concerned with navigating per se, such as Mozilla's Firefox and Google's Chrome.

Mapping space online, however, is not merely a matter of conceiving of cyberspace as space, and navigating through it. The mappings also reflect ways of seeing politics online, and enable their study by new media. The analysis that follows is concerned with the kinds of politics sought online, both in the shapes that have provided space for the politics but also in their mappings, whether manual, semiautomated, or automated. Making a link to associate with the like-minded, joining a web ring (of interlinked sites), or setting up a crawler and graph visualization machine to show the size of the interlinked movement or issue network all do and map politics (without relying on coordinates and location).

I would like to point out first that certain projects (prior to the current locative period) have deployed the coordinates of the geographical map. The Internet's basic root server infrastructure as well as traffic flows through it have been points and lines respectively on Mercator maps. The maps may be made to show politics. For example, Internet traffic maps may be made to display political economies of network engineering. Traffic is routed by peering arrangements that are often more economic than efficient. Run trace routes between Amsterdam and Zimbabwe and note that the packets travel via the United States, instead of in a more direct line from north to south. In another example of political geography online, notice the locations of the thirteen root servers. A root server location map would show north-south divides, and the control of the Internet by the United States and its allies. They "rule the root."[5] Digital divide cartograms show countries resized according to percentages of the population online (figure 2.1). Another digital divide cartogram has country sizes inverted to show what the world would look like if it were mapped not in the progressivist *Wired* style, where worldwide connectivity and usage only appear to expand, but rather in its inverse (figure 2.2). The disconnected world map is a world upside-down, if you will, with countries sized according to nonusage. In a sense the geographical mappings that see politics online are less significant than the politics seen by (linking) association, however that tie is defined. Indeed the focus of this chapter lies in the mappings that show politics in the noninfrastructural Internet and particularly the web: what could be called political web topology. The chapter draws on a study of the politics of web space that I made in parallel to developing a series of political web-mapping devices that form the Issue Crawler project.[6] Instead of placing the Issue Crawler project in the foreground, here I would like to describe, periodize, and critique the ideas that have informed the theorizing of the politics of web space behind the project.

Starry Nights: Tethering Individual Websites to Each Other (by Inlinks) in the Hyperspace Period

Generally, thinking in terms of the web as a universe (to be charted) coincided with early ideas of the web as a hyperspace, where one would *jump* from one site to another at some great, unknown distance. With starry night site backdrops in abundance, the early web looked as if it would "[bring] us into new dimensions."[7] The popularity of random site lists, or generators, is another case in point. They found their best-known expression in Google's "I'm Feeling Lucky" feature, built into the first online version of the engine in 1998. It arguably played upon the famed hyperspace button from the Asteroids arcade game by Atari. "Randomness" as a selection or recommendation mechanism is still in evidence, as with the "Next Blog" button on blogspot.com sites. That current web applications occasionally still build in a jump-to-unknown-site feature, which also could be interpreted in the Blogger case as a variation on an early web ring, shows that vintage ideas about how one may wish to navigate web space remain.

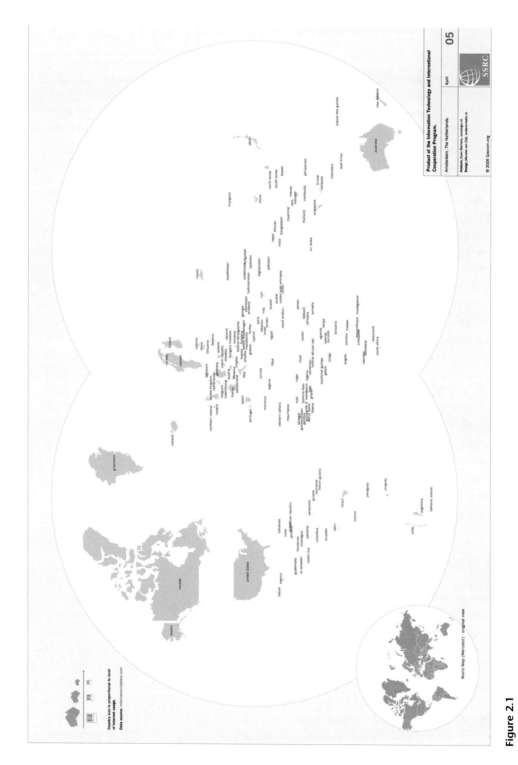

Figure 2.1

Digital divide cartogram, WSIS Tunisia Series, Govcom.org, 2005. © Govcom.org Foundation, Amsterdam, 2005.

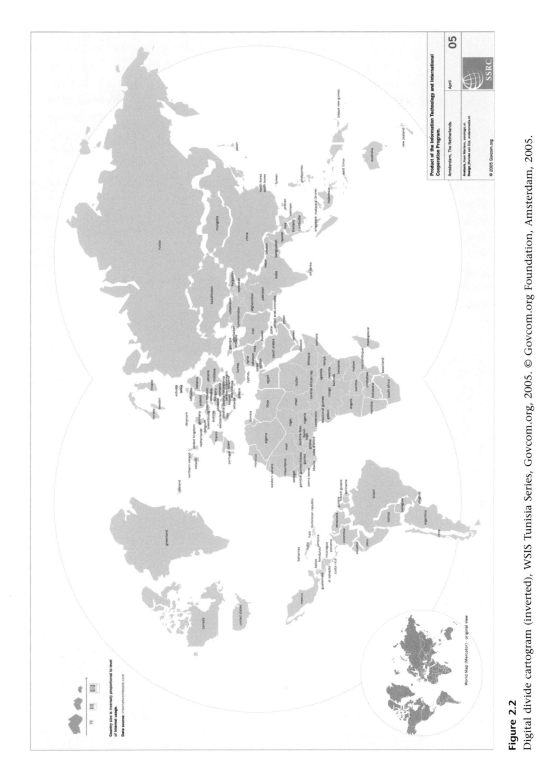

Figure 2.2
Digital divide cartogram (inverted), WSIS Tunisia Series, Govcom.org, 2005. © Govcom.org Foundation, Amsterdam, 2005.

Besides traffic and server location maps, the study of hyperlinks would come to root web space, at least initially, prior to the placement of sites in spaces and networks and to the grounding of users in geographical space. The important insight of the 1990s was that websites (or webmasters) hyperlink selectively as opposed to capriciously. There is a certain optionality in link-making. Making a link to another site, not making a link, or removing a link may be viewed, sociologically or politically, as acts of association, nonassociation, or disassociation, respectively. A Georgia Tech University study on World Wide Web use, published in 1999, found that hyperlinks are matters of organizational policy, especially for corporations and government.[8] Such a "professionalization" of hyperlinking, it may be observed, is to be seen in how domain types tend to link.[9] (See also figure 2.3.) For example, governments tend to link to other governmental sites only. Corporations tend to link only internally, to themselves. Industry alliances, business organization NGOs, or front groups do the web outreach work for corporations, providing "public interest" links.

With the randomness of linking yielding to purposiveness, "mapped" inlinks between *individual sites* became telling. The web could be made to show associations— links between sites professional, organizational, and cultural as meaningful ties. In this prenetwork mapping, individual sites were "evaluated," singly, for reputational purposes as well as for the associations they put on display. For example, in one of our first extended case studies, on genetically modified food, researchers and I pro-

Linking styles

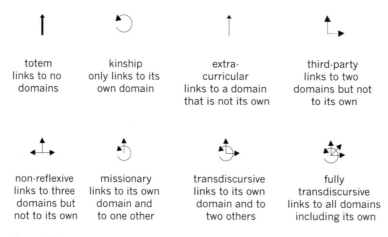

totem	kinship	extra-	third-party
links to no domains	only links to its own domain	curricular links to a domain that is not its own	links to two domains but not to its own

non-reflexive	missionary	transdiscursive	fully
links to three domains but not to its own	links to its own domain and to one other	links to its own domain and to two others	transdiscursive links to all domains including its own

Figure 2.3
Actor hyperlink language, Govcom.org, Design and Media Research Fellowship, Jan van Eyck Academy, Maastricht, 1999. © Govcom.org Foundation, Amsterdam, 1999.

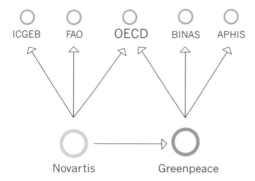

Figure 2.4
Aspirational linking in the GM Food Issue Space. Novartis links to Greenpeace. Greenpeace does not link back. Greenpeace and Novartis link to government. Government does not link back. Govcom.org, Design and Media Research Fellowship, Jan van Eyck Academy, Maastricht, 1999. © Govcom.org Foundation, Amsterdam, 1999.

vided actor profiles according to the *specific* links received and given between organizations and organization types (see figure 2.4). A poignant finding concerned the hyperlinking behavior of Novartis, Greenpeace, and a series of governmental organizations. Novartis linked to Greenpeace; Greenpeace did not link back. Both Novartis and Greenpeace linked to the governmental sites, and no governmental sites linked back to them. The particularities of relationships between three individual actors thus came into view. The work was expanded to look into linking between site types, and how linking may serve more generally as reputational marker for a site type. Three corporate sites were compared; the sites' respective standings differ according to the types of links received, and sites' respective displays of endorsement according to types of links given. One corporation has a different standing by virtue of receiving links from nongovernmental organizations and government, as opposed to from other corporations only (see figure 2.5).

In keeping with the view that not all links are equal, researchers have explored the delicate sociality and temporality of link-making.[10] In exploring what researchers and I called "hyperlink diplomacy," links were classified as cordial, critical, or aspirational.[11] Cordial links are the most common—to project partners, affiliates, and other friendly or respected information sources. Critical links, largely an NGO undertaking, have faded in practice, and aspirational links are made normally by smaller organizations to establishment actors, often by those desiring funding or affiliation. For example, the Soros Foundation, the philanthropic funding organization active among other areas in public health issues in Russia (in the late 1990s and beyond), received links from Russian HIV-AIDS actors and did not link back (see figure 2.6).

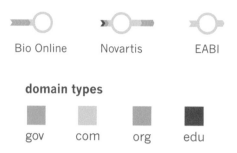

Figure 2.5
Actor reputational profiles by inlink and outlink types. Govcom.org, Design and Media Research
Fellowship, Jan van Eyck Academy, Maastricht, 1999. © Govcom.org Foundation, Amsterdam,
1999.

Crucially, these associations formed by hyperlinks came to be known as "spaces,"
e.g., the "hate space" on the web.[12] The demarcationist, space-making approach (with
space conceived as demarcated and shaped by limited acts of association) had another
important consequence. It performed an important break with cyberspace by suggesting that hyperlinking behaviors dismantle the "open-endedness" of cyberspace,
an idea that had informed "placelessness" and led to what one may call "placeless
space."

From the Politics of Surfer Pathways to the Authority of the List

How do hyperlink spaces showing associational politics differ from other conceptual-
izations of web space? What could be the shapes of the spaces demarcated by link
associations that inform thoughts about the politics of the web? To take up the first
question, in the late 1990s and early 2000s the leading visualizations that colleagues
and I discussed were Plumb Design's ThinkMap Visual Thesaurus as well as the I/O/D's
Web Stalker, followed shortly thereafter by TouchGraph's Google Browser as well as
Theyrule.net by Josh On.[13] All are nondirected graphs, without arrowheads, which is
to say that the items or nodes (synonyms, site pages, board members, and companies)
are associated (and lines are drawn between them) without specifying a uni- or bidirectional association. Undirected graphs, arguably, derive from a path model of the
web, also built into browsers (with the forward and backward arrows), and lead to
ideas about every link being a two-way link.[14] They also lead to ideas about the web
as "small world," where there are measurable distances between sites, described as
degrees of separation.[15] Link maps, thus, would be thought of as surfer pathway maps,
or pathfinders, and the politics in them concerned the distance between official and
nonofficial sites, or between the serious and the salacious.

Figure 2.6

Russian HIV-AIDS virtual roundtable construct. Hyperlink analysis with the Netlocator software, forerunner to the Issue Crawler. Govcom.org, Design and Media Research Fellowship, Jan van Eyck Academy, Maastricht, 2000. © Govcom.org Foundation, Amsterdam, 2000.

Seeing the web in terms of paths is not far-fetched, since one may surf from page to page and use the browser buttons, or the browser history, to retrace one's steps and also move forward again. Two-way links, it may be observed, are less frequent than one-way links; but whichever ways the links were directed, writers found politics in pathways. Viewing any hyperlink as a bidirectional association, we learned at the time, could mean for example that a German ministerial site was accused of "being linked" to a call boy network.[16] The Bundesministerium für Familie, Senioren, Frauen und Jugend hyperlinked to a women's issues information site, and that site linked to a call boy network. To the popular German newspaper *Bild Zeitung*, this web path implicated government. Indeed, it is precisely the perceived political implications of surfer pathways that lead governmental and other sites to place a disclaimer on external links. To government, the surfer should be informed that she is leaving a site, and the outlink that enables the departure should not be considered an endorsement.

From the point of view of dominant device algorithms, outlinks are endorsements rather than stepping stones in a path. Even more strikingly, outlinks are seen, collectively, as website authority measures. Thus, much of the work that would order the web (the Yahoo! Directory and its counterparts such as the Open Directory Project, as well as Google and the other major engines that picked up on its PageRank method) parted ways with the great pioneers of hypertext (and hyperlinks) and the random site generators, who viewed the web as pathway space for the surfer to author a journey, a story, or an adventure.[17] With directories and engines, the web became a space of expert and device-authored lists, where the politics of "making the list" became the concern. In the case of search engines, the lists are generated on the basis of hyperlinks between sites, and ranked according to the sites with the most (authoritative) links in.[18] For engines, the question reads, Which sites are toward the top and liable to be seen and clicked, and which are buried? For directories, the question became, Why are particular sites not listed in a given category? By asking these questions, researchers took up the politics of inclusion and exclusion. They left behind the storytelling, pathway web from hypertext and literary theory, and entered the study of information politics.[19] The politics of search engines (and, less so, of directories) became a dominant line of inquiry.[20]

As links increasingly ordered the web, leading to questions of directory- and device-authored source reputation and inclusion toward the top, it is important to recall how one was able to find the links in the first place, in order to read between them and eventually map sets of them. In the late 1990s, links into sites, referred to as "inlinks" or "backlinks," were not clearly visible. A site's outlinks, of course, most readily in the form of one or more link or resources lists, are viewable to a site visitor. To gain a sense of a site's inlinks, however, requires the use of the advanced search of an engine, access to the referrer logs of a site, or a crawler. Engines that encouraged Boolean queries, like Alta Vista's advanced search of old, enabled sophis-ticated inlink research.[21] For example, one could query the domain-specific inlinks to a particular site, and manually create the organizational profiles discussed above. A site's log files, once considered a promising avenue of Internet studies research, are now routinely out of public view.[22] The trick of adding "/stats" to the end of a host name, and subsequently harvesting one or more sites' log files, including the referrers (showing traffic from inlinks), is no longer workable. Most content manage-ment systems have public viewing of site statistics turned off by default. Researchers may turn to marketing company databases, like Neilsen's BuzzMetrics, or to Alexa's related site feature. "Deep log analysis" generally requires permission from site owners and is fruitful for single-site analysis, or the comparison of a limited number of sites.[23]

Until the creation of "trackback," a feature implemented in the Movable Type blog-ging software in 2002 that shows the links into a posting, inlinks in the late 1990s and early 2000s were not an everyday research concern. Apart from network science researchers and algorithm makers, only the occasional political web researchers with specially constructed crawlers made use of them. Inlinks were found by crawling sets of sites. As in scientometrics, one site's links out (the references) are another set of sites' links in (the citations). Large populations of crawled sites in a particular topic or issue area, as in the work on the Zapatista case and in other information science efforts with affinities to a social science approach to the study of hyperlinks, yielded network maps, discussed below.[24]

More recently, on the web and especially in the blogosphere and in online news, devices recommend pages routinely by counting inlinks, e.g., "most blogged" stories at the *New York Times* and the *Washington Post*. They also count most emailed stories and most searched for (and found) stories, providing further types of authority mea-sures and privileging mechanisms. Breaking with the web as cyberspace and leaving behind politico-geographical mappae mundi of charted and uncharted (dark) webs, concern with inlinks as a marker of page relevance marked a major shift in the under-pinnings of web space.[25] (See figures 2.7 and 2.8.)

For information retrieval, counting inlinks addressed the site authority problem. To those more concerned with the politics of web space, counting inlinks, and espe-cially how they are counted, raised questions beyond inclusion and exclusion in search engine returns.[26] To take up the first point, in the mid-nineties the foremost issue concerning search engine developers had related to how to separate the "real name" from the borrowers of the name, e.g., to return Harvard University at the top of the list when Harvard is queried, and not a deli or a health clinic with the same name. In leading search engine results (such as AltaVista's), the "eminent scientist and the isolated crackpot [stood] side by side," as one leading author put it more generally about search results spaces.[27] In their ranking logics, AltaVista granted site owners the

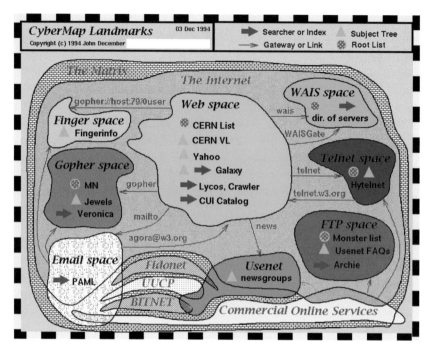

Figure 2.7
CyberMap Landmarks. © John December 1994. Reproduced with permission.

authority to describe the content of their sites (in metatags), and their descriptions became the basis for the engine returns. The web became a space displaying "side-by-side-ness," fitting with contemporaneous ideas about its pluralizing potential.[28] Institutional hierarchies of credibility were challenged; noninstitutional actors found their place toward the top of engine returns.

Google, conversely, granted other sites that authority (hyperlinks and link pointer text). Counting inlinks and having other sites grant authority through linking (and naming their links well) form the basis for most search engine algorithms these days, including Yahoo!'s as well as Microsoft's. Once a major competitor to automated search engines, the directory has declined. The demise of the directory can be viewed (at archive.org's Wayback Machine) by noticing how it has been placed deeper and deeper in Google's search hierarchy—from front page tab to two and now three clicks away, if it can be found at all by clicking. The politics of search engine tabs here lies in setting the work of web librarians in relative darkness. Even Yahoo!'s much-heralded web "library science" of the 1990s, the Yahoo! directory, is no longer its default engine. Thus web space, if conceived as ordered by engines, is no longer expert-vetted. (It is problematic, however, to think of web space ordered by engines as unvetted at

Figure 2.8
Cyberspace. DiploFoundation, 2003. © DiploFoundation, 2003. Reproduced with permission from DiploFoundation, www.diplomacy.edu.

all. Engine companies hire "optimizers" [often a student job] to check results per query. They back-check samples of query results to determine whether they match expectations.)

Search Engine Space and the New Politics of the Sphere

The "sphere" from public sphere theory has reverberated for some time in thoughts about web space.[29] The blogger who coined, or recoined, the term "blogosphere" had in mind rational argument among bloggers.[30] Prior to the growth of networks of the like-minded, and the neotribal school of thought for interpreting web "spaces," the idea of the sphere rested on the web as "great conversation."[31] Mapping conversations (for example, in Usenet) coincided with assumptions of the neopluralist potential, the rich content of public debate online, and the deliberative democratic spirit.[32]

Conceptions of web space, and of how it is ordered, now must take into account how engines are demarcating spheres, and how site owners must cooperate with engines to be well included in a sphere. "Web sphere" analysis, initially, did not refer to search engine space, but rather to a meticulous collection of thematically related sites for further analysis.[33] Nowadays, spheres are increasingly coconstructed by engine algorithms and site owner behavior. Using Google Web Search to look for recent news items, or for recent blog postings, has become inadvisable. The web has separate spheres.

Of course when site owners link improperly, the engines no longer work, if by working is meant the maintenance of real-name (official) results returned from real-name queries.[34] "Miserable failure" is not supposed to place the White House page for George W. Bush's political biography at the top of engine returns, as it did in Google between October 2003 and January 2007. Google-bombing and other forms of lack of cooperation revealed how Google and other PageRank-like algorithms would *like* site owners to link. Engine considerations of proper site owner as well as user behavior have consequences for thinking about the politics of web space. The implications go beyond the study of how Google fixes its engine, and what that may mean generally for the critique of any organic search engine returns, as the nonadvertising search engine results are called in the industry (Cohen, 2007).

Rather, the consequences of site owner and user behavior have to do with the multiplication of web spaces. As a case in point, commentators in the blogosphere (those leaving comments on postings) do not tend to name their links in a fashion ultimately digestible for the ranking algorithms of the dominant engines.[35] Comment links are routinely not counted by search engines, meaning that there is a hierarchy in what counts as a link. When a web search engine is unable to handle site owner and user manners in a new space (in this case, comments in blog postings), the web becomes a series of subspaces. The web sphere, the blogosphere, the news sphere, even the tagosphere (folksonomic spaces) are each searched separately—web search, blog search, news search, social bookmark search. Each sphere engine also has different source-privileging mechanisms, with different combinations of authority and freshness. The study of the politics of web space becomes cross-spherical. How does a source fare for the same query across each sphere? Questions arise of new media effects that go hand in hand with the web's neopluralist potential from public sphere theory. Is one more knowledgeable, or exposed to more points of view, when primarily searching and reading in the web sphere, the news sphere, the blogosphere, or the folksonomic tagosphere?

Apart from the observations made above about the hierarchies of sites found in inlink counts and in search engine returns, now across spheres, the idea of the perceived equality of sources continues to politicize web space. Concern with the underrepresentation or absence of a large portion of sources has its roots in research into the dark or hidden web.[36] Such thoughts about underrepresentation are reflected in the French viewpoints in the literature as well as in the Google counterproject, Quaero.[37] The idea of a Google counterproject is fueled not so much by the urge for a public spirit to counteract the commercial as by U.S. source dominance. In google.com and the other currently dominant search engines, at last count no single French site is in the top 50, according to PageRank.[38] Of course the French would not use google.com but google.fr, which itself is of interest to scholars of media concentration. In country after country the national engines (e.g., exalead.fr) have small market shares compared to Google. In France Google commands approximately 90%, in the Netherlands over 95%.[39] National webs, if understood as those organized by national engines, have grown darker. Thus while Google may wish to organize the world's information (as its slogan goes), it is increasingly organizing at least major countries' and major language spaces'.

Network Mapping and Multiple Site Analysis

That the web would come to be thought of in terms of a network space, as opposed, for example, to a virtual space, initially required a change in understanding about the reality it has on offer. Indeed, when network mapping, it is important to point out that the analysts' focus is on the real. Information from the web no longer is from the virtual or deserving of a special status, having been tainted by virtue of self-publication, or stricken by rumor and the conspiratorial. Web network analysts strive to leave behind the idea of mere representation of a world apart.[40]

Additionally, unlike traffic and click analysis with log files, the work relies not on single- but on discrete or massive multiple-site analysis. Why map multiple sites as networks, and which politics are shown? There are largely two kinds of political network mapping that make use of multiple-site analysis, the social and the issue-professional. In the more popular "social" way of thinking, network mapping on the web has as its goal to make the covert visible, to reveal the deep structure of relationships, to dig for ties and, often, dirt.[41] A search engine query resulted in the newspaper headline: "UN weapons inspector is leader of S&M sex ring."[42] There is a brand of web political work devoted to "outing" and scandalizing, which could be described as a light form of infowar. Put differently, understandings of the web as space that could show a social network, together with the return of the informality of the web (particularly through the blogosphere and more recently social software), have given rise to an investigative outlook. The impulse relates not only to projects to reveal old boys' networks (strong ties with consequences) but also to the web's street proximity, its closeness to the ground, including the "fact-checking," evidential spirit of the political blogosphere. Digging up information, data-mining, and checking up are forms of digital trace mapping.

The work colleagues and I have done in network mapping sought to make a distinction from persistent social network ideas, and instead show public displays of connections. It is important to emphasize the web's capacity to display configured, professional and publicized political culture. Such work also leaves behind the hopeful sphere or deliberative approach, discussed above. Social theorist Noortje Marres prefaces her PhD dissertation with the following remark: "When we [took] to the web to study public debates on controversial science and technology, we [found] issue networks instead."[43] Notions of the web as debate space, as great conversation, as virtual roundtable did not fit with the empirical findings. Even when researchers and I endeavored to *make* the web into a debate space, by harvesting text from organizations' specific, issue-related deep pages, we found only statement juxtapositions—comments by organizations on a particular statement, but scant interorganizational exchange (see figures 2.9 and 2.10). Organizations would release views on an issue on their websites, but forums and other dialog spaces were not used by what could be construed as the parties to a debate. The web could not stand in for a building—or an event where debating parties could gather. The alleged deliberative, conversational, and nonhierarchical spirit of the web could not be found.[44]

With the demise of commitments to deliberative approaches to understanding web-political spaces came an appreciation for forms of network politics, especially those that could be seen as configurations of transnational, highly mobile actors, who are, in a sense, based in networks.[45] Especially global issues may have typical discursive homes, as at (recurring) conferences, summits, and other gatherings. Web mapping became a means to pin down actor mobility in networks, and also to ask questions about commitment and attention span. (See figure 2.11.) As a part of the circulation of people, things, and information, do networked actors move from issue to issue (or do issues move from network to network)? Previous social movement research had raised the idea of a free-floating movement potential, in the sense of a given collection of publics able to form a movement, with particular conditions.[46] Movements, on this view, are not spontaneous uprisings, as in the notion of a smart mob, but more an infrastructural phenomenon.[47] Are networks simply there, like websites under construction, waiting for political content? In a recent case study over an 18-month period on the media justice network in the United States, a core and durable network of approximately 20 media justice actors more than doubled its size when funding was announced.[48] More critically, the notion of actors being based in networks, as opposed to institutions or other rooted settings, raises the question of whether they remember what is happening on the ground. The challenges in the political network mapping of web space currently concerns how the maps of where issues are based (networks) stand in for what is happening not so much offline (as implicit in the real/virtual debate of old) as off-network.

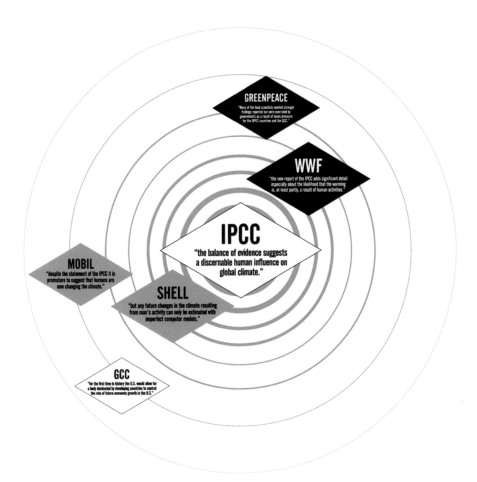

Figure 2.9
Key statement in context map. Discursive affinities (or nonaffinities) between organizations in the use of the Intergovernmental Panel on Climate Change's finding: "The balance of evidence suggests a discernible human influence on global climate." Graphic by Noortje Marres, Richard Rogers, and Noel Douglas, 1998. © the authors, 1998.

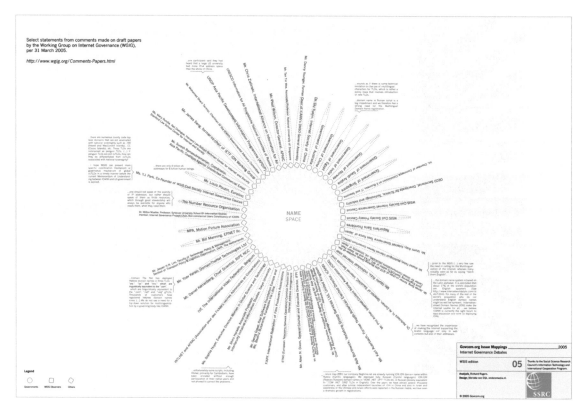

Figure 2.10
Internet governance debates (in the form of statement juxtapositions): Name Space, WSIS Tunisia
Series, Govcom.org, 2005. © Govcom.org Foundation, Amsterdam, 2005.

Conclusion: Questions for the Study of the Politics of Recent Web Space

One could consider the web a network space to be mapped by software. The (mapped)
spatializations I refer to, however, are not ones that are autogenerated by software or
given by algorithm or physics, at least not all of them. Rather, each redoes network
space in ways that are often different from the infrastructural network models that
preceded them, namely the centralized, decentralized, and distributed networks of
communications theorist Paul Baran in the early 1960s, or the chain, star, and all-
channel networks of the security studies scholars John Arquilla and David Ronfeldt
in the 1990s.[49] Each spatialization also reconfigures the network as spaces to do work
that is more than communication flow (maintaining it robustly) or command and
operations (keeping up the fight). Indeed, I am describing the web historically as a set
of political spaces in the making. They are in the making both in their political poten-

Figure 2.11
Where an issue is based: Issue Crawler results plotted to the Issuegeographer, 2005. © Govcom. org Foundation, Amsterdam, 2005.

tial (great conversation, etc.) as well as in their mapping (virtual roundtable, etc.). They have relied not only on the physics of the network map but also on the metaphysics of the nongeometrical sphere.

The purpose of the analysis has also been to periodize these conceptions of web space. During the first period, that of hyperspace, a time that predated search engines, links on websites propelled so-called cybernauts into other dimensions by virtue of random links or later offerings called "Next Blog," a feature still present on blogspot. com sites. With the first mappae mundi of cyberspace, in the cybergeographical turn of the mid to late 1990s, the network gained more contours, with multiple borders inside it, as well as inhabitants (cyberians). It was no longer primarily depicted as matrices and corridors but as territories and islands, including topical ones, with a melding of tree maps and coastal drawings. Autospatialization occurred when network mapping software entered web space, initially with a search engine that performed a kind of network scientometrics. Google's ascendancy could be viewed as a triumph of network science over other approaches in information and library science embodied by Yahoo!'s directory (for example), but the introduction of the graph also interfered with the plotting of circle maps and the virtual roundtable construct. The information equality associated with alphabetical listings, and the egalitarianism of the activists' circle and the NGOs' roundtable, became entangled in link networks and so-called power laws. Here one could think of the artwork by Tomás Saraceno, the sphere enmeshed in the network, shown at the Venice Biennale in 2009, as capturing a specific historical moment in web network topology prior to the geoweb or locative period.[50] The network's more recent locative turn, in the mid-2000s, saw the end of both cyberspace and the virtual as a political space competing for *status aparte*. With cyberspace all but grounded, efforts at retaining its sovereignty were pushed offshore to data haven undertakings, such as Metahaven's *Sealand* project.[51]

The current locative period has seen methods built into tools for outing and scandalizing. It also has seen the return of questions about equality and demographic concentrations in web space. For example, the Wikiscanner, which through IP-to-geo lookups outs the editors of Wikipedia pages, prompted a royal scandal in the Netherlands,[52] when the *NRC Handelsblad* newspaper reported having discovered that a computer at the royal family's home had anonymously edited and embellished a Wikipedia article about itself. (The case concerned the scandal in 2003 in which a Dutch prince renounced his claim to the throne because his princess had provided "incomplete and false" information about her relationship with a drug lord. The "royal edit" on the Wikipedia page removed the word "false.") In another example of the return of well-known politics, online communities have had the tendency to be geographically concentrated and located on a single site, as Hyves in the Netherlands, Facebook versus MySpace in the United States, Orkut for Brazil, Cyworld in South Korea, and Lunarstorm in Sweden. Studies point to the reinforcement of (middle-) class structures in the populations of users (new boys and girls networks) per social software platform per country.[53] Researchers also see a treasure trove of data in the profiles and linked friends be harvested from these spaces for social network analysis.

The question here no longer concerns media and analysts' projections of politics onto web spaces (great conversations, public spheres, deliberative debate, etc.) and how to historicize, empirically support, or debunk them. Rather, the web is increasingly grounded with geographical and linguistic specificity by platform and space. Indeed, how to approach the study of the subdivision of the web into separate spaces? Which politics are in view in which online space? (In order to address the study of separate spaces or spheres online, in chapter 5 I put forward a technique called cross-spherical analysis.)

The domestication of what was once cyberspace appears to bring us back to the classic questions and approaches (e.g., class structures in social media). Is the imaginative association between the Internet and new politics in decline? Generally, inquiries over the past decade into the politics of web space have shifted from the extent to which the online world provides new hierarchies to how they reflect and recreate them as part of social reality. As scholars continue to disaggregate the online (as search engines already have done in providing separate subengines by sphere), the concerns shift away from the study of Internet and politics in general to the politics of separate spaces.

3   The Website as Archived Object

That the web arrived as infrastructure awaiting content, as opposed to content await-ing infrastructure, is not often appreciated. In the early to mid-1990s websites were under construction and databases were yet to be populated. Sites generally needed filling in. (The same could be said these days of people's profiles on social media platforms, a subject of chapter 7. Often fields are empty.) The web's initial emptiness could account for the importance placed upon the precious "content providers," a phrase from the web's early period. As noted in the previous chapter, creative encour-agement for putting up content came in the form of homespun awards, an early form of website analysis. These were granted by self-appointed web editors to websites chosen for their quality (see figure 3.1). Once granted, the seal for the site of the week (or similar) typically would be affixed to the winning front page, with a link back to the originating awards page. At the awards page, a surfer could view other sites that had earned the same distinction. Awards gradually would be granted by category, such as the best education site award, technical site of the day, coolest science site, shiitake enlightened site, etc.[1] To bestow added distinction on them as they proliferated, awards might be given an imprimatur (*Exploratorium*'s ten cool sites or *Popular Science*'s best of the web) or provided with a provenance (the *original* cool site of the day award). Over time, collections of selected sites organized by category became formalized. There are annual awards granted in a ceremony by an "academy," modeled after those of film and TV, providing a seal, reciprocal linking, as well as an actual statuette (the Webby Awards).[2]

Apart from award-making, a second early practice of website adjudication and collection-making was the professional link list (Amnesty International's list of human rights groups, organized by topic and country, for example) and directory (Yahoo! and the Open Directory Project), together with particular methods of website collection-making (such as web archiving), which is the subject of this chapter. Carefully chosen link lists organized by category could be considered the first web guides, or web gazet-teers if one thinks in early cybergeographic (navigational) terms. In the mid-1990s one of the more important listings sites of its kind continually updated an index of

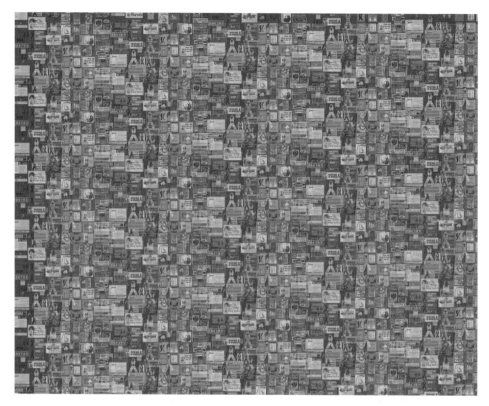

Figure 3.1
Homespun and professional web awards, mid to late 1990s. Collection by the author. © Anja Lutz, 2000. Reproduced with permission.

worthwhile destinations organized by content category. One would submit a URL with description to Yahoo! (originally "Jerry's Guide to the World Wide Web") to have it considered for placement in its directory. (Early search engines also accepted URL submissions; nowadays URL submissions made to Google are less likely for site inclusion than for site removal.)[3] Online editors browsed and sorted websites. Yahoo! as well as the Open Directory Project (formerly "NewHoo"), the volunteer-expert directory, undertook the immense editorial task of choosing, listing, and keeping unbroken the links to sites by category. At the same time Yahoo! Labs in particular could stake claim to having put into place a new content classification system for the web. To an "Internet cataloger" writing a well-known essay in 1998, Yahoo! was making a significant contribution to newfangled online library science, not only by its classification scheme but also by the means of content "navigation" it developed.[4] Yahoo!'s system differed from that of a library, where each book would be shelved by necessity in one location. At yahoo.com the resource could be placed in multiple categories, and linked to (and located from) each.

Soliciting, evaluating, and categorizing websites—not to mention developing navigation schemes to reach them—could be considered an original form of website analysis. As discussed in the next chapter, the rise of the algorithmic search engine has accompanied the demise of this activity: the large-scale collecting, hand-sorting, and display of websites.[5] Link list authors, Internet catalogers, directory makers, and all manner of human editors of the web have been crowded out by the search engine. Directories are ill-maintained, or overcommercialized through paid inclusion models; Amnesty International's link list of human-rights-related organizations is gone. Googlization, though it has many connotations, could be thought of in terms of the commanding position the search engine has assumed in contemporary website analysis. Before turning to that discussion (in chapter 4), I would like to step back and focus on one contribution to website analysis that is still editorial and undertaken at least partly by hand: web archiving.

The Archived Website and the Privileging of Content

In certain areas of web studies, the individual website is privileged over other web objects and spaces because that is where the "content" is. Besides the hyperlink, the search engine, the sphere, and the platform, the website is a fundamental organizing unit of the web. It could be considered what the film is to film studies, the television show to television studies. To take the analogy further, it is the television show (not the television listings) that tends to be saved, just as websites are archived, rather than the search engine results that once returned them,[6] the references contained in them (hyperlinks), the ecology in which they may or may not thrive (the sphere), and the pages or accounts contained therein that keep the user actively grooming his or her online profile and status (the platform).

Website archiving is the preserve of old media (if that term may still be used), in the sense of which elements are privileged. What is archived is the content, stripped of much else: to save its content, the web archivist usually must destroy much of the website, so to speak. The website is archived without the annotations and other gloss that is written onto it, attaches to it, is embedded in it, or surrounds it. Location-aware banner advertisements that are targeted to a particular marketplace normally may not be saved. The same may be said of the more dynamic "plugged-in" minimodules such as a social plug-in (Facebook) with lists of friends or Google adwords, both of which update in more of a cascading fashion than the rotation of a billboard banner. Usually, embedded video is not retained in the archived website, for like banners and adwords it is pulled in from another content provider. Surrounding entities such as cookies as well as interlacing (ad-serving or surveillance) "websites" are not captured.[7] One may view these complex relations as a website loads and ultimately resolves. There may be a series of URLs involved while a website loads, perhaps a tinyurl or bit.ly to begin, redirected to the destination URL, which triggers one or more adservers and the 1x1 pixel market research "web bugs," placing or reading cookies and counting impressions. A list of all the URLs that load for a single website is displayed in the browser's activity log.[8] These appendages to the website are not visible in the everyday browsing experience, and thus would require consideration of an archiving practice (capturing cookies, for example) that has a specific research focus (for instance, a website's advertising entanglements).

Of all natively digital objects, I mention web bugs and cookies not to be obscure but rather to point out that the question of where the website begins and ends—which is a classic one in web archiving discourses—is of a piece with the media theory and historiography that accompanies the practice of archiving, as I come to shortly. Generally speaking, the archived website ends nowadays with the content put up by the site author. In the archiving, that content is freed from the commercial support system (or political economy), second- and third-party material (intellectual property of others), as well as the social apparatus and the talkback (friends' recommendations and visitors' comments). In a sense, the "new media" elements (cookies, embedded material, recommendations, comments, etc.) are eliminated for posterity, and a traditional content container, looking somewhat broken for its missing pieces, remains as the "archived website." The ads, it should be pointed out, will be missed by media historians, who have studied their counterparts in print media such as magazines, with Lynn Spigel, for example, finding how the fireplace (and the piano) yielded to the television as a central object in the ideal domestic family setting.[9]

Surfing the Web as It Was

The web archiving scholar Niels Brügger has written: "Unlike other well-known media, the Internet does not simply exist in a form suited to being archived, but rather is first formed as an object of study in the archiving, and it is formed differently depending on who does the archiving, when, and for what purpose."[10] That the object of study is constructed by the means by which it is "tamed" and captured is a classic point from the sociology and philosophy of science and elsewhere.[11] Indeed, I would like to build upon the proposition that the web archive is to be studied in terms of how it has been made, and also how it is accessed, beginning with the first and still most significant one of its kind, the Internet Archive (archive.org), and its search interface, the Wayback Machine (waybackmachine.org).[12] Following Brügger, of importance here is how a web archive as an object, formed by the archiving process, embeds particular preferences for how it is used, and for the type of research to be performed with it. Which research practices are invited by the specific form assumed by the Internet Archive, and which are precluded?

When they use the Internet Archive (archive.org), what stands out for everyday web users accustomed to search engines is not so much the very existence of an archived Internet (which in itself is remarkable). Rather, the user is struck by how it is queried via the Wayback Machine. The search box contains an "http://" prompt; one enters a single URL, not keywords, into the search box, and what is returned is a list of stored pages associated with the URL from the past, either in a table with columns (in what is termed the classic version) or in a calendar mode (since December 2010). Next to a date, an asterisk indicates that the archived page is different from the one previously archived (in the classic version), which is important for researchers interested in capturing and studying website evolution, as an approach to the study of the website as archived object in a historiographical tradition akin to the biographical.

The Internet Archive came into being in 1996, and its interface and content navigation system, the Wayback Machine, in 2001. Archived websites had been available for viewing earlier through the Alexa toolbar, which indicated whether an archived version of a site was available when one came upon a 404 or "page not found" error. In other words, originally the Alexa toolbar, in tandem with the Internet Archive, was the solution to the broken link, and to interruption in surfing. Arguably the entire means of navigation of the Internet Archive in the Wayback Machine derives from a flow principle of continuous surfing from page to page. In keeping with the principle, it also preserves the Internet as a "cyberspace" which one navigates seamlessly. I would also argue that the Wayback Machine's construction furnishes an *experience* of web history, "surf[ing] the web as it was," as its motto reads, more than it provides a means to study it. Indeed, surfing is arguably a model of web use from the 1990s that has faded in practice, supplanted by search and perhaps by "wilfing," a British acronym for "what was I looking for" that also references ideas about the impact of the web and search engines on cognition more generally.[13] At the Internet Archive, preserving surfing is a manner of doing web history; in fact it also makes history in the sense that the surfing is sometimes smoother in the Wayback Machine than it was on the web, when links were often broken.

The Wayback Machine embraces continuous flow (click-through) over interruption and pages not found by what I would call "atemporal linking."[14] By this I mean that sites linked to one another in the Wayback Machine may not share the same "periodicity," a term for a bounded timeframe employed in scholarly web-archiving circles (e.g., the few months of a media attention cycle for a major disaster, or the campaigning season for elections).[15] In the event, radio buttons, animated gifs and starry night backgrounds may meet big buttons and tag clouds, all in the same surfer's path. Once the available pages of the queried URL are loaded, one may click through the pages returned, and on to other pages of other sites. When a user clicks a link, the page nearest to the date of the originating page is loaded; if there is no archived page available, the Wayback Machine will access the live web page instead. That is, the links from one site to another always "work."

Not every date for every site archived is 100% complete. When you are surfing an incomplete archived site the Wayback Machine will grab the closest available date to the one you are in for the links that are missing. In the event that we do not have the link archived at all, the Wayback Machine will look for the link on the live web and grab it if available.[16]

By loading pages closest in date to the ones surfed away from or by connecting to the live web, the Wayback Machine, with its atemporal linking, "jump-cuts" through time, thus providing the continuous flow of surfing and preserving the web as cyberspace (and improving upon the "old" cyberspace).

Website Biography as Historiographical Approach Embedded in the Wayback Machine

Besides presenting a particular history of the web, the Internet Archive (and particularly the Wayback Machine) also represent a specific historiography: the single-site history, or the site biography. In effect, the Internet Archive, through the interface of the Wayback Machine, has organized the story of the web, for the researcher, into the histories of single websites. With the current form assumed by the Wayback Machine, one can study the evolution of a single page (or multiple pages) over time, for example by collecting snapshots from the dates that a page has been indexed and playing them back like time-lapse photography. (The outcomes of such an approach are discussed briefly below.)

One also can go back in time to a page for evidentiary purposes, which appears to be a primary use according to the literature.[17] The Internet Archive has been used in the evidentiary arena in instances of intellectual-property or trademark infringement, as well as in practices such as cybersquatting and typosquatting. In patent cases, the claim of novelty may be harmed by prior art found online.[18] The archive also would aid in retrieving missing web citations in law as well as medical journals. (There is a literature describing the decay rate of links in recent journal articles, also known as accelerating link rot.)[19]

Outside of the evidentiary arena, what would comprise a website biography? One could peruse the public records for ownership (provenance research), beginning with the birth of the website and following its life as documented records, both from name authorities (ICANN) as well as from the records generated by the website itself (logs).

Sites have a history as a domain name, for each may have been sold and resold. They may have been poached or parked (purchased and never used). They also may have been hacked or vandalized, and those historical moments are not often recorded, unless the site is party to an infowar or other event that is recorded by cybersecurity researchers or hackers. URLs may have had websites that violated guidelines of search engines, or content policies of countries practicing Internet censorship, and been downgraded (in PageRank) or blacklisted, respectively. Of interest in this context is Constant Dullaart's hand-made collection of parked websites, with generic templates and content, awaiting owners; suggesteddomain.com is where his repository of parked sites loops.[20] Websites have histories in terms of visitation, which are logged, however fleetingly. Obtaining the log files for a site may be of interest to researchers desiring to know about the patterns of visitation; by default (in Webalyzer) hit and referral logs older than a year are often erased monthly, and a site owner may have only the past twelve months on file. Thus in the provenance research approach, sites come furnished with (historical "who was") records as well as (relatively short-lived) analytics data in the form of logs.

One could take a "layered" approach (in the sense of graphical or image editing software), akin to *web2DiZZaster* (2007) by the media artist sumoto.iki, who stripped web pages of their content so that only the underlying templates and formats remain (see figure 3.2). It is critical work in that sumoto.iki evacuated Web 2.0 sites of their user-generated content, revealing the sites' emptiness without "users like you."[21] More radically it shows the effects of the dying out of the bees (the "disaster" in the title of the work) in what has come to be known as the "worker bee economy" that is Web 2.0.[22] Other artistic research on the anatomy of a website is Hendrik-Jan Grievink's *Template Culture: Form Follows Format* (2009), an exhibition of well-known company sites reduced to their templates (see figure 3.3). Here one peels websites like proverbial onions, revealing the commonalities in form and structure, and in the critical mode an underlying sameness or blandness.

A related, albeit more social-scientific, approach to the manual study of the website is "feature analysis," in which one creates a codebook of all (or as many as possible) website features and checks a set of sites for their presence or absence, creating a features matrix.[23] Sites are scrutinized for the prominence or obscurity of features, too. Studies of eye tracking show that Western readers are attracted to the upper left portion of a website, so prominence may be thought of in terms of placement on the page; any features residing "below the fold" (beneath the browser window and reachable only by scrolling) are considered obscured. A web page's advertisement real estate provides a guide to placement and prominence analysis. Here one may compare traditional newspaper analysis (units such as headline size, column inches) to their counterparts online. The work required to do so is in the emerging field of web content analysis, a subject of chapter 8.[24]

Figure 3.2
Twitter stripped to template in the set *web2DiZZaster*, by sumoto.iki, 2007.

Once time is introduced to the above types of analysis (and others), the Wayback Machine becomes compelling for website biography. The practice of making a movie of a website, in the style of time-lapse photography, originates with Jon Udell's pioneering *Heavy Metal Umlaut*, which is the story of the evolution of a Wikipedia entry and likely one of the earliest "documentary screencasts."[25] It is instructive for its narrative, beginning as it does with the overall story of the growth and professionalization of a once amateurish encyclopedic entry (on a subcultural practice), and subsequently focusing on a few storylines, including the struggle to "typeset" the heavy metal umlaut online, and the vigilance of the article authors when page vandalism strikes. The movie was made by screen-capturing the history of the revision edits to the article (clicking through Wikipedia itself) and providing a voiceover track.[26] In the following, I relate (briefly) the making of a screencast documentary, not of a Wikipedia article, with its revision history conveniently stored by the wiki, but of a website, using the output of the Wayback Machine.

Google and the Politics of Tabs, the movie, is an alternative history to Google's own tenth-anniversary timeline.[27] As I noted earlier, it is the story of the demise of the Internet cataloguer and the human editors of the web, which can be dated to March 2004, when the once well-placed "directory" was removed from the front-page real estate at google.com. The movie also provides a method for using the output of the Wayback Machine (the google.com pages bearing an asterisk). In doing so it follows the dominant medium device (organizing the web into single-

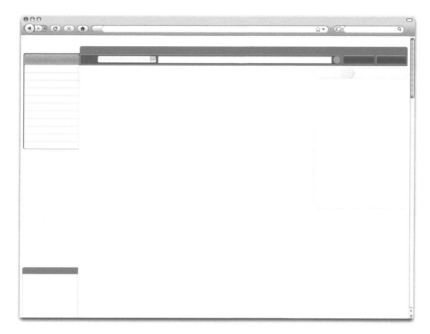

Figure 3.3
Amazon_Template_023 in the set *Template Culture: Form Follows Format*, by Hendrik-Jan Grievink, 2009. © Hendrik-Jan Grievink, 2009. Reproduced with permission.

site histories), and repurposes its output for social study (demise of the online librarian).

All the available and unique pages from http://www.google.com were captured from the Wayback Machine and made into a movie as well as an info-graphic.[28] The analysis focused on the area of the interface above the search box—the tabs—examining which search services (web, images, maps, news, etc.) have been privileged by Google over time on its front-page tabs, where further to the left is always the more preferred placement. It was found that the "directory," the human-edited project by the Open Directory Project (dmoz.org), enjoyed front-page status (third tab from the left) on Google from March 2000 until March 2004, when it was degraded and placed under the "More" button. By August of 2006 the directory had been moved from under the "More" button to under "Even more," and in May 2007 it was removed entirely from the menu of search services, which by that time had moved upper left on the Google front page. One had to search Google to find Google's directory, as the movie concludes. The history, or screencast documentary, provides a long view (a decade in web history) of the decline of the significance of Internet cataloguers and web librarians

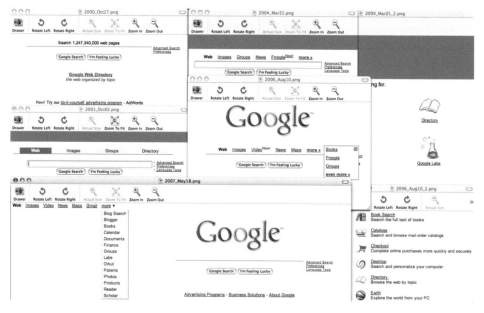

Figure 3.4
The demise of the directory: web librarian work gradually demoted in Google, 2000–2007. Screen shots of front page, and the contents behind the "More" and "Even more" buttons, at google.com, October 27, 2000, to May 18, 2007, showing significant changes to the placement of the Google web directory. Source: Wayback Machine at web.archive.org. (cc) Digital Methods Initiative, 2008.

generally, and the rise of web information organization by algorithm rather than by hand.

Apart from whois genealogies, anatomies, features analysis, and interface politics and epistemology, one may capture and interpret changes in substance on a website, that is, shifting priorities and commitments of the individual, group, organization, or institution that runs the site. Here it is not structures or features that are analyzed but rather the substance of the main menu—lists of issues, campaigns, missions, slogans, services, products, etc. that reside on the front page and organize the content of the website. For example, we have captured and loaded into a movie the historical home-pages of whitehouse.gov, concentrating in particular on the issue list, which is one of the substantive menu items. It is a study of the gradual appearance of the word "secu-rity" in the issue language used after 9/11, reaching its height one year later in Sep-tember 2002 when all issues on the White House agenda (as seen on whitehouse.gov) were security ones: "National security," "Homeland security," and "Economic security" (see table 3.1). All remaining issues were under placed under a "More" button, showing their demotion in standing at that time under the George W. Bush administration (2001–2009).

Table 3.1

Up and Down with "Security" as Prominent Issue Language at Whitehouse.gov, September 2001–September 2009: Main Menu Contents of "Policies in Focus," "In Focus," or "Issues" in the Left Column of the Front Page of the Whitehouse.gov Website

September 28, 2001	**September 29, 2006**	**October 2, 2008**
Education	Budget Management	Afghanistan
Tax Relief	Education	Africa
Defense	Energy	Budget Management
Social Security	Health Care	Defense
Medicare	Homeland Security	Economy
Faith-Based and Community	Hurricanes	Education
	Immigration	Energy
September 28, 2002	Jobs and Economy	Environment
National Security	Judicial Nominations	Global Diplomacy
Homeland Security	Medicare	Health Care
Economic Security	Middle East	Homeland Security
More Issues	National Security	Immigration
	Pandemic Flu	International Trade
October 1, 2003	Patriot Act	Iraq
Medicare	Renewal in Iraq	Judicial Nominations
Iraq	Social Security	Middle East
National Security	More Issues	National Security
Economic Security		Veterans
Homeland Security	**September 26, 2007**	More Issues
More Issues	Budget Management	
	Defense	**September 27, 2009**
September 28, 2004	Economy	Civil Rights
Economy	Education	Defense
Iraq	Energy	Disabilities
Education	Environment	Economy
National Security	Global Diplomacy	Education
Homeland Security	Gulf Coast	Energy and Environment
More Issues	Health Care	Ethics
	Homeland Security	Family
September 28, 2005	Immigration	Fiscal Responsibility
Hurricane Relief	Iraq	Foreign Policy
Homeland Security	Judicial Nominations	Health Care
Judicial Nominations	Medicare	Homeland Security
National Security	National Security	Immigration
Renewal in Iraq	Pandemic Flu	Poverty
Jobs and Economy	Patriot Act	Rural
Social Security	Veterans	Seniors and Social Security
More Issues	More Issues	Service
		Taxes
		Technology
		Urban Policy
		Veterans
		Women
		Additional Issues

In the opening chapter, I discussed the research practice of reading websites, which only menu substance analysis approximates in the discussion so far. The reference there was to the use of the Internet Archive by Dutch investigative journalists, who hand-picked over one hundred right-wing websites via the Wayback Machine and read the changes to their contents in the past ten years.[29] Their approach was word choice analysis: given a range of equivalents, was the term employed more or less harsh/extremist? They found that the right-wing sites gradually began to align in tone and sentiment with the right-wing extremist sites. Dutch society appeared to be "hardening" over the course of the years since the assassinations of Pim Fortuyn and Theo van Gogh, and that impression was made more solid by compiling a list of websites and manually analyzing them. As I mentioned at the outset, that the Internet could be used to ground a claim about a societal condition was not only surprising for those of us familiar with its study as cyberspace and cyberculture, and with ideas of virtual life as distinctive and separate, however much they have been contested empirically. The analysis that confirmed a shift in the language of the right wing toward extremism also led to the notion of "online groundedness"; one could ground claims through website analysis, and seek to apply them beyond the legal (evidentiary) arena. It is worthwhile to emphasize that the analysis was performed by making a list of websites—from the past. Indeed, one could think of it as a new kind of link list to the archive and imagine it as a web compilation or even a special collection, one entitled "Dutch right-wing and right-wing extremist sites, 1997–2007." As an analytical strategy, one would make a list of thematic or period websites *already archived* and provide a means of accessing, querying, and otherwise analyzing them—an approach to the website as archived object with which I will conclude. Before discussing results from analyses made through collections of previously archived websites, and especially from conjuring up a "past state of the web"—which is the specific contribution made here—I would like to consider the larger question of website special collections, a fledgling area with a manual approach to website analysis.

From Biographical to Event-Based and National Historiographies

The suggested citation for the collections of web archives at the Library of Congress (LOC), "Archived in the Library of Congress Web Archives," returned very few results in Google Scholar, Google Web Search, or Google Book Search, with the exception of pages from the LOC website itself and a smattering of other sites.[30] Virtually no one references the dozen special web archives as primary source material in their scholarly or nonscholarly publications, at least in the LOC's preferred style, according to the dominant search engine. The problem posed at the opening of this chapter from the early days of the web has been transformed; instead of websites

awaiting content, there is content now awaiting users, like books in libraries awaiting borrowers.

While the collections of archived websites are underreferenced and (presumably)
underutilized, the Internet Archive itself as well as its Wayback Machine are well-cited.
Queries for the "Wayback Machine" and the "Internet Archive" in the search engine
return copious results. The vast majority of the references are to information and
library science pieces about the methods and techniques of web archiving, including
(on occasion) to certain critiques of their biases toward Western sources and subject
matters—an observation made of Wikipedia, too.[31] Web archiving infrastructure
receives scholarly and nonscholarly attention; the archived materials—the primary
source material—gain less notice.

The question of the lack of "researcher engagement with web archives" has been
taken up by web archiving scholars, where one of the more poignant observations
concerned the kind of web to be archived in the first instance, and in future, so that
the materials would be used.[32] According to one observation, web archives may be
more attractive (to humanities scholars) if the websites they contained were made up
of digitized materials, e.g., websites with photographs, personal letters, and other
materials from World War II. In the event, websites containing primarily digitized
materials have been archived. Here history and web history become separate objects
of study. The web becomes a delivery mechanism for "old media"—albeit with vintage
html code enframing it.

As an approach to the selection of materials to be archived, saving websites containing digitized historical media has its practitioners. In the event, there is a "single-
site" collection at the Library of Congress web archives, one of the special collections
of web archives.[33] Saved in this collection are 23 individual websites, many of which
are themselves online archives of military history materials, making the special collection into a double container. These are website archives of digitized archival
materials.

Apart from the single-site set, the special collections of web archives at the Library
of Congress include ones (in alphabetical order) on the Crisis in Darfur, Sudan, 2006;
Indian General Elections 2009; Indonesian General Elections 2009; Iraq War 2003;
Papal Transition 2005; September 11, 2001; United States 107th Congress; 108th Congress; United States Election 2000; 2002; 2004; 2006; and 2008. At the Internet Archive
there are five additional ones, on the Asian Tsunami (2004–2005), U.S. governmental
sites at the end of G. W. Bush's term 2008–2009, Hurricanes Katrina and Rita (2005),
the U.K. national archives, as well as Web Pioneers, most of which were undertaken
by the Internet Archive without collaboration of the Library of Congress, and at the
time of writing appear somewhat abandoned, with 404 "page not found" errors when
loading the Asian Tsunami collection. Links to archives made so that links do not

break themselves are broken. Making website archives appears to be project-based as opposed to continuous. Activity ends in 2006, and picks up again with the 2009 web archives of the end-of-term U.S. governmental website collection as well as those from the Indian and Indonesian elections.

The U.K. national archives pointer links through to the more recent special collections at the U.K. governmental site, including Volcanic Ash Cloud (2010), U.K. National Budgets (March and June 2010), Financial Crisis (2008), Swine Influenza (2009), and the 2012 Olympic and Paralympic Games and Cultural Olympiad. If one were to characterize the special collections generally, they appear to embody a second historiographical approach to web archiving: event-based history. Indeed, to a leading handbook on web archiving, it has become an established pursuit to capture "events of importance, such as elections or disasters."[34] This historiographical commitment derives from the work of the pioneering webarchivist.org project by Steven Schneider and Kirsten Foot, who, together with collaborators, have created a series of special collections of websites, beginning with the 2000 U.S. elections.[35] "September 11, 2001," as the Library of Congress lists it, is perhaps the most well-known of the collections, and together with their efforts in archiving the 2002 U.S. elections and the Asian tsunami of late 2004, established the web archiving tradition of histories of elections and disasters.[36] Events arguably pose the greatest challenges for archivists, and at the same time also create the "archive fever" for the urgency of the undertaking, as content is continuously being lost to posterity through the combination of the ephemeral nature of web content generally and rapidly changing websites during events more specifically.[37] Without rapid steps taken, content is forever lost. In the case of the September 11 archive, the archivists were putting the necessary pieces together to archive the 2002 U.S. national election websites when the attacks on the World Trade Center struck. They were well positioned so as to begin the special practice of creating what they call a "web sphere," which is treated in multiple articles by the web archivist authors as well as a small circle of scholars engaged in the specialty area of web archiving. Foot and Schneider are remarkably consistent in their definition of a web sphere, which is also a method and research practice. In the original piece of scholarship, they write that "a web sphere [is] a hyperlinked set of dynamically defined digital resources spanning multiple web sites relevant to a central theme or 'object.' The boundaries . . . are delimited by a shared object-orientation and a temporal framework."[38] In the seminal as well as in successive articles, the research practice is also laid out.[39] The web sphere crucially is dynamic in two senses, for the archivists continually locate new websites (or web resources) to be included, and websites continually point to other websites (either new ones or previously unknown ones) which are relevant to the theme. The web sphere is bounded by the theme as well as by a temporal dimension ("periodicity"), which could be thought of as its coverage span or attention cycle (in traditional terms) in relation to the event. The actual research practice of collecting the websites could be characterized as a snowball method, updated for the web. Editors find URLs through searching and surfing the links between the thematically related websites; URLs are also recommended to them through crowd-sourcing (or less grandly termed means), and checked for inclusion. Websites are subsequently tagged or otherwise annotated so as to create metadata. In the subsequent work, they also may be categorized into site types and analyzed for features.

The radical nature of their approach to the selection of materials to be archived (the dynamically evolving collection) is to be appreciated when contrasted with a third archiving method and embedded historiography. In the list of U.S. and U.K. special collections above, one may also take note of the emergence of a normal archiving practice (in the Kuhnian sense of normal science), now applied to the web: the keeping of records for the purposes of national history.[40] Indeed, as the Internet Archive as well as special collection makers using the web sphere method cede their position as the major archivists of the web (in terms of sheer number of projects), national libraries are creating lists of websites to be saved. At the time of writing, the National Library of the Netherlands, for example, is regularly archiving 998 websites.[41] The actual quantity of websites archived, approximately 1,000, is a round number that opens questions of how to pick and hand-sort the websites to be kept for national history purposes, not to mention how many sites to keep. (The web sphere approach would result not in round but in squiggly numbers.)

To begin with, the criteria of what constitutes a Dutch website are of interest here, in order to appreciate why websites are still analyzed manually. Following similar definitions of a national website from archiving projects in other European countries, the National Library defines a website as Dutch if it meets certain tests. It is a Dutch website if it is:

(1) In the Dutch language, and registered in the Netherlands;
(2) In any language, and registered in the Netherlands;
(3) In the Dutch language, registered outside the Netherlands; or
(4) In any language, registered outside the Netherlands, with subject matter related to the Netherlands.[42]

There are national registrars of country domain names, so that each website registered in the Netherlands as .nl is known, in principle. There are libraries (in a software sense) for detecting automatically the language of a website, so one could differentiate for sorting purposes a site in Dutch and a site not in Dutch (that is, between the first and second criteria). Given a very large collection of websites (for example the Internet Archive's collection), one could detect Dutch-language sites outside of the .nl domain (the third criterion) and filter out Belgian (and Flemish) sites if they are .be.[43] To classify those remaining Dutch/Flemish-language sites (which are neither .nl nor .be)

would require a manual intervention. Indeed, that is where the automated identification and sorting would end. To identify for archiving purposes a website of any
language, registered outside of the Netherlands, with a subject matter related to the
Netherlands requires reading websites.

In the realm of web archiving, at least, the Internet cataloguers, web librarians, link
list builders, and other web editors have defined the Dutch website—their object of
archiving, in the sense of Brügger above—so as to necessitate a manual approach. The
web archiving handbook I referenced above recommends the formulation of a collection policy and a collection list (in the example of the Netherlands above, the definition of a Dutch website would be related to the collection policy of archiving the
Dutch web, and the 998 sites would be the selection or list).[44] The sites that are typically archived are governmental, national-cultural, and higher-education—a kind of
establishment, which leaves out not only the self-described challengers to the (media)
establishment such as bloggers but much distinctive web culture, including many of
the top sites in the Netherlands (by traffic), including Google, Facebook, YouTube,
LinkedIn, Wikipedia, Twitter, as well as Google.nl and Nu.nl, the Dutch news aggregator. That the top sites are not archivable or only partially so opens up the larger question of the limits of web archiving for web historical work.

One purpose of thinking through the consequences of manual practices of website
analysis concerns the kind of webs we are left with once archived, and the kind of
research we are able to perform with them, as I have discussed in historiographical
terms: single-site histories or biographies, event-based history, and national history.
When critiquing the practice of Dutch web archiving, as a scholar in the Netherlands, and particularly the actual results (998 websites archived out of 3.5 million
.nl sites and an unknown number of the other "Dutch" sites), I would like to recall
the nary-a-care archiving by the Internet Archive in the 1990s and early 2000s.[45] As
Brewster Kahle, the founder of the Internet Archive, put it in a 1996 *Wired* article:
"I usually work on projects from the you've-got-to-be-crazy stage," by which he
meant envisaging archiving the entire web, or as much of it as possible. As I argued
in the opening chapter, the end of cyberspace as virtual realm apart and the rise of
the institutional and regulatory frameworks for the Internet have not been kind to
web archiving. They also have "damaged" the Archive. To process the quantity of
requests to be removed from the Archive (and the Wayback Machine), the decision
was taken to interpret robots.txt, the robot or crawler exclusion code that may be
built into a website, to mean that the site prefers to be left out of the Internet
Archive altogether, even those pages that were previously in there prior to the placement of robots.txt, or prior to the current ownership of the website domain.[46] As I
noted above, there are more requests these days to have websites removed from
storage than for them to be included (as in the web directories, guides, and awards
pages of old).

Conjuring Up a Past State of the Web

In keeping with the overall digital methods principles, colleagues and I approached the Internet Archive by considering how to repurpose its ordering device (the Wayback Machine) for social research. As discussed, the first outcome followed the output of the Wayback Machine (lists of pages of a single site from the past). Site histories were captured by retaining only the pages with changes to them (the ones marked with asterisks) and loading them for playback in a movie. What could one learn from the history of a single website, apart from seeking evidence from it for legal proceedings? With the screencast documentary-making (or Wayback Machine movie-making), a time dimension is added to website analysis. It also makes explicit what the Wayback Machine implies, with its invitation to tell the history of a website and through it the history of the web—the life and times of Google as being the life and times of a decade of web history, in the example discussed. Website biographies now could stand beside the event-based histories of the special collections (which in the U.S. at least appear in need of reinvigoration) and the national histories of the national web records (as they continue to be built).

The second outcome of applying the digital methods principles to the Internet Archive and the Wayback Machine was to build a collection maker of already archived websites, as mentioned above (see figure 3.3). In a sense such a collection maker would be in keeping with a trend in web archiving toward providing tools for users to archive the web themselves (the Archive-IT project), instead of providing archives in search of users and researchers. The impetus was a desire to add another historiographical approach that also would be sensitive to the needs of web history. To the biographical, event-based, and national historiographies on offer to date, colleagues and I sought to offer a past state of the web, or a portion thereof, that could be reconstructed and studied.[47] The early blogosphere was chosen for its significance in web history, and the Eatonweb, one of the most complete blog directories of its day.[48] The Eatonweb was used to date the end of the early blogosphere: the day, or close to it, that Eaton could no longer keep up with his list of all blogs online, and thus when the blogosphere as sphere ceased to exist. In chapter 5 I treat the notion of the sphere in "blogosphere" as being held together by at least one link list, or core directory site, that links to all sites in it, so that in theory each site is equidistant from the core, in the classic geometrical form of the sphere. The last "complete" list of the blogosphere at Eatonweb (August 15, 2000) serves as the list of URLs for the nominal early blogosphere. Each URL is queried in the Wayback Machine, and the percentage of the early web that is archived is established (see figure 3.4). A remarkable 70% of the early blogosphere, as defined by Eaton, is available in the Internet Archive; a small percentage of websites could be added to that figure, if robots.txt code were removed from certain sites that were once significant in the early blogosphere. These sites are still online

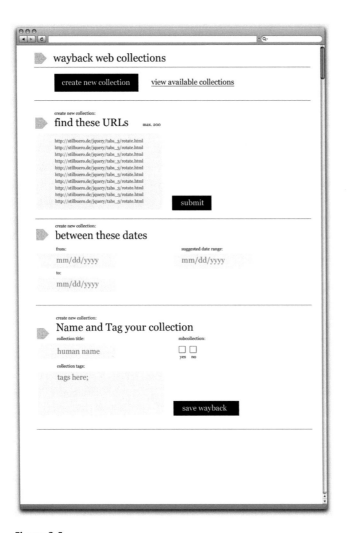

Figure 3.5
Mockup of website collection maker to make a collection of already archived websites from archive.org. (cc) Digital Methods Initiative, Amsterdam, 2009.

Figure 3.6
The archived and unarchived early blogosphere. Depiction of the portion of the blogs listed on Eatonweb, August 15, 2000, archived as well as missing from the archive (in the middle). (cc) Digital Methods Initiative, Amsterdam, 2009.

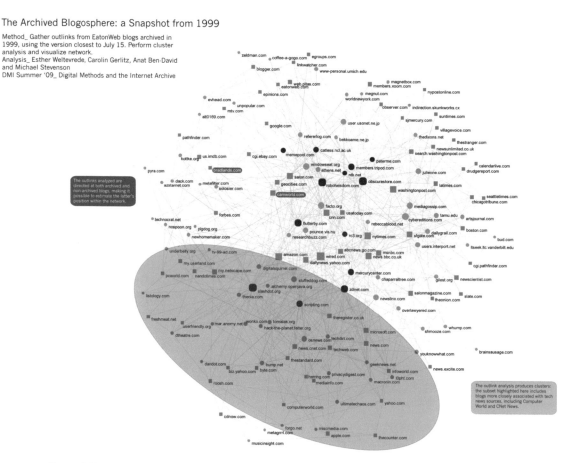

The Archived Blogosphere: a Snapshot from 1999

Method_ Gather outlinks from EatonWeb blogs archived in
1999, using the version closest to July 15. Perform cluster
analysis and visualize network.
Analysis_ Esther Weltevrede, Carolin Gerlitz, Anat Ben-David
and Michael Stevenson
DMI Summer '09_ Digital Methods and the Internet Archive

The outlinks analyzed are
directed at both archived and
non-archived blogs, making it
possible to estimate the latter's
position within the network.

The outlink analysis produces clusters:
the subset highlighted here includes
blogs more closely associated with tech
news sources, including Computer
World and CNet News.

Figure 3.7
Past state of the web, conjured through link analysis of archived websites. Early blogosphere as
network, showing site context in July 1999. (cc) Digital Methods Initiative, Amsterdam, 2009.

but are now parked and owned by domain resellers. (Michael Stevenson, heading up
the project to conjure up the early blogosphere with the Wayback Machine, has considered purchasing the parked sites and removing the robots.txt code, thereby reacti-
vating or reanimating the once missing websites in the Internet Archive.)

Each of the archived websites from the early blogosphere was crawled and its outlinks captured. Using hyperlink mapping software, we created a cluster graph (or map)
of the early blogosphere, including not only those sites that are in the archive but
also the sites that are missing from it. Still lost, these missing blogs from the early
blogosphere now reappear by name on the map, and the links to them are visible,
providing them with a context from the time that had been invisible in the single-site

output of the Wayback Machine (or the categorizations of site types in special collections) (see figure 3.5). The map of the early blogosphere, showing interlinkings between archived and nonarchived sites, is a means of conjuring up a past state of the web, and appears to be a method of working with web archives (historical link analysis) that has stuck.[49] Among other things, it shows a sense of the relevance of the site at the time, and thus also the significance of the sites in the collection (and those missing). Perhaps it also could put a value on the missing sites so as to aid with their recovery.[50]

4 Googlization and the Inculpable Engine

Googlization and the Service-for-Profile Model

The illustration of Google by Jude Buffum may be read as a shorthand reference for googlization, a term introduced in 2003 to describe the growing "creep" of the media company's search technologies and aesthetics into more and more web applications and contexts, not to mention tradition-rich institutions such as the library.[1] (See figure 4.1.) In a post on his book-in-progress blog *The Googlization of Everything*, the media scholar Siva Vaidhyanathan writes that Google has "altered the rules of the game for at least six major industries: Advertising, software applications, geographic services, email, publishing, and web commerce itself."[2] Googlization connotes media concentration—an important political-economy-style critique of Google's taking over of one service after another online. Within the study of media, more specifically, googlization also could be interpreted as an analysis of Google as mass media, inviting thought about how broadcast media of old are classically critiqued. For example, is there a strict separation between the producer/distributor and the consumer of the media? Engine users generally do not provide feedback about the query returns. Are the financial and technical barriers of entry into the area so high as to forestall newcomers from entrance? New search engines emerge, but the industry has matured. And every major engine employs an algorithm that seeks to emulate Google's PageRank. There is what could be termed algorithmic concentration. Is the programming, or content delivered, seeking to appeal to the largest possible audience? Search engine returns, as argued below, do not necessarily put on display a plurality of viewpoints from a diversity of voices. Rather, the sources often appear quite familiar and established. From those characteristics and others, one could begin to consider the value of mass-media critique applied to Google.[3]

What else is googlization? Vaidhyanathan points out that the services appear to be gratis. Yet when we use "web search, email, Blogger platforms, and YouTube videos, Google gets our habits and predilections so it can more efficiently target advertisements to us."[4] To googlization and other Google scholars, especially in surveillance

Figure 4.1
Stopping Google by Jude Buffum, 2008. © Jude Buffum, 2008. Reproduced with permission.

studies, the search engine company's is a personal information economy business, where the standard exchange is service for profile.[5] Thus googlization, as a process, implies the fanning out of the service-for-profile model both by Google, into its other, nonsearch areas, as well as by its followers and emulators. The question for googlization scholars is the extent of such "creep" as well as its consequences.

That is, to study googlization, and its further spread, one would enquire into whether the service-for-profile model is transforming other media, including the "older" media and perhaps offline trades. Building on the work of the communications scholar Joseph Turow as well as the surveillance studies scholar David Lyon, I described one consequence of the phenomenon of the personal information economy as retailers having to know you in order to sell to you.[6] The questions surrounding the increasing mediatization of retail, including customer relationship management and especially loyalty cards, relate to giving discounts only in exchange for profilable information. Coupons yield to cards swiped. In department stores, geo-identifiers (e.g., zip code) are keyed in prior to check out. Preferences are increasingly saved.

In his study of niche economies, Turow argues that, with the Internet, advertising is gradually turning away from the mass broadcast of the television age to "direct," a form of salesmanship that historically has relied on the personal attention of the door-to-door seller or the visiting market representative.[7] Without the human contact, building a relationship now lies in the form of technology chosen to collect user data, and subsequently to personalize salutations, alerts, adverts, as well as recommendations. The customization code referred to here is distinct from more mundane means of making the desktop, avatars, and mobile communications environments one's own through modification, where the user places her own skins and templates on a page, or associates a ringtone with a particular individual. Google's "direct" is an algorithmic, relational design approach that places relevant information in precious spaces. In a sense, the software also enters the user into personal communication with the database. Here "the personal" should not be understood in the customary, official sense, such as one having to enter date and place of birth, gender, etc. into form fields. Rather, the database contains one's "flecks," content about interests and habits (e.g., from search queries) that are employed to glean a profile on the basis of a small collection of information pieces.[8] Crucially, piecing it together only partially de-anonymizes the user. That is, there is no army of salesmen becoming acquainted with the customers, as deployed by modern "direct" companies such as Amway. Rather, the profiling of tastes follows from one's keywords (from search history) and geography (from the postal code associated with one's account). The question for googlization scholars thus concerns the uptake of such identifiers into more and more services.

What else happens when an industry has been "googlized"? More conceptually, there occurs what may be described as a mode switch from consultational to registrational interactivity.[9] In consultational interactivity, the user queries and chooses from preloaded information, as in a library catalog. One consults what is already there, and user anonymity does not come into play (unless books are borrowed, and anonymity is dealt with through data retention policies and laws). There are no dynamic recommendations. With registrational interactivity, the information delivered is dependent on one's personal settings, preferences such as language, safe search, and the quantity of results (in a lighter version), or on one's histories of sessions, searches, purchases, etc. (in a deeper variation). As personal settings and personal histories fuse, the search engine's acquaintance with the user would ultimately provide returns that seem uncanny, as if it knew what you were looking for and desiring all along. The effects, and affect, of personalization on search may be studied by striving to train a logged-in Google account to return only sources that are desired, such as only anti-fur groups for a fur query, instead of purveyors of the pelts and hides.

Back-End Googlization

Research into what may be termed the uncanniness of search engine returns suited to one's predilections and desires has found forms of the familiar, albeit somewhat different from the expected. In early research, which has been followed up by Daniel van der Velden's design research group Metahaven, engine results are scrutinized not only for what they include and exclude (the classic info-political critique of levels of source plurality and diversity in the medium once celebrated for its egalitarian spirit) but for the kinds of stories search engine results tell.[10] The idea of fashioning a story from search engine returns recalls the writings of literary hypertext theorists (following the lead of a short story by Jorge Luis Borges) in which the path the surfer takes is considered a means of authorship.[11] Here, however, the search engine is the authoring device, as it provides the current sources considered relevant and timely. In the journalistic sense of the term, "timely" news should be on top of events. Similarly, but in a web-specific sense, "timeliness" refers to an acceptable refresh or posting frequency. What do all these timely sites with high inlink counts add up to? Examining the specific set of sources delivered in the returns, what stories do they tell?

As discussed in chapter 1, I interrogated Google by comparing the results of a query for [terrorism] to the source set one is accustomed to hearing on the evening news.[12] Instead of providing a collision space for alternative accounts of reality, Google furnished the familiar: just as the storyline about the war on terrorism has been repeated frequently on television by showing clips from the U.S. White House, so whitehouse .gov was among the top results for the query [terrorism] in 2003, together with cia .gov, fbi.gov, and other establishment sources, including CNN and Al Jazeera. The familiarity of results put paid to the notion of a reputational free-for-all on the web. Google had become journalistic, sourcing like established media and well-resourced agenda-setters. The findings became starker in an experiment by Metahaven. In July 2008 a google.com query for [Karadzic] furnished, in the following order, "Wikipedia, BBC News, Google News, Yahoo! News, *The Guardian*, Reuters, MSNBC, Interpol, YouTube and Google Blog Search."[13] With the exception of Interpol, the entire source set are mainly news sources, and leaning toward the self-referential, with three Google properties toward the top of returns as well as the ever-present Wikipedia, a subject of chapter 8. The online sources delivered appear not only familiar and newslike but also fresh.

Thus the crucial question is, Which kinds of sources are being recommended for a particular query? Put differently, how may one think through the kind of recommendation engine Google is? One may argue that Google, for its majority of user types (searchers and webmasters) as opposed to its advertisers, always has provided an indication of the state of source dominance per area of inquiry. Google is a status-authoring device.[14] Given all the pages that do reference a keyword, the search engine delivers those "deserving" to be listed as the top sources. Thus, apart from seeing the source set as the story, one also may view the engine results as telling a second kind of story— that of the current status of the topic or issue in question through the organizations currently representing it, on the record, in the engine returns. Compare queries made in Google in 2004 for ["climate change"] and for [RFID], in terms of the types of actors present in the top returns (see figure 4.2). For climate change, there are U.N. scientists, governmental agencies, and other establishment actors. For the RFID (radio frequency identification) query, the actor types are the trade press, corporations, lone activists, and electronics tinkerers. A comparison of the actor composition provides an indication of the maturity of the issue, with RFID in an emerging, more polarized discursive space (hopes and fears), and climate change a more settled one (policy processes). By 2008 the RFID engine return space contained a somewhat different population of actors, with nongovernmental organizations (epic.org and eff.org), mainstream media, as well as a governmental agency making an appearance. Comparing the actor composition in engine returns for the same query over time shows changing states of play for an issue, according to the sources at the top of the returns.

Generally speaking, the lesson for googlization scholars is the resonance of such novel status-making across other platforms. Have the back-end algorithms taken over from the traditional status makers, the publishers, editors, and other classic adjudicators? One case study to build upon concerns the web directories, the human-edited projects, including Yahoo!'s and the Open Directory Project's, that have sought to organize the web by topic. Yahoo!'s web directory is the archetypal example. From the mid-nineties to Wikipedia's entry onto the web in 2001, it was a model to emulate, not only for the entire web but also nationally, with such efforts as Startpagina in the Netherlands. For all the innovation and imitation that it spawned, the Yahoo! directory met its fate in October 2002, when it was replaced as Yahoo!'s default engine—by Google returns. Subsequently, in February 2004, Yahoo! cut the ribbon on its very own algorithmic machine, designed by in-house engineers, to yield results not so unlike Google's. Giving way to the familiar "organic" results of the dominant engine, it put its handmade directory aside. Was Yahoo, in a sense, googlized?[15]

Front-End Googlization

On the front end, Yahoo!'s portal approach remained, with its bountiful services, text, and images (or clutter, if one's sensibilities are trained by Google's aesthetics). What had changed at Yahoo? Casting an eye not on the front page but on Yahoo!'s engine results page, Search Engine Watch writes:

How does the new Yahoo! search engine differ from Google? The presentation of the results is very similar. Yahoo! has wisely opted to keep things looking mostly the same, with a few exceptions. There's a link to the cached copy of each indexed page—now being served from Yahoo, not Google. Just about everything else on search result pages looks the same.[16]

Having the same look as Google was thought desirable, certainly in terms of the single search box, front and center. In his lament about the loss of the butler at Ask Jeeves as well as the longer march of engines joining the "logo, form, button" aesthetic, Derek Powezek, a designer of Technorati's interfaces, argues that too many engines have asked the question, "What would Google do?"[17] His argument could be interpreted as a concern for interface googlization. Indeed, in describing the "googlization meme," John Battelle, author of a well-known book on Google, argues that attention should be paid to the increasing homogeneity on the homepage.[18] Reducing it to a single search box could be construed as the pinnacle of the merging of usability and functionality.

Intergovernmental Panel on **Climate Change**
... IPCC Third Assessment Report - **Climate Change** 2001. ... Integrating Sustainable
Development and **Climate Change** in the IPCC Fourth Assessment Report. ...
www.ipcc.ch/ - 36k - Cached - Similar pages

UNITED NATIONS FRAMEWORK CONVENTION ON **CLIMATE CHANGE**, UNFCCC
What's New. 16 August 2004 New version of CRF Software. 9 August 2004 International day
of the world's indigenous peoples Statement ...
unfccc.int/ - 21k - 24 Aug 2004 - Cached - Similar pages

Global Warming:The Pew Center on Global **Climate Change**
... Coping with Global **Climate Change**: The Role of Adaptation in the United States (June
2004) Pew Center Report. The Day After Tomorrow: Could it really happen? ...
www.pewclimate.org/ - 28k - 24 Aug 2004 - Cached - Similar pages

ClimateArk -- **Climate Change** Portal
Climate Ark -- **Climate Change** News & Information Portal and Archive. Full Text Searches
& Information Archive of Reviewed **Climate Change** Internet Content. ...
www.climateark.org/ - 33k - 24 Aug 2004 - Cached - Similar pages

US Global **Change** Research Program
Our Changing Planet The Fiscal Year 2003 US Global **Change** Research Program and
Climate Change Research Initiative [PDF, 1.6 Mb] Also available in hardcopy from ...
www.usgcrp.gov/ - 11k - Cached - Similar pages

Climate Change, Government of Canada
On the Government of Canada **Climate Change** web site you can learn about the science,
impacts and adaptation to **climate change** and how you can take action by ...
www.climatechange.gc.ca/english/default.asp - 14k - 24 Aug 2004 - Cached - Similar pages

Climate Change Programme
WWF **Climate Change** Programme, ... Sharing **climate change** experiences, © WWF-Canon
/ Cat HOLLOWAYCoastal flooding, widespread coral bleaching ...
www.panda.org/about_wwf/ what_we_do/**climate_change**/index.cfm - 54k - 24 Aug 2004 -
Cached - Similar pages

New Scientist | Environment Report | **Climate Change**
Climate change - Burning fossil fuels and using the atmosphere as an open sewer has turned
out to be a recipe for disaster. The ...
www.newscientist.com/hottopics/**climate**/ - 33k - 24 Aug 2004 - Cached - Similar pages

Climate Change Solutions: Greenhouse gas emission reduction ...
... **Climate Change** Awareness and Action The **Climate Change** Awareness and Action
Education Kit is a complete teaching resource designed specifically for use in ...
www.climatechangesolutions.com/ - 11k - Cached - Similar pages

Figure 4.2
Issue maturity indications from actor composition in top search engine results. Google results
for the queries [RFID] and ["climate change"], 2004, compared.

RFID Journal
The only source for timely, objective news and information about **RFID** and its many business applications. ... Putting **RFID** Know-How to Work. ...
www.**rfid**journal.com/ - 26k - 23 Aug 2004 - Cached - Similar pages

>   RFID Journal - Frequently Asked Questions
>   For answers to frquently questions about **RFID** technology and consumer privacy, see Privacy FAQs. ... What is **RFID**? How does an **RFID** system work? ...
>   www.**rfid**journal.com/article/articleview/207 - 95k - 23 Aug 2004 - Cached - Similar pages
>   [More results from www.**rfid**journal.com]

AIM - The global trade assocation for automatic identification
... Covering technologies such as barcode, radio frequency Identification (**RFID**), card technologies (magnetic stripe, smart card, contactless card, optical card ...
www.aimglobal.org/technologies/**rfid**/ - 37k - 23 Aug 2004 - Cached - Similar pages

Spychips: **RFID** Privacy Website
Order Katherine Albrecht's video "**RFID**: Tracking Everything Everywhere." Sign up for our free weekly newsletter ... **RFID** PRIVACY ISSUES AND NEWS. What is **RFID**? ...
www.spychips.com/ - 17k - Cached - Similar pages

RFID, Inc. Radio Frequency Identification Products....!
RFID Inc. features radio frequency identification products, also offering ISO standard interchangeable products. ... Looking for a 5 or 10 cent **RFID** Tag? ...
www.**rfid**inc.com/ - 15k - Cached - Similar pages

RFID tags: Big Brother in small packages | Perspectives | CNET ...
RFID tags: Big Brother in small packages | CNET News.com's Washington watcher Declan McCullagh says that retailers may love the concept of miniscule ...
news.com.com/2010-1069-980325.html - 46k - Cached - Similar pages

RFID - Wikipedia, the free encyclopedia
RFID. From Wikipedia, the free encyclopedia. Radio frequency identification (**RFID** ... [edit]. History of **RFID** tags. Perhaps the first work ...
en.wikipedia.org/wiki/RFID - 35k - Cached - Similar pages

EPIC **RFID** Privacy Page
EPIC logo. Radio Frequency Identification (**RFID**) Systems. ... 1). Introduction. Radio Frequency Identification (**RFID**) is a type of automatic identification system. ...
www.epic.org/privacy/**rfid**/ - 37k - Cached - Similar pages

RFID Tags in New US Notes Explode When You Try to Microwave Them
RFID Tags in New US Notes Explode When You Try to Microwave Them Adapted from a letter sent to Henry Makow Ph.D. Want to share an event with you, that we ...
www.prisonplanet.com/022904**rfid**tagsexplode.html - 40k - Cached - Similar pages

The **RFID** Weblog - **rfid**.weblogsinc.com
... A New Alternative to Bluetooth/**RFID**/NFC on the Horizon. ... FDA Looking at Wireless/**RFID** Solutons to Combat Against Counterfeit Drugs. ...

Figure 4.2
(continued)

Everybody loves using Google. Therefore, doesn't everybody want the same simple design on every site they visit? . . . People are calling this approach Home Page Googlization.[19]

The fascination is with Google's simple search box, including its two main buttons, web search and its homage to hyperspace, "I'm Feeling Lucky." That second button is an anomaly for the googlization critique, in the sense that it has neither spread across engines nor is linked up with the source of revenue, advertising. "I'm Feeling Lucky" skips the results page.

Where the second interface, the results page, is concerned, a critical study should include what could be dubbed results page googlization. Despite the arrival of Kartoo in 2002 and other engines "visualizing" returns, listed results dominate, with a default of ten per page and each entry comprising title, description or teaser text, and hyperlink.

Studying the input field (search box) and the output (the list) has detracted attention from the tabs, however. In its first ten years, recently celebrated, Google has made subtle changes to its front-page real estate. There have been upgrades and downgrades of such services as Froogle and Groups, as Google Labs and other acquired projects see the light of day, only to be deemphasized later. Paying attention to the tabs, in a longitudinal study, is one way to step backstage, and also to come to grips with Donald Norman's classic Google critique: "Is Google simple? No. Google is deceptive. It hides all the complexity by simply showing one search box on the main page."[20] Norman, the design and usability scholar, is referring to the absence of transparency in two respects—the interface lacks an overview of the services on offer and also, perhaps more to the point, masks the organizational structure. Google thus becomes a new case of a "social hieroglyphic."[21] In a variation on the Marxist language, one could argue that it makes invisible the social relations behind its commodity, and at the same time naturalizes them, making it all seem like second nature.[22] Search engine returns, at least those that are not sponsored, are "organic." Here the contribution of Henk van Ess, the investigative journalist and search engine observer, is of special interest. The URL discovered in 2005, http://eval.google.com, prompted a cause célèbre and exchanges with company representatives, posted online, for Van Ess found that Google hires humans (students) to check the search engine results for reliability.[23] Finding that the results are manufactured arouses excitement, and not only because of its association with the Mechanical Turk or the climax of *The Wizard of Oz*, when the curtain is drawn back to reveal a human behind the supernatural effects. It also complexifies the simple search box, removing its reductionism. As pure algorithmic logic recedes, Google's back end becomes messier.

Where another of its significant relationships with humans is concerned, Google more generally has been in sync with Yahoo! on one project, of crucial importance to librarians and editors. Google followed Yahoo! by downgrading its directory. As discussed in the previous chapter, in March 2004 Google moved its directory (the engine built on top of the Open Directory Project, dmoz.org) off of its front page, demoting the directory tab to the "More" button, and in 2007 to "Even more," before it eventually disappeared altogether.

Googlization studies are thus inquiries into how subtle interface changes imply a politics of knowledge, in particular the deprivileging mechanisms through the relegation of editorial services to further depths of a website. The burying of the directory in both Yahoo! and Google signals a much larger transformation—the demise of the expert human editors of the web. (Paid "Internet cataloguing" positions also disappear.) Just as poignantly, for library scientists, is another consequence of the rise of the back-end algorithm for directory innovation, very much unlike in the alphabetical, egalitarian spirit and also unlike Ranganathan's top-level categories with constitutive elements forming a whole. By 2007 Yahoo! had changed the default output of its directory. The alphabetical listing was replaced by a ranking of sources based on "popularity."

By default, Directory site listings are presented sorted by popularity and relevance. Sites that are most popular with users or the most relevant to the category appear at the top of the site listings. The order of websites or web documents is based upon Yahoo! Search Technology.[24]

That search has supplanted browsing (and surfing) is a larger web phenomenon, often attributed to usefulness and the sheer volume of websites rather than to googlization. The users are sorting (and tagging) more content than the cataloguers.[25] In another of the many inversions brought about by new media, the audience has taken over from the tour guide. Everybody holds the red umbrella. But for the googlization project the further question has to do with the impact of user empowerment as against editorial expertise or algorithmic purity.[26] Search is becoming personalized, based on search history and the results clicked. To achieve this, the search engine user is being "recorded," also in the sense of the words Google has chosen for the settings. One pauses search history, and resumes it. Playing back one's history is encapsulated in the feed option. As the veteran search engine observer Danny Sullivan writes, one of the greater significances of personalized search is that "the days of everyone seeing the same results for any particular query are growing more numbered."[27] The story authored by the search engine results is now partly of one's own writing, as certain sites that one visits frequently are boosted a few places upward. Sullivan tells of his gratification in seeing his own articles rather high in the rankings for certain favorite queries, and wondering if his work is as highly ranked for other users.

The Inculpable Engine

For media scholars, one question has been how to reinterpret the idea of the gatekeeper—the powerful editor controlling the stories that are fit to print—in light of the link networks determining rankings, and search histories boosting favorite sources in personalized search. Without taking algorithmic tweaks and major overhauls into account, a discussion of new forms of gatekeeping might start from cases of sites being deindexed. Matt Cutts of Google blogs about them, telling readers about "webmaster best practices," with admonitions about baiting crawlers with "engine spam" such as back-door pages (also known as one-way link pages, or pages a user cannot visit by navigating through a website). Perhaps of greater import are particular glimpses Cutts provides into the workings of the Google bots. Writing about a mother crawl in 2006 called bigdaddy, he relates that there are "sites where our algorithms had very low trust in the inlinks or the outlinks of that site. Examples that might cause that include excessive reciprocal links, linking to spammy neighborhoods on the web."[28] The valuation of one hyperlink as one vote no longer applies; not all links are of equal value. It is a useful corrective.

As a case in point concerning the varying values of links, in 2007 researchers and I began logging Google results for the query [9/11], with a focus on 911truth.org, a

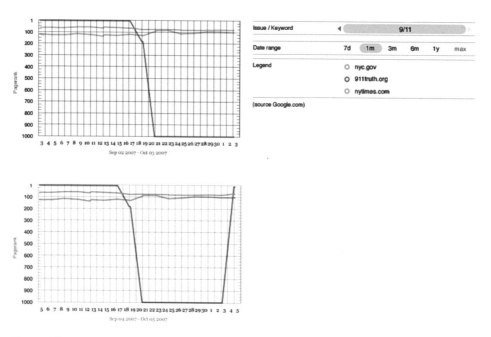

Figure 4.3
Drama in search engine space. At the top, a website is gone: the apparent removal of 911truth .org from Google results for the query [9/11], September-October 2007. In the lower figure, a website returns. After a two-week hiatus, 911truth.org returns to its usual top-ten placement in Google returns for the query [9/11], September-October 2007. Issue Dramaturg by Govcom.org. © Govcom.org Foundation, Amsterdam, 2007.

source that is considered a conspiracy site (see figure 4.3). Two other sites' rankings were also highlighted, the *New York Times* (nytimes.com) and the New York City government (nyc.gov). In 2007, from March through September 11, 911truth.org routinely made the top ten in the results for the query. The *New York Times* and the New York City government were well below the fold, coming in under result rank 50 and 100, respectively. One of the purposes of the work was to put on display particular organizations' rankings in the results for a query, in an effort to think through the cognitive changes that Google has brought about. (Thus googlization studies also become interested in the evolution of one's ideas about relevant sources.) Normally, the top ten results (or the top 20, 30, 50, 100, depending on one's preferences) constitute the population of sources one would consult. One does not normally ask oneself why the *New York Times* or the New York City government is not present on one's results page. Or, having figured so significantly in the event itself, shouldn't the New York City Fire Department be there? Such questions are precluded, for the Google results themselves make up the world of relevance.

Of greater importance, the research project documented the sudden disappearance of 911truth.org from the results. Some ten days after September 11, 2007, 911truth.org dropped precipitously from a top 5 source, to 200, and then off the chart, returning some two weeks later to its usual top placement.

One possible explanation is that 911truth.org, as a franchise site with chapter affiliates such as ny911truth.org, sf911truth.org, and vancouver911truth.org, routinely link to the parent site, and did so with a flourish around the 9/11 anniversary, signaling what Matt Cutts called excessive reciprocal linking. For researchers and me charting the sudden drop in ranking, the question arose of the stability of the source set in search engine returns. Is there volatility in the returns in the sense that what one receives today may be rather different tomorrow? (That results change over time is of interest to those researching the current status of the subject matter, according to the source set or actor composition returned, as argued above.)

I would like to conclude with a major implication of personalization. To Danny Sullivan's point that customized search removes returns common to all searchers for the same query, I would like to add that personalization takes the search engine off the hook, because the "blame" or responsibility for the results is partly one's own. Critical examinations of search results for their politics of information provision, such as the ones above, are replaced by studies of the effects of personalization. There is another implication for scholarly critique. For those considering Google as the new mass media, the user feedback previously lacking has now been built in. The user coauthors the results.

5 Search as Research: Source Distance and Cross-Spherical Analysis

Search Research versus Search as Research

In the web-epistemological search engine critiques put forward in the previous two chapters, the analysis concerns both front-end and back-end politics. On the engine's front end, the changes in the menu items from 1998 to 2007 show the promotion of algorithmic search over the human-edited directory. Beginning in 2004 it became difficult to find the directory at Google, as it was gradually demoted and placed multiple clicks away from the front page.[1] The demise of the human-edited web was seen through the gradual changes to the interface of Google (with the implication that the history of Google could tell in part the history of the web). The carefully edited web, with link lists, also tended to become unkempt, as I related in the discussion of the website as archived object. Link lists are disappearing (the example of Amnesty International's), and directories are becoming neglected (the Open Directory Project, dmoz. org). At the time of writing, the "About" section of the Open Directory Project has not been updated in nearly ten years. The section refers to the web-editing project as being the product of the "Internet brain" and to the editorial standards set by "net-citizens," terms now long displaced by notions of collective intelligence and the wisdom of the crowd.[2]

Yahoo!'s original directory project also has witnessed the creep of algorithms that displace the human editor and rank sources according to relevance (or "popularity," as it is termed there). A query made at Yahoo!'s directory results in a list of sources that is no longer alphabetical by default, but rather is ranked according to popularity. Default settings are important markers of what is considered normal, or strives to be. The end of the alphabetical listing of sources heralds the decline of information egalitarianism in the style of the encyclopedia.[3] Now there is a hierarchy of sources provided by an algorithmic directory. The new, ranked source list also may infiltrate the realm of the subject matter experts, whose special acumen now competes with recommendation systems as authors of expertise.

With respect to the back end, algorithmic authority, a (critical) term popularized in the discourse of Internet research by Clay Shirky, means trust in the epistemological value of engine output.[4] While I seek to rehabilitate or in fact apply the notion in the following, I would like first to touch on how such faith in the back end is often critiqued. In critical search research, one inquires into the exclusionary mechanisms of engines. Engines may not index the entire web, as was found and decried in the late 1990s.[5] They may neglect orphan websites (those sites that do not receive links), which also illuminates how crawlers work. A decade ago the inability to crawl all the web led to notions like the dark web, alluding to the intriguing terra incognita of cyberspace and harkening to the hand-drawn mappae mundi of cybergeography, with territories populated by all manner of outcasts and others, alive and well online—pirates, pornographers, rumormongers, and conspiracy theorists.[6] More to the point, this was also a critique of the lack of reach (and ultimately the exclusionary work) of search engines. Engines darkened the web.

Engines boosted sources that received many links; the results were termed "organic" (inviting the critique that engines "naturalize" their privileging mechanisms). Engines still darken the web, or certain sources, though there is less critique and more understanding now of the rationale for privileging some over others. The reason is that content of infomercial quality continually seeks to rise toward the top of engine returns. One such example is the YouTube video "How to Pack for a Trip to Spain," uploaded by eHow and the subject of a critical *Wired* article in 2009 on the growth of a new, sweat-content economy, whose business model is to flood the top of engine returns with cheaply made articles and videos, attract hits, and thus interest online advertisers.[7] Google reminds us that it continually changes its algorithms, and the weighting of their great number of variables (or signals). It does so not only to obfuscate the workings of the engine to spammers, but also to address the manipulators of automated engine results, who create made-for-engine pages (such as backdoor pages) as well as made-for-engine content. Google results need to maintain their quality because the web gradually has become divided into good neighborhoods and spammy ones, some whose content is authored for readers and others whose content is scraped from sites and repeated, or is spam authored for engines.[8] Google's algorithmic changes have aimed to penalize sites that are prepared first and foremost for engines.[9] "Content farms" have been lowered in the rankings, joining "link farms" as a leading source of web pollution from the point of view of search engines. Content farms are more recent but link farms persist, as witnessed by a long exposé about an American department store chain in early 2011, which apparently made use of the black art of search engine manipulation. The department store's high PageRanks for all manner of general product queries (e.g., [dress]) went undetected for months, including throughout the Christmas shopping season. "Someone paid to have thousands of links placed on hundreds of sites scattered around the web, all of which lead directly to JCPenney

.com."[10] In short, together with all manner of recommendation systems online (including Amazon.com's seminal one), Google's and other search engines' orderings have given rise to a skein of optimization practices so that sites can rise toward or remain near the top. In what I have termed the hyperlink economy, the higher rungs of engines' output are of some considerable value.[11] As such, search engine space invites stratagems to game it, prompting questions about which types of results can be trusted, and when. Which queries result in made-for-engine content at the top of the returns? Which query results are free of such "engine artifacts" (the high placement of sites through optimization as well as "hard-coding," such as Google properties—news, images, videos—appearing in the top ten results)? Indeed, Fairsearch.org, an industry group allied against Google, points to the artificiality, or artifactuality, of engine results as an unfair trade practice (see figure 5.1).

Given websites optimized in one form or another to make them rise in the rankings, is it worthwhile even to consider the use of engine results for more than everyday information gathering? Can we conceivably employ the engine for research? There has been preliminary work to answer such questions, and the purpose of this chapter is to fill out the contours of it, describing how to analyze search engine results for certain social research purposes, or at least make the case for using search as research.[12]

Search Engine as Research Machine or Consumer Appliance

To begin with, I would like to briefly change the terms of search engine critique, away from the cognitive and social effects of search engines (as valuable as this critique is) to their algorithmic authority, or the type of authority authored by the engine. From this viewpoint search engines become socio-epistemological machines, authoring source standing for a given subject matter. Generally speaking, sources seek standing in all manner of ways, from provenance and origins stories over letterhead and seals to partnerships with others of standing (to name a few). Online standing is built upon direct, named association (receiving inlinks with your name in the anchor or underlined, hyperlink text), but also on a set of other analytics—hits, freshness, posting frequency, age, likes. In certain online metrics, so-called offline standing also is important. The key combinations applied to author standing differ somewhat for each space or sphere on the web. The web sphere ranks by a "relevance" based on inlinks received by sites, and by users' clicking on engine returns. The blogosphere ranks by inlinks together with posting regularity and freshness. The news sphere ranks based on freshness, but also strives to respect journalistic culture, including the scoop, or the source first with the news. It also appears to be more hard-coded, with news organizations boosted on the basis of their history and staff size. (Social media, though not discussed further in this chapter, also have different ranking formulae, such as Facebook's Edge-Rank for ranking friends' posts and Twitter's trending topics for ranking tweets. A

GOOGLE'S CONDUCT THREATENS CONSUMERS AND INNOVATION

Google is abusing its dominant position in search to stifle competition and capture more control over the flow of information and commerce online. Officials charged with protecting innovation, economic growth, and consumers must step up and enforce existing laws that will prevent Google from further stifling competition on the Internet.

"SEARCH IS CRITICAL. IF YOU ARE NOT FOUND, THE REST CANNOT FOLLOW" -Google Executive
Santiago de la Mora 8/23/09

ON AVERAGE, 34% OF GOOGLE'S TRAFFIC WENT TO THE NO. 1 RESULT

about **twice** the percentage that went to No. 2. [*NYT* 2/12/11; *Chitika Insights* 5/25/10]

Links below the fold receive less than 1% of users' attention. [*CNN Money* 3/8/11]

GOOGLE DOMINATES SEARCH & SEARCH ADVERTISING

 Google, **controls more than 79% of all searches in the U.S.** Advertising accounted for almost 96% of Google's total revenue in 2010, or about $28 billion. [*StatCounter* 9/20/11; *comScore* 4/13/11; *Google IR* 4/20/11]

 Search advertising is the largest source of online advertising revenues. As of April 2011, Google has over 79% share of paid search in the U.S. The ad revenue split for search advertising is **Google 49%,** publishers 51%. [*Efficient Frontier* Q1 2011; *eMarketer* 3/1/11; *Google Adsense Blog* 5/24/10]

 Google controls 98% of the U.S. mobile search market and 97% of the mobile search advertising market (a market that is predicted to reach $1.1 billion in 2011). [*SearchEngineLand* 3/7/11]

 Google has a dominant position in almost every EU country, with an overall search market share of **94%** in Europe. [*StatCounter* 9/20/11]

 Google has a 90% share of Europe's online advertising market. [*The Guardian* 12/6/10]

✱NOT TO MENTION:
Google is growing stronger in the **$10.1 billion U.S. display advertising market** – its share is up 49.2% since 2010. (This figure will likely increase with Google's acquisition of AdMeld.) [*eMarketer* 3/1/11]

THIS DOMINANCE ADDS UP TO POWER.
(IN FACT, GOOGLE CALLS ITSELF "THE BIGGEST KINGMAKER ON THIS EARTH") -Google Executive
Amit Singhal 5/17/10

POWER OVER: **1** Where sites rank in search results. **2** How search results are displayed.

3 Who can advertise on its search page. **4** What price advertisers must pay.

GOOGLE IS ABUSING ITS DOMINANCE IN ORDER TO STIFLE COMPETITION

SEARCH MANIPULATION

Google can program its algorithm to exclude, penalize, or promote specific sites or whole categories of sites. In 1998, Google's founders wrote: "[A] search engine could add a small factor to search results from friendly companies, and subtract a factor from results from competitors. This type of bias is very difficult to detect but could still have a significant effect on the market."

UNFAIR TREATMENT OF ADVERTISERS AND PARTNERS

Google's ubiquity has made it a "must-buy" platform for advertisers and other technology partners. However, Google can manipulate paid search to limit competition and Google imposes exclusivity restrictions on its partners' use of software such as the Android mobile operating system.

DECEPTIVE DISPLAY

Users expect search results to be presented in order of relevance. However, Google now favors many of its own pages by displaying them at the top or in the middle of the results page as if they were natural search results, without clearly identifying them as Google results.

CONTENT SCRAPING

Google scrapes content developed by other websites, such as user reviews, without permission and displays that content on its own pages. This keeps users on Google's pages, enabling Google to earn even more money while depriving competing sites user traffic and revenue.

ACQUISITIONS OF COMPETITIVE THREATS

Google acquires companies that threaten its dominance in search.

Figure 5.1
Fairsearch.org's fact sheet as search engine critique, June 2011. Source: Fairsearch.org.

cross-platform ranking is the Klout score, which measures a user's impact across several sites.) Source standing, then, respects spherical culture, in the sense that it relies on the distinctiveness of the practices of website owners in the web sphere, bloggers in the blogosphere, and news organizations in the news sphere.

The question becomes whether one can make use of the source standing authored by engines as a research practice, and to which ends. Could Google be made into a research machine? In the late 1990s, the engine's creators and company cofounders described it as a "research tool," by which they also construed search as research, both in the foraging sense of finding sources as well as in an adjudicative one of allowing the engine to preevaluate (rank) the sources found.[13] Can one perform source standing research with Google, or is one always only studying Google itself? How to take into account Google artifacts, or those results that rely less on web publishers and web users than on the engine to rise to the top? Does the engine's battle with spammers (broadly defined) and privileging of its own properties, to name two engine practices, downgrade its capacities as research machine?

For search to become research, the larger questions concern how to query engines and how to read results. Just as important perhaps is how to distance oneself from everyday search practice and rethink engine inputs and outputs. The questions follow from Google's features, such as search in one's own language, search within sites, or search each sphere separately (the web sphere, the blogosphere, and the news sphere) and compare the results. With respect to searching in one's own language, a researcher could seemingly make country- or language-specific queries and perform cross-country analysis with the local-domain Googles. Making use of Google's indexing of individual websites, one might query one or more organizations or groups and gain an indication of their partisanship or their commitment to particular issues through frequency analysis of keyword use. A third research practice that compares the outputs of web search, blog search, and news search could be thought of in terms of cross-spherical analysis: one compares the presence and absence as well as the ranking of sources across multiple spheres (web sphere, blogosphere, and news sphere).

In judging whether we can use search engines as research machines that return the most relevant sources per query, the constitution of relevance is crucial. Since at least the mid-2000s, it has been argued, search engine companies gradually have changed the definition of the relevance of a source from an evaluative scheme based on inlink count (and the content of the link) to one that combines inlink with click count and freshness.[14] Thus sources are boosted in the rankings if users have clicked them in previous searches, thereby allowing the users to decide in part on importance. They rise if they are fresh, thereby elevating the epistemological status of presentism. As pointed out in the previous chapter, with the demise of the universal search engine and the rise of local-domain Googles and personalization that return sources (and ads) tailored at least to location and language, the relevant sources returned have changed.

In place of the webby form of citation analysis, sources are now relevant because they are consumed (clicked) and recently uploaded. That is, in the type of search engine critique I am pursuing here, one line of inquiry becomes the extent to which the engine is more a consumer information appliance than a research machine, owing to the algorithmic changes.

There are numerous other hurdles for Google's capacity to serve as a research machine. The initial one concerns certain regularities in the returns that appear to be more Google artifacts than adjudicated results. Google properties (Google Maps, Google Places, Google Images, YouTube videos, and Google News) are often returned in the top ten, meaning other sources must make way for Google in that valued space. Similarly, Wikipedia articles are often atop the returns for substantive as opposed to navigational or transactional queries (as those for web navigation and e-commerce are called). This example is more complicated, for Wikipedia's appearance at the top could be construed as a Google artifact, a web artifact, a relationship between two top web properties, a computer engineering hard-coded shortcut, some combination of these, or something else entirely. That is, Wikipedia's appearance may be afforded by Google's allowance of its heavy interlinking (facilitated by bots), by its high inlink count, by user clicks, or by its treatment as analogous to a Google property. However one accounts for its standing online (a theme I return to in chapter 8), a researcher considering Google as a source adjudication device would be right to ask why a Wikipedia article would be placed higher in the results for the query ["climate change"] than the U.S. Environmental Protection Agency and the U.N.'s Intergovernmental Panel on Climate Change. A third critique of Google artifacts is the question of using Google to undertake source research about the engine itself. Does Google swamp the searcher with Google-authored sources as results when researching German criticism of Google Street View, for example? Here the questions about Google as research machine begin to resemble those put forward by the industry alliance in their fair trade discourse (figure 5.1).

Google's Definition of the "Local"

A second set of observations should be made about when Google's sense of the local may be deployed for social research purposes, especially in terms of the local-domain Googles (google.fr, etc.) and its evaluation of sources. Can one perform cross-country and comparative media analysis with local-domain Googles? If one were to use Google as a research machine for source adjudication work by country, it would be worthwhile to investigate its notion of the local as well as its ability to author ranked lists of local sources for a query. Another way of expressing the concern is the question of Google as localizing or globalizing machine (or something else). Does Google, in its work as local search engine, only return results from area sources, however defined? Or is it a device that primarily returns results in the local language (wherever their origin) with advertisements? Thus here I discuss the tension between Google's local domain as organizing the national or the language web (a theme I discuss in chapter 6).

It is important not to dismiss lightly (in the research into Google as research machine) the extent to which the local is not about local sources, but about market reach into national search markets. With its 150 or so local-domain Googles, Google may be considered a globalizing machine, and analyzed through such concepts as the postcolonial, the transnational, and the glocal. I allude to these terms so that they may be filled in, or tested, empirically. In the work discussed below, it was found that queries in Latin American local-domain Googles routinely return sources from Spain, whereas Latin American sources do not appear in the results in Google Spain (google.es). Thus Google's sense of the local is an object of study that is included in the larger question of Google as research machine. In the work that follows from an analysis of Google's sense of the local, the question for cross-country analysis is whether a study has as its corpus (or realm of inquiry) any or all local-domain Googles, the local-domain Googles where languages are relatively country-specific, or the local-domain Googles that are able to organize local results (where the definition of the local remains problematized).

In a series of (exploratory) projects in this area, entitled *The World According to Google*, the first of these queried ["human rights"] in over 150 local-domain Googles, with the query translated into the main language of each, and found that only 25 local-domain Googles returned a majority of results from "their" country, according to the sites' respective whois information (though four—google.de, google.no, google.si, and google.ua—had nine of the top ten from their country).[15] In other words, Google generally is not defining "local" as sources originating from the country associated with the local domain, and thus could be said to have another sense of the local, at least according to this preliminary undertaking. In the second such study, which had more iterations, the analysis sought to tease out a Google notion of the local further by querying issue language pinpointed to matters of concern in the Amazon River basin, thus putting forward the question of which sources have the privilege (so to speak) of discussing local concerns. It first queried [diversidad] or diversity in local-domain Googles of three countries in the Amazon River basin (Colombia, Peru, and Venezuela), finding that the vast majority of the results were from sources in Spain, providing middle and secondary school educational materials. Sources from Spain were identified from country domain, the contact information located on the websites, and the type of conjugation of the Spanish language on the sites. A more elaborate exercise of this sort followed with the querying of [diversidad] in a larger series of Spanish-language local-domain Googles, with the number of sources returned in the top twenty from each country in parentheses: Spain (9), Mexico (6), Argentina (5), Chile (4), Colombia (3), Cuba (2), Peru (1), Honduras (1), Venezuela (1), Costa Rica

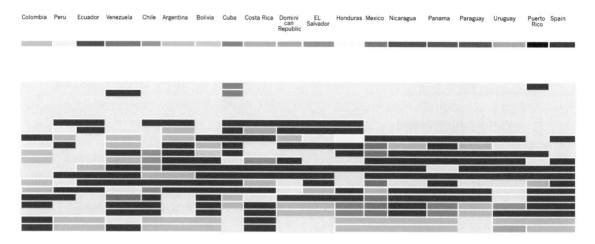

Figure 5.2
Comparison of source origin of results for the query [diversidad] or diversity in Spanish-language local-domain Googles, December 2010. Color indicates source origin. Analysis by Natalia Sánchez Querubín, Digital Methods Initiative, Amsterdam.

(1), Bolivia (1), Uruguay (1), Dominican Republic (0), El Salvador (0), Ecuador (0), Nicaragua (0), Panama (0), Paraguay (0), and Puerto Rico (0) (see figure 5.2). Here Google's returns are ranked according to each country's (or territory's) success in being able to provide information in its "own" Google, with a distribution that for the top slots is akin to a list of Spanish-speaking countries by population. In order to consider Google as research machine for cross-country or comparative media studies, however, the origins of the sources are of less interest than their interpretations. A subsequent project compared the URLs returned for the query [Amazonia] in the Spanish-language local-domain Googles. For Google Spain, the results originated largely from that country's own sources (see figure 5.3); for each of the other countries, Google provided some sources from Spain, with the remainder being regional or perhaps translocal, all from Latin America, without any one country supplying a majority in any country's result set. That is, Google's local is here a Latin American blend, with sources from Spain always present in the minority. Most importantly, the results are very similar across all the Latin American countries: it is as if there is one result set for all of Latin America. Thus Google's "local" is much broader than a definition based on country domains. Google is not a national web maker, generally. It also is not necessarily a language web maker, by which is meant that the results would have been the same (or similar) across all local-domain Googles sharing the same language. Rather, at least for the Spanish-speaking space in our limited exploration, Google privileges sources from Spain overall, and provides Spanish-speaking countries outside of Spain with largely one result set.

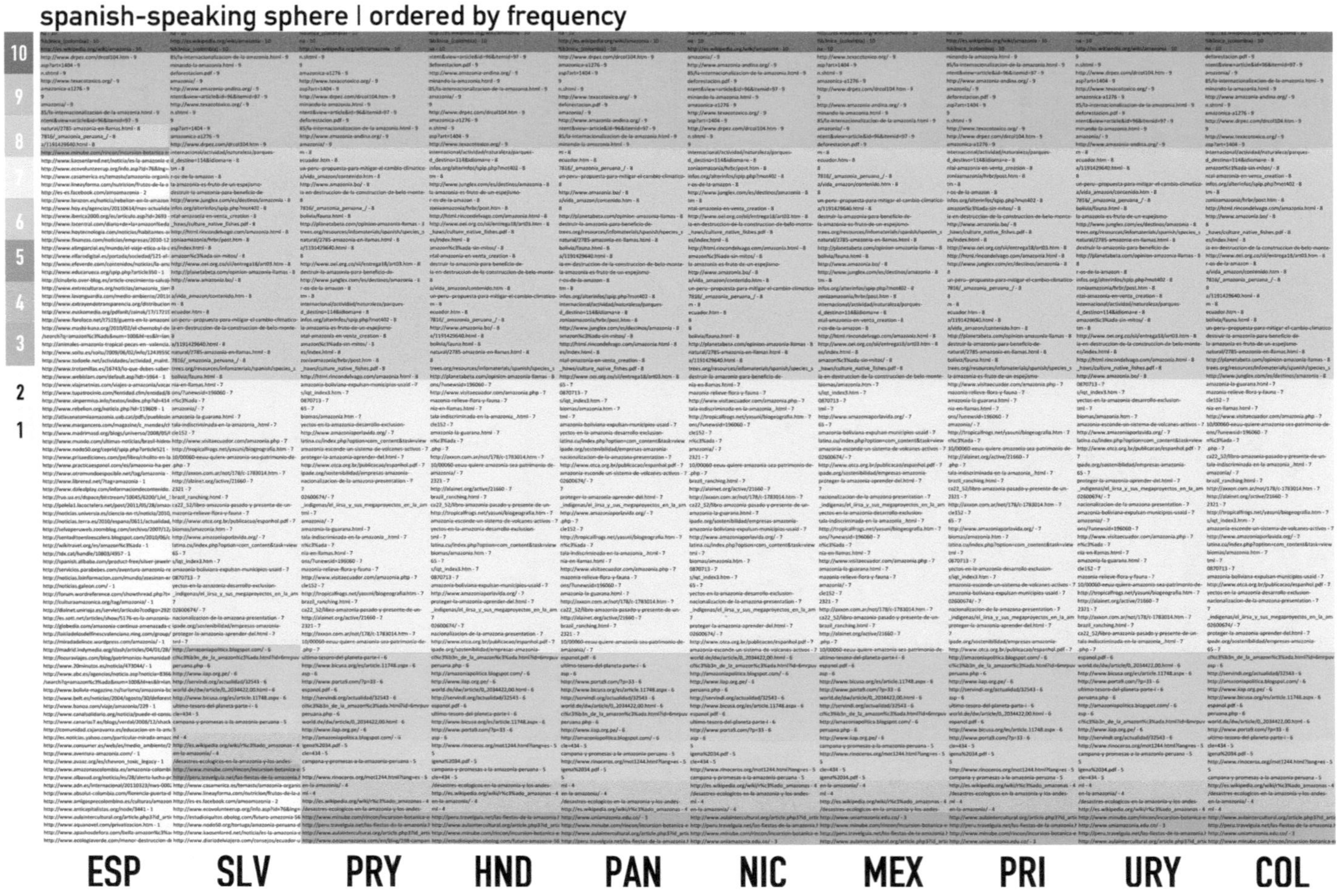

Figure 5.3
Similarity of results in Spanish-language local-domain Googles for the query [Amazonia], July 2011. Shadings indicate quantity of same results across local-domain Googles. Analysis by Natalia Sánchez Querubín and Diana Mesa, Digital Methods Summer School, Amsterdam.

The work that differentiates local-domain Googles according to the types of sources returned informs another question. When does the study of Google only concern Google, and when does it move beyond to social research? A similar question applies to the larger undertaking of digital methods: the study of the Internet to make findings that are not only about the Internet. Figure 5.4 illustrates a cross-country study of the results for the query [rights], where the query chosen is underspecified, allowing the algorithm to do its most work, and the local-domain Googles are selected for the country specificity of the languages (though not exclusively). Country-specific local-domain Googles are queried and results saved so as to have ranked lists of relevant rights types per country: for example the Finnish engine returns the right to roam (dear to Finns), the Dutch prostitutes' rights, and the Italian the right to oblivion (forgetting).

The steps as well as special considerations for this study were as follows. The local-domain Googles were queried for the word [rights] in the respective languages, then the rights types (one per site in the results) were lifted and left in the order Google returned them. The search engines were asked to output ranked societal concerns, as opposed to information only, through the open-ended query formulation. Also one might choose particular settings (results only in a particular language, results only from a particular country) to facilitate a research outlook that is distinctive from Google diagnostics or the study of Google, as discussed above. The Google properties were removed, including Google News, Google Images, YouTube videos, and Google Books; Wikipedia, given its relationship with Google (however defined), was also removed. Another type of artifact results from search engine optimization research, e.g., Google's privileging of the site's name or page's title. Thus a website called R.I.G.H.T.S., an acronym for the slogan Redistribution In Graphics Has To Stop, was returned in the top ten for the query [rights]. It is a tricky case, for the site is concerned with artists' copyright and unattributed reuse; this result can thus be construed as a rights issue wrapped in an engine-friendly publicity strategy.

The Study of Queries

Search as research relies on query design, so I would like to pursue the study of queries briefly. Engine queries are built in ways that may be surprising, and query research, as I discuss in the concluding chapter, has as one of its goals the coping with peculiar or irregular queries. That is, when querying an engine, some users fill in sentences, pose fully punctuated questions, or make remarks in search engine input fields, as if in conversation with the engine. Additionally, it was found that engine users fill in (portions of) URLs so as to access them via the search engine as opposed to directly.[16] (These are called navigational queries.) Other queries of interest to search engine analysts may be characterized as an alternative use of a search engine. One subject of analysis has been the "Google bomb," which brings to the top of Google results a website that normally would not be returned for the query in question, as discussed in chapter 2. Among the many cases are ones where engine manipulation is undertaken for political rather than commercial purposes, as with the 2003 Google bomb that pushed the George W. Bush campaign website to the top of the returns for the query [miserable failure]. (The technique was for webmasters to create hyperlinks to the campaign website with the pointer or link text "miserable failure.") It is important to point out that queries for "old" Google bombs have returns that discuss the notion as well as individual cases, and no longer yield the bombs (or blasts) themselves.

Another query that has been researched is the one that returns the offensive result. The query for [Jew] returns the anti-Semitic site Jewwatch.com in its top results. It interests search engine analysts because this is perhaps the only instance where Google's interface (rather than its blog) has supplied built-in commentary, with its own banner ad placed above the results: "We're disturbed about these results as well."[17] In that Google retains it, the offensive result also could be seen (and marketed) as general evidence of the lack of handcrafting of its engine's results. Along these lines it is instructive that the Anti-Defamation League, linked to in the explanation by Google of the offensive result, also puts forward the idea that Google results are not "authored" but rather automated. In the short item on its website titled "Google Search Ranking of Hate Sites Not Intentional," the group explains the Google returns as follows:

While it is true that hate sites do appear when certain search terms are used, their appearance and rank are not controlled by Google. Google employs technology that automatically ranks sites based on a complicated formula called an algorithm. The ranking of Jewwatch and other hate sites is in no way due to a conscious choice by Google, but solely is a result of this automated system of ranking.[18]

I would argue that Google does author results at least in the sense of source standing per returns list, albeit not by hand (with the possible exceptions of Wikipedia and special cases of delisting). For the current purposes, however, it is instructive to point out that the search engine will output the offensive result, as one of Google's founders explained to the Anti-Defamation League in a letter concerning the results, as long as the offending website has followed webmaster guidelines (and not used techniques considered to be engine spam).[19] "The longevity of ownership, the way articles are posted to it, the links to and from the site, and the structure of the site itself all increase the ranking of 'Jewwatch' within the Google formula" is how the Anti-Defamation League explained Google's algorithm in its press release.[20] I touch on the sensitive subject matter here not only to show how Google was able to transform the situation of an offensive result into an opportunity to explain that its algorithm is complex and its returns are not hand-picked or hand-censored; Google notes as much in its

The Nationalities of Issues

Most significant rights types per country according to local Google results of the query for rights in the local languages.

RESEARCH STRATEGY
Employ Google to show most prominent types of rights per country.

METHOD
Query the term "rights" in the local languages in the local Google versions, e.g., "oigused" in Google.ee and "direitos" in Google.pt. Manually, read the results and make lists of the top ten, distinctive rights types, leaving them in the order that Google provided.

Google.se with query "rattigheter" (13.07.09)
Google.fi with query "oikeudet" (13.07.09)
Google.ee with query "oigused" (15.07.09)
Google.lv with query "tiesibas" (16.07.09)
Google.co.uk with query "rights" (13.07.09)
Google.nl with query "rechten" (13.07.09)
Google.be with query "rechten van" (15.07.09)
Google.be with query "droits" (14.07.09)
Google.lu with query "rechte" (15.07.09)
Google.de with query "rechte" (15.07.09)
Google.at with query "rechte" (15.07.09)
Google.ch with query "rechte" (15.07.09)
Google.fr with query "droits" (14.07.09)
Google.pt with query "direitos" (14.07.09)
Google.es with query "derechos" (13.07.09)
Google.it with query "diritto al" OR "diritto all" OR "diritto alla" (13.07.09)
Google.ro with query "drepturile" (13.07.09)
Google.mo with query "drepturile" (13.07.09)
Google.ru with query "prava" (13.07.09)
Google.com.tr with query "haklari" (17.07.09)
Google.jp with query "権利" (16.07.09)
Google.hk with query "權利" (17.07.09)
Google.com.ph with query "karapatang" (16.07.09)
Google.ci with query "droits" (17.07.09)
Google.com.au with query "rights" (14.07.09)
Google.ca with query "rights" (15.07.09)
Google.ca with query "droits" (15.07.09)
Google.com with query "rights" (14.07.09)
Google.com with query "derechos" (15.07.09)
Google.com.mx with query "derechos" (15.07.09)
Google.com.br with query "direitos" (15.07.09)
Google.ar with query "derechos" (15.07.09)
Google.pe with query "derechos" (15.07.09)

DATA STORAGE
The top 100 results per query are stored for validation purposes. In Firefox, save page as, web page, complete. Data sets available at http://wiki.digitalmethods.net/Dmi/NationalityofIssues/.

Note the local Google versions were chosen on the basis of the language skills of the participants of the Digital Methods Summer School, 2009. Note too that when faced with a large quantity of Google versions for a single language, a further selection was made, e.g., the top three Spanish-speaking countries according to population.

For those local Google versions where multiple languages are spoken, the two dominant languages were queried. We queried google.be (Belgium) in Flemish and French, and queried google.ca (Canada) in English and French.

FINDINGS
Countries could be said to have distinctive concerns, compared to other countries, as read from Google results. For example, everyman's rights in Finland, prostitutes' rights in the Netherlands, computer programmers' rights in Japan and the right to oblivion in Italy (not saving everything) are unique to the respective countries. The specific rights language per country has been retained, meaning that LGBT rights in the United States, and homosexual rights in Hong Kong, are not regarded as equivalents. Also, given the limited sample of countries and the method for selection, the most widely shared rights across countries are not the subject of analysis.

ANALYSIS: Vera Bekema, Liliana Bounegru, Andrea Fiore, Anne Helmond, Simon Marschall, Sabine Niederer, Bram Nijhof, Richard Rogers and Elena Tiis.
DESIGN: Vera Bekema and Anne Helmond.
A product of the Digital Methods Initiative, Summer School '09, http://www.digitalmethods.net/.

 Right type

 Right type unique to the country (in this sample)

Figure 5.4
Rights types: the nationalities of issues. Top rights types per country, according to the results of queries for rights in the respective languages of local-domain Googles. (cc) Digital Methods Initiative, Amsterdam, 2009.

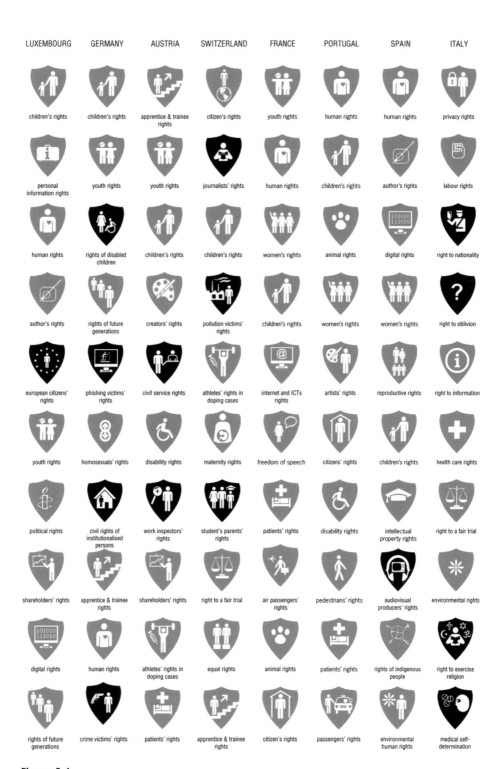

Figure 5.4
(continued)

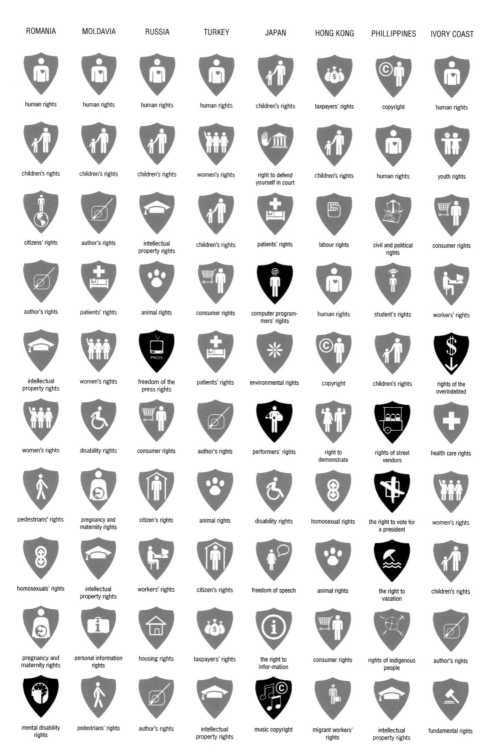

Figure 5.4
(continued)

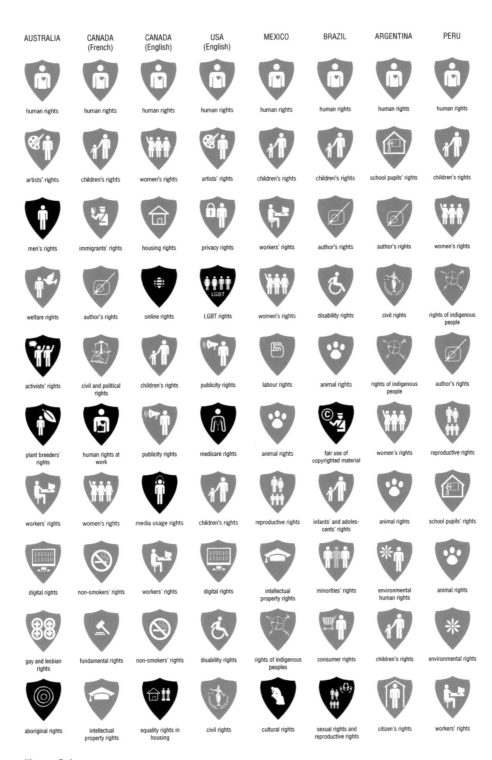

Figure 5.4
(continued)

webmaster guidelines: "Google prefers developing scalable and automated solutions to problems, so we attempt to minimize hand-to-hand spam fighting."[21] More importantly for present purposes, I would like to point out that engine placement is hard-earned and long-term, high engine placement even harder. Such an epistemology would open the way for search engine use in source research, and critique of Google as research (epistemological) machine would lie in any slippage in it. As I come to shortly, personalization would constitute such a weakening, for it would mean that the user coauthors the results. Therefore, in one's preparation for using the engine as research machine, and in one's query design, one must clear the engine of personal settings, and also seek to turn off localization and personalization.

Engine query analysis often concerns deviance (irregular or odd query-building) and anomaly (results that amuse or offend). The analysis especially relies on optimization and manipulation cases, including the commercially significant (JCPenny.com) as well as political Google bombs. Indeed, in each case the work touches on and elucidates in part the workings of the search engine as link counter, whether these links have been planted by activists practicing tactical media or black-hat search engine optimizers disguising advertising. In each case the search engine becomes embroiled in a debate about its role as both adjudicator of sources and author of a list of them, whether the contents of the websites are mundane or offensive. Each case concerns the top returns of the engine, and how long the top ranking has been retained (for years or only the holiday season). In the event, standing is not earned through short-term antics (where Google responds in a somewhat fatherly manner by grounding a website, and providing means to atone through good behavior and a URL resubmission form). Rather, it is the product of spherical culture as well as long-term webmaster or site owner dedication to contents and upkeep, as experiments have shown on the latency in search engine ranking (the time it takes for a new site to climb to the top of the results).[22] It takes time to become established online (in engine returns) and to maintain standing.

Societal Search: Interpreting Engine Results

In an extreme formulation, the point of departure of search as research, or societal search, may be summarized as follows: we look at Google results and see society, instead of Google.[23] That is to say that, including its "artifacts," engine results put much on display—from source competition and standing to longevity and commitment. How, then, to begin to make such interpretation more apparent? How to read engine results so that they are more than information? How to query engines so that the results begin to answer research questions, however preliminary or exploratory?

I would like to proceed in a practical manner. "Query design" is the practice of formulating a query so that the results can be interpreted as indications and findings (however cluelike), as opposed to mere information retrieved or optimization and manipulation exposed (however fascinating). In preparation, digital methods researchers consider the installation of a clean research browser, like the purchase of a new field notebook. The general purpose of the preparation, in this case, is to eradicate traces. The researcher prepares a clean slate, free of cookies and other engine entanglements such as history and preferences. One signs out of the engine (by logging out of gmail, yahoomail, etc.) and uninstalls toolbars, which are incidentally one of the leading means by which engines study users. To be clear, here we are turning the tables and are making studies of engines, or more precisely social studies via or on top of engines. If one has a Google account, it is desirable to disable customized results, an option in one's web history. If one does not have a Google account, the Google cookies should be cleared and not allowed to be set. An alternative to the discomfort of uncoupling oneself from the search engine (and its continual study of the user), and spending time in one's cookie folder, is to employ a Google scraper (such as the erstwhile scroogle.org) that returns google.com results without placing a cookie or allowing Google to keep a query log history. The scraper would query the "ncr" or no country redirect version of Google, a purist's google.com in a world of gradual personalization. The second step is to learn the search operators, and think about them (again) less from an information retrieval and more from a research point of view. How to use the [site:] query, for example, and the date ranges? Third, consider the query not as a question but as a research question posed to the engine, and carefully craft it. Query design, more specifically now, is the stringing together of search operators with keywords in order to answer a (research) question put to one or more sources. The question may be posed in the no country redirect Google, across local-domain Googles, or in the various sphere engines (for the web sphere, blogosphere, news sphere), as I come to shortly, in the discussion of the sphere as engine-demarcated space and its comparative study as cross-spherical analysis. There may be multiple queries, launched individually or batched. The crucial point is to consider the keywords, with the search operators, and which source sets for them to be queried in. Also of importance is the use of quotation marks. Without quotation marks, queried keywords may return results for synonyms or other inexactitudes, providing equivalents as opposed to matches. In this case, engines seeking to be helpful to all users may become less so for the researcher.

The research I describe relies precisely on the properties of search engines most often critiqued, both historically as well as in contemporary network culture critique: indexing (which recalls the lack of complete indexing of all the web, and the notion of the dark web) as well as ordering and ranking (which recalls ideas of the exclusionary engine, burying sites low in the returns). Here the purpose is to emphasize the engines' capacities as indexer as well as author of the order of things. Where indexing is concerned, research work especially relies on the engine's ability to index individual websites, so that the researcher is able to count the number of mentions of a particular term on a website, where helpfully one mention is one page. For example one is able to query Greenpeace.org (Greenpeace International) for all of its campaigns, and count the number of pages on which Greenpeace mentions each, thereby beginning the study of each campaign's (internal) resonance. Which campaigns have the most pages on the Greenpeace site? This is a [site:] query, together with a list of campaign keywords, carefully extracted from the website. What is returned is a ranked list of campaigns. Here, with the aid of the search engine, the web is turned into a site of research into issue resonance in an organization; with date ranges employed, one can begin to detect changes to campaigning behaviors and perhaps strategies over time, in advance of an interview with the Greenpeace campaign director, for example, or after that same encounter to better understand the history that was told.

Before describing the workings and the principles behind the Lippmannian Device, the software made for issue resonance analysis, I would like to move to how one may interpret search engine results' rankings manually, without automated techniques, and to the more formalized study of search engine results called "source distance," in which the researcher saves engine results for particular queries, and inquires into the distance of particular sources from the top of returns are particular sources for significant queries.

Search engine results can be read and interpreted for the composition of source types returned in the top results, for the familiarity of the sources returned compared to other media such as television, and for the absence of (significant) sources, where the exercise is to estrange oneself from the symbolic world (so to speak) that the source list invites one into, and consider which other sources could and perhaps should be present, as in the Issue Dramaturg project discussed above. How to consider search engine results as compositions of actors currently occupying an issue space? As discussed in chapter 4, for the [RFID] queries made in 2004 and 2008, the engine results showed how the RFID space had changed significantly over the course of the four years. In 2008 there were governmental agencies and established nongovernmental organizations in the top ten, which may be contrasted with the doom-saying activist, lone tinkerer, and ebullient trade press high in the rankings in 2004. From the engine results, one could tell that the issue had matured.[24]

Source Distance: The Epistemological Study of Search Engine Returns

For any given subject matter, including any social issue, certain sources are winning the competition to be the top sources returned. Which sources are returned at the top for the query ["climate change"]? How to study and characterize the sources close to the top, compared to those toward the bottom? Critiques of the new hierarchies of credibility authored by engines have led to new media art projects, such as Shmoogle, which randomizes the results of a Google query: "[what] if the result you were looking for was hiding in page 53?"[25] There is less work, however, on the epistemological consequences of algorithmic authority. How to capture and analyze source-privileging mechanisms, that is, which sources are recommended highly for a given subject matter? How to study engine returns? I would like to discuss a method called "source distance." It is web epistemology applied, in that it addresses the question of how to characterize the privileging of sources by search engines. As the term suggests, it is the study of the distance of a source from the top of the rankings. How far from the top are certain sources per query? Do the top sources share a particular type or bent? It also has a longitudinal element. Are the top sources stable? Does the top of the web (per query) exhibit volatility? The implications of the work could be thought of in relatively straightforward terms. For example, whose voice is well organized online, in the sense of being highly present for particular matters of concern, and whose is absent or less audible? It also puts forward a study of engine output without a sole focus on the top rankings, and especially their optimization and manipulation, while remaining aware of Google artifacts.

In the opening of the book, I discussed how source distance as an analytical technique was conceived. There are sources and issues at the top of the news: Are those same sources at the top of the web (for the particular issue in question)? How to conceptualize the top of the web, and how to measure the distance between it and the sources that could be the ones informing the issue? The Google Scraper for source distance research—later also called the Lippmannian Device for partisanship and issue resonance analysis—was developed to transform search into research by capturing search engine results for any query and saving the results for further study, including source prominence per query as well as questions of the stability or volatility of sources in query results over time. As I have pointed out above, through the study of engine results over time one is able to inquire into the time it takes for sources to become established, and similarly to be dislodged from top placements.

The source distance analytical technique relies on a two-step process in which one first queries the search engine, for example, for ["climate change"]. The top 100 or more results are stripped of description text and all else, so that only the URLs remain.[26] Each URL (or each unique host) is inserted into the Google Scraper and is queried (for example, for the names of the climate change skeptics, so as to identify skeptic-friendly sites or sites with other reasons for mentioning them, such as watchdog sites). The Google Scraper queries each website for each keyword. It outputs the results in the form of a source cloud, with the http or www removed from each clouded source, so that only the colloquial domain name remains, such as Greenpeace.org. The cloud is a Google-ordered source cloud, meaning the results are in the same order as returned by Google. (One may wish to have an alphabetical source cloud for locating particular sources, or a ranked ordered cloud, where sources with the greatest frequency of results appear first.) Each domain name is resized according to the number of times it mentions the keyword.

The seminal work with the Google Scraper, as described in the opening chapter, was concerned with the climate change skeptics, who were receiving press attention and air time on the television news. How are the skeptics faring on the web? This work also introduces the renamed Scraper as Lippmannian Device, named after Walter Lippmann and his call for a coarse means to detect bias, partisanship, or more generally alignment.[27] The Lippmannian Device is meant to be an everyday piece of equipment for the analysis of issue spaces by issue professionals and other publics. It sits atop the search engine and relies on its capacity to index individual websites. One queries a set of websites for keywords, showing in tag clouds which websites mention which words. The tag clouds are renamed issue clouds or source clouds, depending on which output the user chooses (see figure 5.5). The Device may be used for mapping or positioning actors and their issue language in controversies thought difficult to disentangle:

> The problem is to locate by clear and coarse objective tests the actor in the controversy who is most worthy of public support. . . . The hardest controversies to disentangle [are when] the public is called in to judge. Where the facts are most obscure, where precedents are lacking, where novelty and confusion pervade everything, the public in all its unfitness is compelled to make its most important decisions. The hardest problems are those which institutions cannot handle. They are the public's problems.[28]

Here the example used was again climate change, where the objective was to identify skeptic-friendly sources. Three lists of skeptics were triangulated, and those skeptics' names appearing on at least two of the lists were retained. ["Climate change"] was queried in the software, and 100 results retained. In the second step, each of the skeptics was queried in each of the unique hosts from the 100 results retained in step one. In the source clouds of the leading climate change sites on the web, according to Google, the skeptics found relatively scant voice and were not close to the top of the web, which for climate change in July 2007 included epa.gov (the U.S. Environmental Protection Agency) and ipcc.org (Intergovernmental Panel on Climate Change) in the top five. There were skeptic-friendly sites where the names of the skeptics resonate, such as Marshall.org (Marshall Institute), and there were watchdog sites, such as Sourcewatch.org, where the skeptics too received a great deal of scrutiny.

A decade ago search engine companies competed by algorithm (among other things). Algorithmic variety, however, declined gradually (at least among the larger engines) with the growth of Google worldwide, and the closure or repositioning of national search engines (the Dutch Ilse and the Austrian AON as portals with vertical or specialized search engines). Some notable exceptions are in China (Baidu operating since 2000), the Czech Republic (Seznam since 1996), Japan (Yahoo! since 1996), Russia (Yandex since 1997 and Rambler since 1996), and South Korea (Naver since 1999). As discussed in the previous chapter, Google arguably has ushered in a form of media concentration that could be called algorithmic concentration—large engines largely following Google's PageRank. While the account of the similarity of engines may be well known or experienced in everyday use, what are perhaps less appreciated are the differences across web spaces. Engines rank sources distinctively by sphere, as I discussed briefly above. Search engines have different ranking logics for the web sphere, the blogosphere, and the news sphere, where sources are privileged according to different mixes of the variables or signals: inlink count, click-through, freshness, age, updating regularity (and for the news sphere certain offline variables such as size of the news staff of the organization). Here I also would like to put forward a comparative analytical practice, whereby search engine returns are captured from engines across the spheres (web sphere, blogosphere, and news sphere), and the rankings of the sources (and source types) across them are compared. Thus I would like to introduce a comparative media studies approach that is based on the subdivision or partitioning of the web into distinctive adjudication cultures. By interpreting search engine logics across spheres (through empirical findings), one may ask which engines (and spheres) introduce hierarchies of credibility for information sources similar to others, and which introduce unfamiliar rankings? Here one is performing critical source analysis that concerns the reproduction, across media spaces, of the familiar and the official, where the familiar may be predefined or newly defined. One may pose the questions in classic terms of spheres as more or less critical, more or less diverse, more or less generous in the materials they allow to rise to the top, or still circulate in the reachable results pages. The larger questions of source plurality and diversity per sphere as well as the organization of critical and oppositional voice remain crucial, and analyzable through the technique put forward here. Of interest in the following is the question of the web's proximity to publicity culture and to media icons, such as one views on television and on portals, too. Which spheres are prone to creating media icons, and which less so?

Cross-Spherical Analysis

How is comparative media analysis often done? The use of the term "comparative" in research usually refers to cross-country comparisons, such as in comparative media law. In media studies, the term "comparative" may refer to analysis across media forms, such as comparisons between print and web, or across different news media (TV news, newspaper, news magazines). Generally this kind of comparative media analysis also takes into consideration how attention or significance is

Climate Change Sceptics on the Web (S. Fred Singer)

Research Question_To what extent are climate change 'skeptics' present in the climate change spaces on the Web?
Findings_There is distance between the skeptics and the top of the search engine returns.

epa.gov (0)   bbc.co.uk (0)   defra.gov.uk (0)   unep.org (0)   born.gov.au (0)   ipcc.ch (0)   pewclimate.org (0)
davidsuzuki.org (0)   panda.org (0)   mfe.govt.nz (0)   ec.gc.ca (0)   exploratorium.edu (0)   climatechange.com.au (0)
greenpeace.org (1)   climatechallenge.gov.uk (0)   guardian.co.uk (0)   iisd.org (0)   g8.gov.uk (0)   campaigncc.org (1)
foe.co.uk (0)   state.gov (0)   scidev.net (0)   eea.europa.eu (0)   whoi.edu (0)   cbc.ca (0)   energy.gov (0)
marshall.org (0)   climateark.org (1)   un.org (0)   dar.csiro.au (0)   theglobeandmail.com (0)   acfonline.org.au (0)
gcrio.org (0)   nature.com (0)   grida.no (0)   nature.org (0)   ecokids.ca (0)   royalsoc.ac.uk (0)
climatechangecentral.com (0)   iea.org (0)   ecn.ac.uk (0)   ecy.wa.gov (0)   worldwildlife.org (0)

realclimate.org (14)   faqs.org (0)   metoffice.gov.uk (0)   open2.net (0)   scienceagogo.com (0)

eldis.org (0)   ft.com (0)   who.int (0)   climatecrisis.net (0)   ltscotland.org.uk (0)   abc.net.au (0)   climatechange.ca.gov (0)
envirolink.org (0)   mofa.go.jp (0)

sourcewatch.org (64)

iucn.org (0)   dfat.gov.au (0)   ncdc.noaa.gov (0)   # climatescience.gov (11)
climatechangecollege.org (0)   ciel.org (0)   ucar.edu (0)

Source_google.com
Query_"Fred Singer"
Method_Search for query "Fred Singer" in top 100. Organized in order.
Tools_Google Scraper and Tag Cloud Generator
Date_30 July 2007

Product_of the Digital Methods Initiative, dmi.mediastudies.nl. **Analysis**_by Bram Nijhof, Richard Rogers and Laura van der Vlies. **Design**_Anne Helmond.

Climate Change Sceptics on the Web (Sallie Baliunas)

Research Question_To what extent are climate change 'skeptics' present in the climate change spaces on the Web?
Findings_There is distance between the skeptics and the top of the search engine returns.

epa.gov (0)   bbc.co.uk (0)   defra.gov.uk (0)   unep.org (0)   born.gov.au (0)   ipcc.ch (0)   pewclimate.org (0)
davidsuzuki.org (0)   panda.org (0)   mfe.govt.nz (0)   ec.gc.ca (0)   exploratorium.edu (0)   climatechange.com.au (0)
greenpeace.org (0)   climatechallenge.gov.uk (0)   guardian.co.uk (0)   iisd.org (0)   g8.gov.uk (0)   campaigncc.org (0)
foe.co.uk (0)   state.gov (0)   scidev.net (0)   eea.europa.eu (0)   whoi.edu (0)   cbc.ca (0)   energy.gov (0)
marshall.org (6)   climateark.org (2)   un.org (0)   dar.csiro.au (0)   theglobeandmail.com (0)
acfonline.org.au (0)   gcrio.org (0)   nature.com (0)   grida.no (0)   nature.org (0)   ecokids.ca (0)   royalsoc.ac.uk (0)
climatechangecentral.com (0)   iea.org (0)   ecn.ac.uk (0)   ecy.wa.gov (0)   worldwildlife.org (0)

realclimate.org (55)

faqs.org (0)   metoffice.gov.uk (0)   open2.net (0)   scienceagogo.com (0)   eldis.org (0)   ft.com (0)   who.int (0)
climatecrisis.net (0)   ltscotland.org.uk (0)   abc.net.au (0)   climatechange.ca.gov (0)   envirolink.org (0)   mofa.go.jp (0)
sourcewatch.org (0)   iucn.org (0)   dfat.gov.au (0)   ncdc.noaa.gov (0)   climatescience.gov (0)
climatechangecollege.org (0)   ciel.org (0)   ucar.edu (0)

Source_google.com
Query_"Sallie Baliunas"
Method_Search for query "Sallie Baliunas" in top 100. Organized in order.
Tools_Google Scraper and Tag Cloud Generator
Date_30 July 2007

Product_of the Digital Methods Initiative, dmi.mediastudies.nl. **Analysis**_by Bram Nijhof, Richard Rogers and Laura van der Vlies. **Design**_Anne Helmond.

Figure 5.5

Climate change skeptics' presence in the leading climate change websites, according to google.com, July 2007. Source distance analysis by the Google Scraper. (cc) Digital Methods Initiative, Amsterdam, 2007.

Climate Change Sceptics on the Web (Timothy Ball)

Research Question_ To what extent are climate change 'skeptics' present
in the climate change spaces on the Web?
Findings_ There is distance between the skeptics and the top of the
search engine returns.

epa.gov (0)   bbc.co.uk (0)   defra.gov.uk (0)   unep.org (0)   bom.gov.au (0)   ipcc.ch (0)   pewclimate.org (0)
davidsuzuki.org (0)   panda.org (0)   mfe.govt.nz (0)   ec.gc.ca (0)   exploratorium.edu (0)   climatechange.com.au (0)
greenpeace.org (0)   climatechallenge.gov.uk (0)   guardian.co.uk (0)   iisd.org (0)   g8.gov.uk (0)
campaigncc.org (6)   foe.co.uk (0)   state.gov (0)   scidev.net (0)   eea.europa.eu (0)   whoi.edu (0)   cbc.ca (0)
energy.gov (0)   marshall.org (2)   climateark.org (0)   un.org (0)   dar.csiro.au (0)   theglobeandmail.com (0)
acfonline.org.au (0)   gcrio.org (0)   nature.com (0)   grida.no (0)   nature.org (0)   ecokids.ca (0)   royalsoc.ac.uk (0)
climatechangecentral.com (0)   iea.org (0)   ecn.ac.uk (0)   ecy.wa.gov (0)   worldwildlife.org (0)   realclimate.org (0)
faqs.org (0)   metoffice.gov.uk (0)   open2.net (0)   scienceagogo.com (0)   eldis.org (0)   ft.com (0)   who.int (0)
climatecrisis.net (0)   ltscotland.org.uk (0)   abc.net.au (0)   climatechange.ca.gov (0)   envirolink.org (0)   mofa.go.jp (0)
sourcewatch.org (0)   iucn.org (0)   dfat.gov.au (0)   ncdc.noaa.gov (0)   climatescience.gov (0)
climatechangecollege.org (0)   ciel.org (0)   ucar.edu (0)

Source_google.com
Query_"Timothy Ball"
Method_ Search for query "Timothy Ball" in top 100. Organized in order.
Tools_ Google Scraper and Tag Cloud Generator
Date_30 July 2007

Product_of the Digital Methods Initiative,
dmi.mediastudies.nl. **Analysis_**by Bram
Nijhof, Richard Rogers and Laura van der
Vlies. **Design_**Anne Helmond.

CC_BY-NC-SA

Climate Change Sceptics on the Web (Willie Soon)

Research Question_ To what extent are climate change 'skeptics' present
in the climate change spaces on the Web?
Findings_ There is distance between the skeptics and the top of the
search engine returns.

epa.gov (0)   bbc.co.uk (0)   defra.gov.uk (0)   unep.org (0)   bom.gov.au (0)   ipcc.ch (0)   pewclimate.org (0)
davidsuzuki.org (0)   panda.org (0)   mfe.govt.nz (0)   ec.gc.ca (0)   exploratorium.edu (0)   climatechange.com.au (0)
greenpeace.org (0)   climatechallenge.gov.uk (0)   guardian.co.uk (0)   iisd.org (0)   g8.gov.uk (0)   campaigncc.org (2)
foe.co.uk (0)   state.gov (0)   scidev.net (0)   eea.europa.eu (0)   whoi.edu (0)   cbc.ca (0)   energy.gov (0)
marshall.org (4)   climateark.org (1)   un.org (0)   dar.csiro.au (0)   theglobeandmail.com (0)   acfonline.org.au (0)
gcrio.org (0)   nature.com (0)   grida.no (0)   nature.org (0)   ecokids.ca (0)   royalsoc.ac.uk (0)
climatechangecentral.com (0)   iea.org (0)   ecn.ac.uk (0)   ecy.wa.gov (0)   worldwildlife.org (0)
realclimate.org (27)   faqs.org (0)   metoffice.gov.uk (0)
open2.net (0)   scienceagogo.com (0)   eldis.org (0)   ft.com (0)   who.int (0)   climatecrisis.net (0)   ltscotland.org.uk (0)
abc.net.au (0)   climatechange.ca.gov (0)   envirolink.org (0)   mofa.go.jp (0)   sourcewatch.org (0)   iucn.org (0)
dfat.gov.au (0)   ncdc.noaa.gov (0)   climatescience.gov (0)   climatechangecollege.org (0)   ciel.org (0)   ucar.edu (0)

Source_google.com
Query_"Willie Soon"
Method_ Search for query "Willie Soon" in top 100. Organized in order.
Tools_ Google Scraper and Tag Cloud Generator
Date_30 July 2007

Product_of the Digital Methods Initiative,
dmi.mediastudies.nl. **Analysis_**by Bram
Nijhof, Richard Rogers and Laura van der
Vlies. **Design_**Anne Helmond.

CC_BY-NC-SA

Figure 5.5
(continued)

analyzed for each medium, e.g., headline size, column inches, and section for news-papers, the number of minutes politicians are on screen for television, etc. In cross-media studies, one is concerned with how the story or narrative remains the same, despite the different packages or media containers. Here the aim of cross-spherical analysis is to build upon comparative media analysis, in the sense of comparing substance, coverage, and storyline across media forms, and to apply what is learned to the web.

A sphere is a device-demarcated source set, i.e., the pure PageRank of all sources on the web (most influential sites by inlink count), or indeed analogous "page rank-ings" of all sources as granted by the dominant engines for each sphere, i.e., Google Web Search for the web sphere, Technorati or Google Blog Search for the blogo-sphere, and Google News for the news sphere.[29] (One could add Delicious or Stumble-upon for the social bookmarking or tagosphere, and perhaps other sphere engines, too, such as the image sphere organized by Google Image Search.) Thus, to study a sphere, the proposal is first to allow the engines to demarcate it. In sphere analysis one considers where sources are ranked in each sphere, per query, and compares them. Importantly, with cross-spherical analysis one may consider the consequences of each sphere's or engine's treatment of links, freshness, etc. Do particular sources tend to be in the core of one sphere and absent from others? What do comparisons between sources, and source distances, across the spheres tell us about the quality of the spheres? In the empirical case study, the focus is again on climate change, in the project titled *Issue Animals*. As with the climate change skeptics source distance research, one locates reputable lists of keywords (or names) for the object of study in question, and triangulates them. The keywords in this case are animals associated with climate change, the term which is queried in the dominant engines of the web sphere, blogosphere, and news sphere, in the same procedure described above for the skeptics research. The animals are queried one by one in each of the individual results (returned in step one). In addition to the resonance of the keywords for each sphere, the analysis also captured, counted, and resized images (in a manual proce-dure), creating what could be called image clouds to accompany the issue or keyword clouds. The results for the cross-spherical analysis are counterintuitive to a degree (see figure 5.6). The news delivers the polar bear as the top issue animal, a result that is amplified in the blogosphere, suggesting a strong relationship between the two spheres. This much is well known.[30] In the web sphere, however, the issue animal keywords are more distributed, displaying the web as a more info-egalitarian sphere, less prone to focusing on one animal as poster or icon. The image analysis produces similar findings: the blogosphere portrays not only the polar bear but also activists dressed as polar bears, thereby strengthening its dominance as issue animal (see figure 5.7).

Conclusion: Search as Research

This chapter proposes a shift in the focus of search engine critique, away from Google as hegemon, monopolist, and surveillance machine (however crucial) to its rehabilitation as research machine. The introduction of source hierarchies and exclusionary practices into an allegedly democratic or egalitarian medium was among the earliest, critical work on search engines.[31] More recently, algorithmic authority, or the belief in the epistemological value of search engine results, became a way to phrase the power of Google. Here, instead, I have first recalled the search engine's origins as a research machine and asked whether it may be used as one again, and under which conditions. May we apply the engine's work in how it demarcates web spaces and orders sources? The answer is not straightforward, for the user and the engine increasingly coproduce results, and unplugging from Google (so to speak) and preparing a clean slate are part of the research practice. Once the groundwork is laid, the researcher is asked to rethink engine use, including the foreign-language engines, advanced search features, and the subengines—not an easy task for anyone using it as a consumer on an everyday basis! How to employ the local-domain Googles, the [site:] query, and the individual web, blog, and news engines attuned to the cultures of the separate spheres online?

For cross-country comparison through the use of the local-domain Googles, one may wish to familiarize oneself with Google's sense of the local. To do so, inquiries are made into the large language areas online, describing each's sense of the local. As reported above, the general finding (from the small cases) concerning Google's local-domain engines is that there is a hierarchy in the sense of which ones provide more local results and which fewer, with the global north furnishing more local sources in the results for the query ["human rights"]. Such a general observation of Google as machine of the north is complicated by the experiments conducted with Spanish-language local-domain Googles, where two locals were distinguished. Sources from Spain were furnished in Google Spain for the query [diversidad]. In the Latin American local-domain Googles the local is comprised of a somewhat uniform regional result set. While intriguing, the findings are more in the realm of Google diagnostic work, making way for a research practice that builds atop the engine for other purposes.

While Google's sense of the local becomes research work in itself, a second practice is more in keeping with the larger effort of doing research with the web (as opposed to only about the web). The Lippmannian Device harnesses the engine's indexing capacities of individual websites so as to query them for keyword mentions. It is a simple impact-measuring device, which charts presence and absence as well as frequency (and thus resonance), without any coding of usage as positive, negative, or neutral, and without any sentiment or emotive indications. Which sources mention

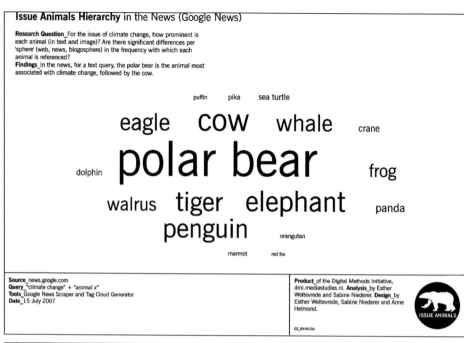

Source_news.google.com
Query_"climate change" + "animal x"
Tools_Google News Scraper and Tag Cloud Generator
Date_15 July 2007

Product_of the Digital Methods Initiative,
dmi.mediastudies.nl. Analysis_by Esther
Weltevrede and Sabine Niederer. Design_by
Esther Weltevrede, Sabine Niederer and Anne
Helmond.

CC_BY-NC-SA

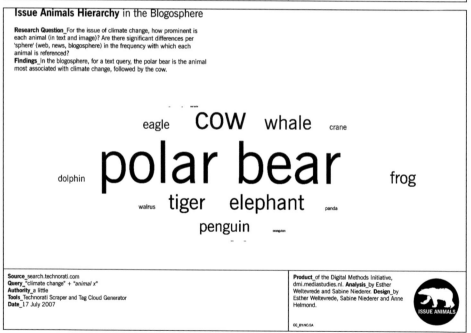

Source_search.technorati.com
Query_"climate change" + "animal x"
Authority_a little
Tools_Technorati Scraper and Tag Cloud Generator
Date_17 July 2007

Product_of the Digital Methods Initiative,
dmi.mediastudies.nl. Analysis_by Esther
Weltevrede and Sabine Niederer. Design_by
Esther Weltevrede, Sabine Niederer and Anne
Helmond.

CC_BY-NC-SA

Figure 5.6

Cross-spherical analysis. Distribution of mentions of animals associated with climate change ("issue animals") in top 100 sources returned by Google News, Technorati Blog Search, and Google Web Search for the query ["climate change"], July 2007. (cc) Digital Methods Initiative, Amsterdam, 2007.

Issue Animals Hierarchy on the Web (Google)

Research Question_For the issue of climate change, how prominent is each animal (in text and image)? Are there significant differences per 'sphere' (web, news, blogosphere) in the frequency with which each animal is referenced?
Findings_On the web, for a text query, results are distributed across all the animals not particularly favoring one issue animal.

puffin pika sea turtle

eagle cow whale crane

dolphin polar bear frog

walrus tiger elephant panda

penguin orangutan

marmot red fox

Source_www.google.com
Query_"climate change" + scrape top 100 results for "animal x"
Tools_Google Scraper, Compare Lists and Tag Cloud Generator
Date_15 July 2007

Product_of the Digital Methods Initiative, dmi.mediastudies.nl. **Analysis**_by Esther Weltevrede and Sabine Niederer. **Design**_by Esther Weltevrede, Sabine Niederer and Anne Helmond.

CC_BY-NC-SA

Figure 5.6
(continued)

the climate change skeptics by name, and which do not? There are two overall methods. In a method dubbed "source distance," the question is how far from the top of ranked climate change sources are those sources that make mention of the skeptics. The source distance method is a means of media monitoring and media criticism, inviting comparisons with other (traditional) media, such as the news, and measuring source distance there ("top of the news"). The second approach, broadly speaking, is "issue alignment," which is one answer to Lippmann's call for a coarse, simple, and objective means to detect an actor's side. The work on the climate change skeptics is again illustrative. Which sources mention the skeptics by name, with what frequency? The source clouds that are outputted are for insertion into presentations, and in that sense are considered equipment for issue professionals and other publics. The clouds are also navigational (clickable), where the users are directed to the context of use of the keyword.

The third research practice discussed above follows the engine culture of disaggregating the web into spheres: web sphere, blogosphere, and news sphere. (In principle, one may expand the spheres to include other spaces online organized by a dominant engine, device, or platform.) Spheres are considered engine- or device-demarcated

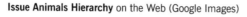

Issue Animals Hierarchy on the Web (Google Images)

Research Question_For the issue of climate change, how prominent is each animal (in text and image)? Are there significant differences per 'sphere' (web, news, blogosphere) in the frequency with which each animal is referenced?
Findings_On the web, for an image query, results are distributed across all the animals not particularly favoring one issue animal.

Source_images.google.com
Query_"climate change"
Method_count and scale similar animals by frequency of appearance
Result_all (1,420,000 images in 107,000,000 web results, 918 presented by images.google.com)
Date_17 July 2007

Product_of the Digital Methods Initiative, dmi.mediastudies.nl. Analysis_by Esther Weltevrede and Sabine Niederer. Design_by Esther Weltevrede, Sabine Niederer and Anne Helmond.

ISSUE ANIMALS

Issue Animals Hierarchy in the News (Google News Images)

Research Question_For the issue of climate change, how prominent is each animal (in text and image)? Are there significant differences per 'sphere' (web, news, blogosphere) in the frequency with which each animal is referenced?
Findings_In the news, for an image query, results are distributed across few of the animals, favoring the polar bear and introducing the cow.

Source_news.google.com Image Version
Query_"climate change"
Method_count and scale similar animals by frequency of appearance
Result_all (3.095 images in 25,933 articles, 782 presented by news.google.com)
Date_17 July 2007

Product_of the Digital Methods Initiative, dmi.mediastudies.nl. Analysis_by Esther Weltevrede and Sabine Niederer. Design_by Esther Weltevrede, Sabine Niederer and Anne Helmond.

ISSUE ANIMALS

Figure 5.7
Cross-spherical analysis. Distribution of images of animals in all of the returns in Google News, Technorati Blog Search, and Google Web Search for the query ["climate change"], July 2007. (cc) Digital Methods Initiative, Amsterdam, 2007.

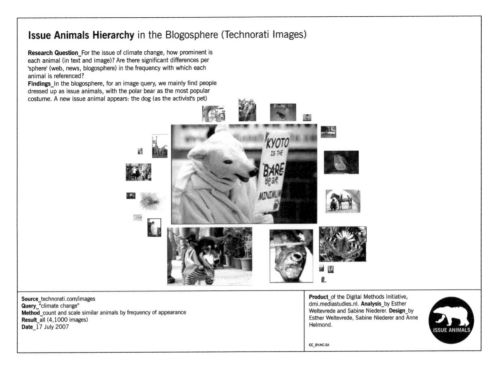

Issue Animals Hierarchy in the Blogosphere (Technorati Images)

Research Question_For the issue of climate change, how prominent is each animal (in text and image)? Are there significant differences per 'sphere' (web, news, blogosphere) in the frequency with which each animal is referenced?
Findings_In the blogosphere, for an image query, we mainly find people dressed up as issue animals, with the polar bear as the most popular costume. A new issue animal appears: the dog (as the activist's pet).

Source_technorati.com/images
Query_"climate change"
Method_count and scale similar animals by frequency of appearance
Result_all (4,1000 images)
Date_17 July 2007

Product_of the Digital Methods Initiative, dmi.mediastudies.nl. **Analysis**_by Esther Weltevrede and Sabine Niederer. **Design**_by Esther Weltevrede, Sabine Niederer and Anne Helmond.

CC_BY-NC-SA

Figure 5.7
(continued)

source sets, ordered and delivered as query results, however broad and underspecified. (The next chapter discusses how one uses engines as well as other device cultures to secure sources at other levels of aggregation.) The research approach called "cross-spherical analysis" expands the single-sphere analysis made available by the Google Scraper to one enabled by comparing the outputs of other scrapers too, including the Google Blog Search Scraper and the Google News Scraper. The work reintroduces comparative media analysis, now applied to the web, where the question, in each sphere, concerns composition of sources and their substance for a given issue area.

6 National Web Studies

The work described in this chapter offers an approach to conceptualizing, demarcating, and analyzing a national web. Instead of defining a priori the types of websites to be included, the approach put forward here makes use of web devices (platforms and engines) that purport to provide (ranked) lists of URLs relevant to a particular country.[1] Once gathered in such a manner, the websites are studied for their properties, following certain common measures (such as responsiveness and page age) and repurposing them to speak in terms of the health of a national web. Are sites lively, or neglected? The case study in question is Iran, which is special for the degree of Internet censorship undertaken by the state. Despite the widespread censorship, the Iranian web appears to be highly responsive. There is also a relationship between blockage, responsiveness, and freshness, i.e., whether blocked sites are still up, and whether they have been recently updated. Blocked yet blogging, portions of the Iranian web show strong indications of an active Internet censorship circumvention culture. In seeking to answer, additionally, whether censorship has killed content, a textual analysis shows continued use of language considered critical by the regime, thereby indicating a dearth of self-censorship, at least for websites that are recommended by the leading Iranian platform, Balatarin. It concludes with the implications of the approach put forward for national web studies, including a description of the benefits of a national web health index.

National Web (Domain) Studies

In 2007 Ricardo Baeza-Yates and colleagues at Yahoo! Research in Barcelona published a review article on characterizations of national web domains, where they sketched an emerging field which I would like to call national web studies. Of particular interest in the article is the distinction the authors made between studies in the 1990s on the characteristics of *the web* to those a decade later on *national webs*.[2] The term "national web" is useful for capturing a historical shift in the study of the Internet, and especially how the web's location awareness repositions the Internet as object of study. The national web is one means of summing up the transition of the Internet from "cyber-space," suggesting a placeless space of email and packets, to the web of identifiable national domains (.de, .fr, .gr, etc.) as well as websites whose contents, advertisements, and language are matched to one's location. The notion of the national web, it is argued here, also enables the study of the current conditions of a web space demar-cated along national lines, as Baeza-Yates and colleagues pointed out in comparing one national web with another. It may be useful, moreover, for the study of conditions not only of the online but also of the ground. That is to say, national web studies are another example of country profiling.

Building upon the web characterization work, this approach to the study of national webs both engages a series of methodological debates (how to study a national web) and provides an overall rationale for their study (why study a national web). Where the former is concerned, the approach is cognizant of the multiplicity of user experi-ences of the web as well as the concomitant web data collection practices (which users may actively or passively participate in). Search engines and other web information companies such as Alexa routinely collect data from users who search and use their toolbars, for example. Platforms where "crowds share" by posting and by rating are also data collection vessels and analysis machines. The outcomes of these data gather-ing and counting exercises are often ranked lists of URLs, recommended to users. When location is added as a variable, the URL lists may be country- or region-specific. The same holds for language: the websites served may be in whole or in part in a particular language. Thus in practice one is able to speak of country-specific and/or language-specific webs organized by the data collected and analyzed by engines, plat-forms, and other online devices. There is a caveat. Users of these devices draw upon their own data, and are recursively provided a selection of considered URLs. Person-alization may influence the country- and language-specific URLs served, however much to date the impact on search engine results appears to be minimal.[3] Conse-quently, the effects of personalization are not treated here.[4]

I term the interaction between user and engine, the data that are collected, how they are analyzed, and ultimately the URL recommendations that result "device cul-tures." In the case study below, a series of device cultures are discussed, together with the kinds of national webs they organize. Discussed are bloggers', advertisers', surfers', searchers', and crowd-sourced webs, each formed by the online devices and platforms that collect their data and ultimately purport to represent or provide in one manner or another a country-specific and/or language-specific web. Put differently, the research practice makes use of web devices that "go local," i.e., devices that not only collect but serve web content territorially (which is usually nationally) or to a par-ticular language group. Going local has these two distinct meanings, which in certain cases are reconcilable and in other cases are not. An engine may serve language-specific websites originating from inside the country as well as from outside the country in question. For example, in returns for a query the Bolivian local-domain Google (Google.com.bo) may just as well serve results from Spain or from Colombia as from Bolivia, all being in Spanish. Thus in discussing the demise of cyberspace and the rise of a location-aware web, there is a tension between two new dominant ways of interpreting the object of study: national webs versus language webs. The aim is to remain sensitive to the tension between the two. That is, "the local," as Google terms its national domain engines, may refer to either a national web, a language web, or both.

There also needs to be a general discussion of approaches to demarcating a national web, including sampling procedures. Of interest is the fruitfulness of research outcomes that both keep separate as well as triangulate the various parts of a national web—the bloggers', the advertisers', etc. Are the URLs listed as "top blogs" by blog aggregators similar to the URLs listed as interesting by crowd-sourcing platforms? Does the list of URLs with high traffic and available advertising space for speakers of a particular language (e.g., Persian) resemble that of the most visited websites in a related country in question (Iran)? Keeping the parts of the web and the lists of URLs separate may be beneficial, it is argued, as a national blogosphere may have different characteristics than a national crowd-sourced web.[5]

Where the overall rationale for studying a national web is concerned, not only does it imply a critique of the web as placeless and universalized space; it is also a means to develop further analyses of relationships between web metrics and ground indicators. Thus another aim of this study is to consider digital methods for understanding the significance of national web space. By digital methods in this context are meant algorithms and other counting techniques whose inputs are digital objects, such as links and website response codes, and whose applications pertain to, but ultimately move beyond, the study of online culture. I discuss metrics for analyzing the health of a national web, such as its responsiveness, freshness, and accessibility. The work builds upon previous experiments that sought to diagnose the condition of Iraq (in 2007, some four years into the Iraq War) by looking at "its web." It was a broken web: Iraqi university websites were down, or had their domains poached and parked; Iraqi governmental sites were suffering from neglect, with the exception of the Ministry of Oil (oil.gov.iq), which was bilingual and regularly updated. In that brief foray into the state of the Iraqi web, the aim was to develop a series of metrics for the health of a web which were both conceptual and empirical. These metrics are fleshed out in the following, as is an overall approach and purpose for national web studies.

Blocked yet Blogging: The Special Case of Iran

The case study in this chapter is of Iran.[6] It is in many respects a special case, not least because the term "national web" itself may be interpreted to mean the separate

Internet-like infrastructure that is being built there.[7] It is also a special case for the scale and scope of Internet censorship undertaken by the state, which is coupled with the repression and silencing of voices critical of the regime. In other words, the Iranian web is experienced differently inside Iran than it is outside of Iran, which is of course the case for all countries where state Internet censorship occurs. It is also seemingly authored differently from outside than from inside Iran. As a consequence many Iranians online, either site visitors or authors, whether inside or outside the country, need to cope with censorship. Inside the country, coping could mean being frustrated by it and waiting for a friend or relative to bring news about a VPN or another means of getting around blockages. It could mean routinely circumventing censorship through VPNs, proxies, Google Reader, and other means. Both inside and outside the country, coping could mean actively learning about (and consciously not using) banned words, and perhaps employing code words and misspellings instead. It could mean self-censorship. The degree to which Iranians online express themselves in times of censorship is of interest here. Dealing with online thuggery is another matter, which is not covered in any detail here. For example, one may be warned or pursued by the Iranian cyberarmy.[8] One protects oneself through the careful selection of one piece of software or platform over another, based on which one provides safeguards and forms of anonymity. One may use wordpress.com for the ease with which one may choose a new email address as a login, or Friendfeed for the capacity to change usernames.

While it may be a special case, it should be pointed out that certain general metrics such as site responsiveness and freshness may be put to good use when studying countries such as Iran. For example, if sites are blocked by the state yet still responding and updated, one may have indications of a reading audience, both outside but also inside Iran. One may have indications of widespread censorship circumvention, as is reported. Here in particular the retention of the separate webs in our sampling procedure is beneficial. That is, the Iranian blogosphere, or the Iranian bloggers read through Google Reader and indexed by Likekhor, are roundly blocked by the state, yet remain blogging. "Blocked yet blogging" may be the catchphrase for at least certain vital parts of the Iranian web.

Perhaps not often recognized as such, national webs are nevertheless routinely created. It may be said that national webs come into being through the advent of geolocation technology, whereby national (or language) versions of web applications (such as Google) are served nationally (google.gr for Greece) together with the advertisements targeted to locals and information in compliance with national laws.[9] One of the earliest and most commonly used examples by Google executives (and by the search engine industry more generally) is that, as pro-Nazi material is illegal in Germany (and France), Google omits those websites in its local-domain search engines, google.de and google.fr.[10] Google.cn is the best-known as well as most controversial instance of localization (and legal compliance), in which Google's Chinese engine once filtered results drastically. A novel relocalization approach in 2010 redirected users of google.cn (China) to google.com.hk (Hong Kong), where Google does not filter, according to the company.[11]

There is of course further literature to draw upon when studying national webs, from the pioneering ethnographic study of the national web of Trinidad and Tobago, where not global but rather Trini culture is performed, to well-known works on media as organizing national sentiment and community more generally.[12] In policy studies, too, national webs, or portions of them, are increasingly "mapped" to inform debates about the extent to which the web, and especially the blogosphere, organizes voice.[13] Of interest is the related work that seeks to build tools to circumvent censorship so that this voice is still heard.[14] In library science, national webs are routinely constructed by national libraries and other national archiving projects, which also have considered how to define such a web.[15] There are variously sized national web archives. Countries that have legal deposit legislation not only for books but for web content (such as Denmark) tend to have notably larger web archives than countries that do not (such as the Netherlands).[16]

Defining National Websites, and the Implications for National Web Capture

Archivists' definitions of national webs and national websites are of special interest in the demarcation undertaken here. How do national libraries define national webs and websites? What may we learn from their definitional work? Earlier I discussed the approach by the National Library of the Netherlands. Following similar definitions of national websites from archiving projects in other European countries, theirs defines a website as "Dutch" if it is in the Dutch language and registered in the Netherlands; is in any language and registered in the Netherlands; is in Dutch and registered outside the Netherlands; or is in any language, is registered outside the Netherlands, and has a subject matter related to the Netherlands.[17] The above scheme for what constitutes a Dutch website, or at least one deemed relevant for a national archiving context, has consequences for their collection. Here, following on the discussion in chapter 3 on the website as archived object, I would like to discuss how a definition affects the collection technique, whether automated or by hand. One might begin with sites from the national domain (.nl), whether in Dutch or other languages, which can be automatically detected with software; one would remove from the list .be sites (from Belgium, where Dutch, or Flemish, is also spoken), unless they treated Dutch subject matters. (Dutch national web archive users likely would be surprised to come upon Belgian websites stored in it for whatever reason!) The National Library's could be described, however, as an editorial approach, for websites related to Dutch subject matters and websites in Dutch but registered outside of the Netherlands (outside of

.nl) pose particular challenges to automation, and to working at scale. (In other words, the National Library does not take a big data approach.) As a research practice, one would not be able to automate the detection and capturing of those sites; one would more likely create a list of them, before routinely capturing them over time. In the national web characterization studies reviewed by Baeza-Yates in 2007, the national domain (known as the country code top-level domain, or ccTLD) is the organizing entity. In practice, however, many countries (or nationals) use URLs outside of their national domains, such as .com, .net, and .org. As noted below, in Iran's case sites with the .ir ccTLD in fact may not be the preferred starting points for demarcating a national Iranian web. In the project data set, the percentage of .ir sites that are blocked is very low compared to .com's, for example. Thus .ir seems to have characteristics that differ from other sites authored and/or read by Iranians.

We are particularly interested to contrast definitions of a national web that are "principled" (a priori definitions of what constitutes a national web and a national website, such as the librarians' above) with those based on device cultures (webs that are formed by collecting and analyzing user data, and outputting leading sites of a country and/or language). Above, the discussion focused on some of the consequences of demarcating a national web when national websites of interest to archiving are based on formalist properties of their content. It becomes difficult to make a collection at any scale.

In preliminary research about the very notion of an Iranian web, a small survey, undertaken by a new media M.A. student at the University of Amsterdam, was made of Iranian bloggers using Google Reader (Gooder) in the student's Gooder network (n = 141).[18] A variety of definitions of a national web were put forward, and the respondents were asked to choose which definition was best suited. (They could choose multiple answers.) From the beginning, the question was met with suspicion, as the term itself was seen as a possible ruse by the Iranian government to create its own Internet, and further isolate the country and the people, as the student reported. Comments on the question stated that the Internet is a "free sphere" and that ideas of a national web would "limit" such freedom.

The questions read as follows:

What is an "Iranian website"? It is an Iranian website if it is:

a. Only in the Persian language
b. In Persian and other languages (and dialects) spoken in Iran
c. Authored by Iranians
d. Related to Iranian issues
e. Accessed by Iranians
f. National domain (.ir)
g. Returned by a Google search

Note first the expansion of considerations for what would constitute a national web beyond what we have related so far, both in the national domain characterization studies but also in the case of the constitution of the Dutch web by the National Library. In particular, sites accessed by Iranians and those returned by Google are newly added candidate constructs of an Iranian web. The former treats the Iranian web like a traditional media consumption survey. (Which sites are most visited?) The question about Google's relationship with the Iranian web is more ambiguous. Google could be equated with the web generally, as its entry point. Or one could find the Iranian web with Google.

Of the survey's respondents, twelve percent believed that only Persian websites could be considered national websites. Thirty-one percent checked the box for websites in Persian and other languages and dialects spoken in Iran. Forty-five percent thought that when Iranians produce the content, it could be counted in the area of a national web. Twenty-nine percent were of the opinion that everything related to Iranian issues is in the area of the Iranian national web. Nineteen percent were of the opinion that the websites accessed by Iranians make up their national web. It should be noted that some people were very much opposed to this definition, since every website can be accessed by anyone. Only four percent of the respondents chose websites with the Iranian domain (.ir), implying that national web studies relying on the domain alone would prove unrepresentative. Nine percent thought that websites shown in Google search results make up the (Iranian national) web.

In a follow-up question addressing whether there was any difference between writing from inside or from outside the country, approximately one-third of the respondents seemed to agree with the communications scholar Gholam Khiabany:

If Iranian blogs are defined in terms of language, this means omission of a large number of Iranian bloggers who write in other languages, most notably English, while including a number of bloggers from Afghanistan or Tajikistan who write in Persian. Focusing on Iranian bloggers writing inside the country also leads to excluding a large number of Iranian bloggers writing in Persian outside Iran.[19]

On the basis of these survey findings, and extending Khiabany's thought, the analyst concluded that a national web could be defined as one that is authored by Iranians, no matter their location or the language in which they write, and no matter the subject matter. In all, the definition of the national web appears to include sites with content authored by Iranians outside of Iran in languages other than Persian, on issues that may not be related to Iranian affairs. This definition makes it nearly impossible to demarcate an Iranian web! In any case, detecting sites authored by Iranians outside of Iran in languages other than Persian would require manual work. It may be worth noting that the definition adhered to by the National Library of the Netherlands also required manual work, but did not expand its definition of Dutch sites to sites authored by Dutch people abroad in languages other than Dutch, unless the subject matter was Dutch-related.

Having considered what I have termed principled approaches to defining national websites and webs, the choice for another course of action (an analysis of the outputs of significant devices for Iranians) has a clearer rationale. That is, methodologically one resists the temptation of a priori definitions of what constitutes an Iranian website, or the Iranian web, however fascinating in a formal and ontological sense. Instead one relies upon the URL recommendations made by dominant web devices and platforms, which through different algorithms and logics are deemed relevant for a specific country and/or language.

The attempt to define the national web informs the literature on national web characterization as well as on policy (and political science) studies of the organization of voice online. It also contributes to media theory and web studies by putting forward the national web as object of study. The overall approach is not only conceptual but also empirical, in that it seeks properties of national web spaces that are indicators of conditions on the ground. Such properties could include how responsive a national web is at any given time, and how accessible. Are responsive sites also fresh, or recently updated? Are sites that are blocked still responsive and fresh? The research is about more than the technical web data sets, and how they may be repurposed for social study. For Iran in particular, the content of websites is carefully monitored by the state; websites may be blocked and website authors may be pursued. In the following, I put forward an approach to demarcating a national web in order to study its current conditions, including analysis of changing degrees of expression and voice (2009–2011).

Demarcating the Iranian Web: Studying the Outputs of Device Cultures

The purpose of the research is to demarcate a nominal Iranian web and analyze its condition, thereby providing indications of the situation on the ground. By nominal web is meant one predicated on the means by which it is organized by online devices and platforms as well as retrieved, both by the user and by the analyst. Here the demarcation of an Iranian web follows multiple, dominant online approaches for indexing and ordering that "go local" and privilege language, location, and audience, broadly speaking. Working in July 2011, colleagues and I found that the web given by three crowd-sourcing platforms aimed at an Iranian audience differs from that yielded by a marketing tool for Persian-language advertisers, a surfer pathway aggregator of users in Iran, and a search engine delivering .ir sites as well as other top-level domain sites from the "region," even though each of these purports in some general or specific sense to provide the Iranian web. Ultimately I have chosen to write about the Iranian webs in the plural and discuss each web's characteristics. Such an outlook addresses an issue faced by the analyst when formulating where to start collecting URLs, whether by compiling seed URLs to crawl, stringing together keywords and operators to form a query, or consulting lists of top blogs by inlink count, top URLs by rating, or top websites by hit count, etc. The Iranian web under study here is comprised of the outputs of the well-known aggregators of Iranian or Persian-language websites. Thus no one starting point is chosen, but rather all have been retained (or at least a number of significant ones).

In national web research, one may be expected to know the population of a web and be able to make a sample from it (in terms of the number of websites, and some categorization of their types). One might port-scan the Iranian IP ranges, for example, and establish whether IP addresses respond to the standard HTTP and HTTPS ports 80, 8080, or 443. One would count how many web servers are active within a specific IP range, and in a second step roughly estimate the number of domains. Alternatively, one might consider approaching the Iranian Internet authority or Iranian ISPs for their data. Or one could crawl a seed list of URLs, or multiple lists, in snowball techniques, and subsequently sift the large catch by language detection software and/or whois lookups. When one begins to rely on web services that have ceilings or have issues with spammers and scrapers (which means most if not all of them), the challenges of (relatively) big online data become apparent. One is unable to run batch queries without permission from corporate research labs, Internet administrative bodies, and others. Just when it is becoming interesting, the research focus turns to the administrative, legal, and social engineering arenas, bringing everything to a standstill. Merely to gain the access and finish the large collecting and sifting project becomes a great achievement in itself. While one medium-scale scraping and querying exercise has been undertaken for this research project, I largely avoid the techno-administrative arena referred to above, and instead seek to make use of what is available to web users. A conscious choice is made in favor of relatively small data, an issue discussed in more detail in the concluding chapter.

I make a case also for a method to demarcate a national web (or webs) that is sensitive to the variety of ways one enters web space by belonging to particular device cultures, which is largely equated with engine and platform operations rather than used in an ethnographic sense (where an object may have a spirit, for example). Generally, the effort is to introduce national web demarcation methods that repurpose web devices that not only "go local" but also capture device cultures. In short, they capture national device cultures. Repurposing web devices has two methodological advantages. First, popular devices may be viewed as mediating and quantifying specific usage. The devices do so by recursively soliciting user participation in content production and evaluation. They calculate the most relevant websites by aggregating links, clicks, views, and votes, thereby outputting collectively privileged sources. Second, the definition of an Iranian web is outsourced to the big data methodology used by devices to order content, which combines algorithmic techniques with large-scale user participation. Relatively small data sets are obtained from the output of these big data devices. Put differently, the repurposing of web devices is both a strategy for the small data researcher to sample from a big data set as well as a means to have samples that represent specific outlooks on how to organize and order web content, as I explain in the discussion of the privileging of hits, links, location, likes, and other measures by the platforms and devices under study.

In the analyses, the purpose is to chart language and other formal features in each Iranian web. More conceptually, the particular approach to national web studies put forward here concerns the health of each web, in the sense of whether it is (still) online and active or unresponsive and broken. Also of interest is the extent to which each is censored or filtered by the state, and whether there is a relationship between responsive (and fresh) websites and filtered websites. The question is whether censorship kills content, one formulated in a previous (and preliminary) project on the Tunisian web prior to the "Arab Spring" of 2011. To approach the success of censorship (from a censor's point of view, if you will), I use time series data from Balatarin, a leading crowd-sourced platform which was scraped, comparing the significant URLs voted up around the presidential elections in 2009 with those of the same time period in 2010 and 2011. First the hosts are run through proxies in Iran so as to check for indications of blocking. Generally it was found that Balatarin's collection of URLs is particularly susceptible to blocking. I also analyzed the use of particular words ("fiery language") in order to make findings about voice online in times of suppression and repression. Of particular interest is the relationship between the use of that language on websites and the blocking of those same sites. Do the authors of the web pages continue to use language that would have their sites blocked? Generally, the findings are discussed in terms of the strength, clarity, and volume of voice. Prior to reporting on the longitudinal analyses, the indexing and ordering mechanisms of the web platforms and devices relevant to the Iranian space are first described. The data culled from these platforms and engines are employed to characterize the web types on offer.

Device Cultures: How Websites Are Valued, and Ranked

The early web was organized by amateur as well as professional link list makers, who took on the mantle of librarians or specimen collectors and made directories of websites, organized by category. Such website categorization by topic remains, in the larger-scale directories such as Yahoo! as well as in smaller-scale collections, though the practice arguably has declined in the face of the other methods (described here) that have become increasingly settled as dominant approaches online for valuing websites.[20] These approaches may be couched in technical as well as politico-economic terms as the "hit economy," "link economy," "geoweb," "crowd-sourcing," and the "like economy," which highlights what is counted, by whom and/or where. Crowd-sourcing, a term coined by the Internet trade press, derives from the practice of out-sourcing, where not only the so-called wisdom but also the labor of the crowd serves the beneficiary, often a Web 2.0 company or service.[21] Another term employed, the geoweb or locative web, has less of the connotation of a particular kind of economy, yet indicates the means by which sites are sourced.

The hit economy, once exemplified by the hit counter on early websites, ranks sites by the number of hits or impressions, where unique visitors count. Such a view is represented by DoubleClick Ad Planner by Google (referred to here as Google Ad Planner), which is a service that ranks sites by audience for the purposes of advertisers. While "Iran" is not among the countries listed there (likely owing to a combination of the lack of a .ir local-domain Google as well as the U.S. economic sanctions against Iran), Persian-speaking is among the site type categories in the available audience analytics. Thus one Iranian web would be comprised of those sites that reach a Persian-speaking audience, as collected and ranked by Google Ad Planner. Using the options available, 1,500 unique hosts for a Persian-speaking audience were collected from Google Ad Planner.

The "link economy" is a term that describes the rise of PageRank and other algorithms that value links.[22] It also captures a shift in URL ranking logics away from an advertiser's model (hit-counting) to a more bibliographic or scientometric manner of thinking (citation- or link-counting). The link economy characterizes Google Web Search, however much the other main component to its algorithm is user click-throughs. Searching Google for .ir sites (including .ir's second-level domains) as well as Iranian sites in generic top-level domains in Google's regional search yielded some 3,500 hosts.[23]

Alexa, like other companies offering browser toolbars, collects user location data such as a postal code upon registration and, once the toolbar is installed, tracks websites visited by the user (see figure 6.1). It thereby keeps records of the sites most visited by user location. Alexa furnishes a list of the top 500 sites visited by users in Iran.

Crowd-sourced sites such as the best-known Iranian example (Balatarin) and its emulators (Donbaleh and Sabzlink) require registration before the user may suggest a link, which is then voted upon by other registered users. Those URLs with the most votes rise to the top. For this exercise approximately 1,100 different hosts from Balatarin, 2,850 from Donbaleh, and 2,750 from Sabzlink were collected.[24] In the following analyses Donbaleh and Sabzlink are grouped, for they share the device culture (crowd-sourcing). Together they resulted in 4,579 unique hosts. The other platform, Balatarin, is treated separately because of its status as highly significant Iranian website. Launched in 2006, Balatarin is considered the first Web 2.0 site in Persian, and has been recognized as one of the most popular Persian websites in 2007 and 2008; it also has been

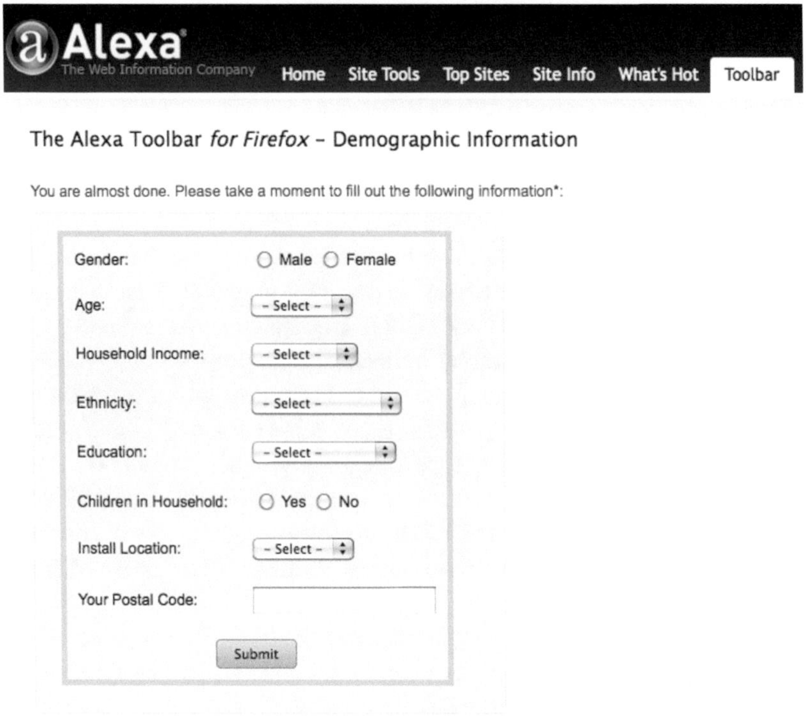

Figure 6.1
Alexa toolbar installation and registration process, with field for user's postal code, August 2011.
© 2012, Alexa Internet (www.alexa.com).

pivotal for the green movement in the opposition before and after the Iranian presidential elections in 2009.[25] The recognition of Balatarin as a platform for the opposition also provides the opportunity to employ it as a barometer in studying the continuing strength, clarity, and volume of that voice. Do the websites that are recommended on Balatarin continue to express themselves critically, or have they discontinued the use of language critical of the regime? By strength of voice is meant whether they continue to use certain critical words. Clarity is thought of as words that are fiery and side-taking rather than coded (which are the categories of the words we study). And volume is whether there are more and more voices using the words. Is the chorus (so to speak) growing louder?

The introduction of the "Like" button and other social counters in social media has brought with it what one may term the "like economy," which values content based on social button activity.[26] Likekhor, as the name suggests, ranks websites by likes; the likes are tallied from Google Reader users who have registered with Likekhor.

Google Reader, or Gooder (as some Iranian users call it), is of particular interest because through it one has been able to read the contents of websites that are otherwise filtered by the state. Google Reader thus effectively acts as a proxy to access filtered websites. At Likekhor the focus is on blogs, pointing up a relationship between Google Reader users and bloggers, or blog readers. From Likekhor we extracted a list of 2,600 hosts, which are collected from a page where all blogs on Likekhor are listed.

Thus, in July 2011 over 10,000 unique hosts were collected through platforms and devices significant to Iranian users (Google Reader, Google Web Search, and the crowd-sourcing platforms) and two that provide ranked lists of Iranian or Persian-speaking sites (Alexa and Google Ad Planner) on the basis of data collected from users located in Iran (Alexa) or from Persian-writing users (Google Ad Planner). These Iranian webs are subsequently characterized individually as well as collectively. I have chosen not to triangulate them, for very few websites recur across them.

Analyzing the Characteristics of the Iranian Web: Language and Responsiveness

One area of research to be built upon is web characterization studies, where one of the main difficulties repeatedly discussed is how to obtain a representative sample of a national web or other web types. According to Baeza-Yates and colleagues, the three common types of sampling techniques used in web characterization studies are "complete crawls of a single web site, random samples from the whole web, and large samples from specific communities."[27] For national webs, which the authors consider to be specific communities, the list is comprised of websites with the same ccTLD. For many national webs, however, such a delimitation would be too partial, certainly for countries where generic top-level domain use is prevalent. Here the approach seeks to retain the .coms, .orgs, .nets, etc. when deemed relevant for Iranians and Persian-speakers by the devices and platforms under study.

To the sampling techniques described above, I thus would like to add a fourth type which could be called multiple-aggregator site scraping, or, more conceptually, device cultures. Google Ad Planner, Alexa, Google Web Search, Likekhor (Google Reader), as well as the crowd-sourcing platforms (Donbaleh, Sabzlink, and Balatarin) make available either through query results or (dynamically generated) listings websites that are relevant for Iranians and Persian speakers. In this case, with the exception of the searchers' web (gained through .ir and generic TLD queries in Google's region search), the percentages of .ir sites among the significant hosts outputted by the devices are relatively low (see table 6.1). The crowd-sourced web references the fewest .ir sites, at just over 10 percent, while the advertisers' web as well as the geoweb, or web of surfers in Iran, have the highest percentage at about 25 percent each. As noted earlier, the .ir sites in the overall collection of URLs are much less likely to be blocked than the .com sites. Of the websites that were tested and found blocked from inside Iran, 80 percent

Table 6.1
Percentage of .ir Sites in Top Websites Collected from Device Cultures Relevant to Iranians and Persian Speakers, July 2011

Percentage	Iranian Web	Absolute Numbers
25%	Alexa (geoweb)	126 of 496 hosts
24%	Google Ad Planner (advertisers)	370 of 1,525 hosts
16%	Likekhor (bloggers)	397 of 2,541 hosts
12%	Donbaleh/Sabzlink (crowd-sourced)	535 of 4,579 hosts
11%	Balatarin (crowd-sourced)	116 of 1,102 hosts

Table 6.2
Metrics Commonly Used in National Web Characterization Studies According to Baeza-Yates et al., 2007

Content	Link	Technology
Language	Degree	URL length
Page size	Ranking	**HTTP response code**
Page age	Web structure	Media and document formats
Pages per site		Image formats
Sites and pages per domain		Sites that cannot be crawled correctly
Second-level domain		Web server software
		Programming languages for dynamic pages

Note: Boldface indicates metrics also used in this study, but we analyze the top-level domain over second-level domain.

were .com, followed by .net with 6 percent and .org with 4 percent. The ccTLD .ir had 3 percent of all censored hosts.

Having reviewed how samples are generally made, Baeza-Yates and colleagues compared ten national web studies in order to arrive at a core set of measures that are shared across many of them (see table 6.2). The characterization of the Iranian web (or webs) in our study has a particular point of departure that benefits from the metrics on offer. In reference to table 6.2's metrics, in the category of content our project shares interest in language, page age, and domain analysis (albeit top-level), and in the category of technology it relies on HTTP response codes. The codes yield what is referred to as "responsiveness," which is considered a basic health metric, together with page age, the freshness measure. There are other metrics that are not employed, though I would like to mention how to do so. Brokenness could be gleaned from link validators, where it would refer to broken links on a site. Additionally, establishing whether websites are "parked" or "hacked" may serve as measures of abandonment by previous owners. Compared against proxy data, parked or abandoned site analysis may be used to make claims about the effectiveness of censorship, or suppression of voice. Fitness could refer to the "validity" of code or correct implementation; Baeza-Yates and colleagues refer to site structure and its "correctness" for a crawler. Other metric types more in the realm of political economy are available that are of interest in expanded undertakings. For example, media, document, and image formats could give an indication of the extent to which a national web is proprietary or open-source, which from certain perspectives is a health issue.

The Iranian Web and Its Languages

One basic metric seeks to measure the composition of languages on the Iranian web (see figure 6.2). Persian is of course the official language in Iran; the Unicode system incorporated Persian script in 2001, and it can be detected.[28] For language detection of websites the research team built a custom tool that makes use of alchemyAPI's language detection functionality; this tool is able to detect Persian as well as other languages, though not all languages spoken in Iran, as I come to.[29] In a second step, the results are manually checked.[30] About two-thirds of the sites in the Iranian web are in Persian, and English is second with one-fifth. Of interest are the proportions of Persian used in the various webs. The results show that the bloggers' space, Likekhor,

Languages on the Iranian web

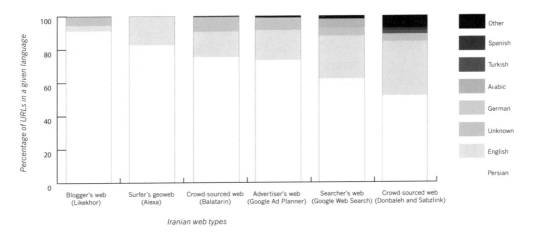

Figure 6.2
The distribution of languages on the Iranian web, August 2011. (cc) Digital Methods Initiative, Amsterdam, 2011.

has 91 percent of its sources in Persian, followed by Alexa's Iran-based surfers' web with 83 percent and the crowd-sourced web with 73 percent. At the bottom are the advertisers' web with 62 percent and Google Web Search with 52 percent. Balatarin, the special case, has 75 percent in Persian. Thus there is significant difference between the webs, including, notably, a Persian-dominant blogosphere (if the Likekhor list may serve as a shorthand reference to such).[31]

Here I would like to return briefly to the kinds of webs that one would capture and analyze if one were to define the Iranian web or an Iranian website a priori, according to a formal definition, a subject raised earlier with respect to the web archivist's formal conditions of a national website (in the Dutch example) as well as the survey respondents' ideas of a national web (for Iran). The blogosphere and to a slightly lesser extent the geoweb (based on surfers in Iran) are most closely related to ideas of an Iranian web as Persian-speaking only, though between them there still would be an average of over 10 percent of non-Persian websites to be reckoned with. The Iranian webs with largest percentages of non-Persian sites are the advertisers' as well as the regional web (from Google's advanced search region option). The advertisers' is the web accessed by Persian speakers as detected by the signals Google compiles on its users and the content it indexes (Google Ad Planner). Both have far higher percentages of non-Persian sites, especially English, though I did not attempt to investigate whether these sites are authored by Iranians or concern Iranian affairs, however that may be defined.

There is another web one could conceive of a priori, which also would have implications for the method by which one would construct the object of study. To include all the languages spoken in Iran (Armenian, Assyrian Neo-Aramaic, Azeri, Kurdish, Lori, Balochi, Gilaki, Mazandarani, Arabic, and Turkmen) would have consequences for the capturing techniques; of the secondary languages spoken in Iran, the language detection tool employed in this study detects only Armenian, Arabic, and Azeri, and not Assyrian Neo-Aramaic, Kurdish, Lori, Balochi, Gilaki, Mazandarani, or Turkmen. To compile sites in those languages, one would rely on specialists' link lists, though the matter was not pursued further.

The Iranian Web and Responsiveness

To analyze the responsiveness of the Iranian webs, the HTTP response status codes (of some 10,000 unique hosts) were retrieved from the Netherlands with a custom-built tool. The inputs to the tool are the lists of hosts in each web that were previously collected. Analyzing the results returned by the response code tool, it was found that there are eight commonly returned codes in the Iranian web spaces (see figure 6.3). The 400 class of status codes indicates that the client has erred; of these, "404 Not Found" is considered the strongest indication of unresponsiveness. Where "400 Bad Request" means that there was an error in the syntax, "403 Forbidden" indicates that

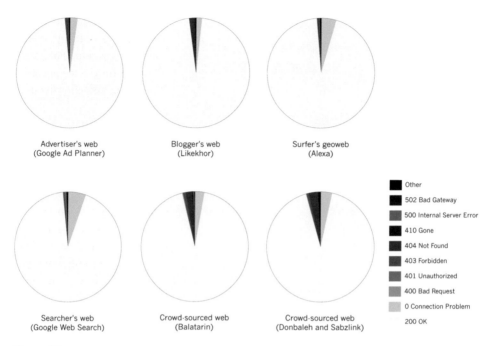

Figure 6.3
The health of the Iranian web measured by HTTP response codes in the Netherlands, August 2011. (cc) Digital Methods Initiative, Amsterdam, 2011.

the server is refusing to respond. "404 Not Found" means that the content is no longer available.[32] Commonly returned response codes besides the "200 OK" status are two redirecting response codes: "301 Moved Permanently" and "302 Found." Redirecting is not necessarily an indication of unresponsiveness and can have a range of reasons, including forwarding multiple domain names to the same location, redirecting short aliases to longer URLs, and moving a site to a new domain.[33] It also may be an indication of a parked website. However, redirects also may be "soft 404" messages to hide broken links.[34] In the current study both 301 and 302 were followed if a location header was returned, which mostly resolved in 200 and 404 response codes. "0 Connection Problem" indicates that the tool was unable to connect to the server; the server may no longer exist, or it may mean that the site did not respond within sixty seconds.

The findings of this portion of the study in the first instance indicate that the Iranian webs are relatively healthy overall. The crowd-sourcing webs of Donbaleh/Sabzlink and Balatarin have 92 and 94 percent of the sites resolving, respectively. The advertisers' space, followed by the bloggers' space, delivered by Google Reader users, have the cleanest bills of health, with 96 and 95 percent of the websites resolving.

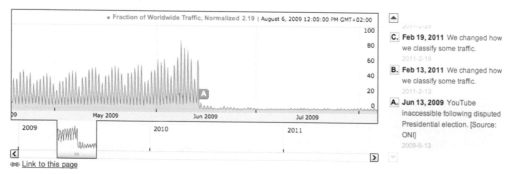

Figure 6.4
Iranian traffic to YouTube comes to a standstill after the 2009 presidential elections. Source: Google, 2011a.

The Iranian Web and Internet Censorship

Arguably, web devices are among the best-informed censorship monitoring instruments. Search engines and platforms receive requests for deleting content—either specific URLs, specific queries, or more general instructions—thereby inviting the creation of an ongoing blacklist as well as a censorship index. For example, it has been reported that to adhere to Chinese government censorship instructions (prior to the redirect to .com.hk), Google engineers "set up a computer inside China and programmed it to try to access websites outside the country, one after another. If a site was blocked by the firewall, it meant the government regarded it as illicit—so it became part of Google's blacklist."[35] In the case of the Iranian web, which is among the most aggressively censored webs in the world, there are no reported requests to Google for removal from the government.[36] The graph in figure 6.4, however, shows how Iranian traffic to YouTube increased in the run-up to the presidential elections in June 2009, before coming to an almost complete standstill one day after. The question of interest in this study is the extent to which blocking important sites has had implications for the health of the Iranian web. In the following, the various Iranian webs collected are checked for availability inside Iran by using proxies. Subsequently, these findings are compared against the basic health measures of responsiveness and freshness. As mentioned above, one of the more remarkable findings is that a large portion of the Iranian blogs is blocked, yet continues to be responsive and is fresh.

The Censorship Explorer tool, which is available at http://tools.digitalmethods.net/ beta/proxies/, lists (fresh) proxies by country, and may be used (with some care) to check for censored websites. The tool returns website response codes and loads the actual websites in the browser as if you were in the chosen country in question. As a starting point in the censorship research procedure, one often checks website responsiveness in a country that is not known to censor (Iranian) websites (in this case, the Netherlands). Subsequently, one runs lists of hosts through proxies in Iran, and logs the response codes. If the response code is "403 Forbidden" while the response code is "200 OK" when connected from the Netherlands, it is understood as a strong indication that a site is blocked in the country in question.[37] Although testing via proxies does not guarantee a replication of average user experience, response code checks through proxies give indications of specific types of Internet censorship, i.e., URL and IP blocking through techniques such as TCP/IP header filtering, TCP/IP content filtering, and HTTP proxy filtering.[38] (There are other known filtering techniques that are more accurately detected by other means, including DNS tampering and partial content filtering.) Often multiple proxies are used, allowing the researcher to triangulate proxy results and increase the trustworthiness of the results. For example, "0 Connection Problem" may be a proxy problem, but may just as well be that the censors return an RST package, which resets the connection, effectively dropping it.[39] Comparing the response codes for multiple proxies can aid in confirming that it is not a proxy problem. Here 12 proxies are used, which are hosted in six different cities in Iran and operated by a variety of owners, including Sharif University of Technology and the popular Internet service provider Pars Online. Concern has been voiced that it is "false to consider Internet filtering as an homogeneous phenomenon across a country," considering that both the implementation and user experience of censorship may vary by city, ISP, or even by computer.[40] Taking note of this concern, the proxies that were selected were from different cities and ISPs, and the findings are based on the response code returned by the majority.

The proxies used for this research were:

217.219.115.133:80—ITC, Tehran, Esfahan
91.98.137.196:80—Sharif University of Technology, Khuzestan
78.39.55.11:3128—ITC, Fars, Shiraz
91.98.137.196:3128—Pars Online, Tehran, Esfahan
80.191.120.129:3128—ITC, Tehran
213.217.43.82:8080—Pars Online, Pars, Tehran
217.219.115.137:80—ITC, Tehran, Esfahan
217.219.97.11:3128—ITC, Shiraz, Fars
80.191.122.11:3128—ITC, Shiraz, Fars
80.191.227.243:3128—ITC, Ahwaz, Khuzestan

188.136.241.2:3128—Ariana Gostar Spadana, Esfahan,
188.136.156.116:3128—Ariana Gostar Spadana, Gostar, Hamadan

The results show that approximately 5 percent of the searchers' web (179 out of 3,547 hosts), 6 percent of the geoweb (29 out of 496), and 16 percent of the advertisers' web (238 out of 1,525) are blocked. The crowd-sourced web has just over 50 percent of the web blocked, with 2,382 of 4,579 hosts. Balatarin is the most aggressively censored Iranian web space with 57 percent blocked, or 623 of 1,102 hosts, followed by the other two crowd-sourcing platforms—Donbaleh and Sabzlink—with more than half of the hosts blocked. Google Reader's web, which in the research work thus far is standing in for the Iranian blogosphere, has 1,127 of 2,541 sites (44 percent) returning the "403 Forbidden" code (see figure 6.5).

As discussed above, the bloggers' web is largely Persian-language and is one of the most responsive of all the webs under study, with 95 percent of the sites returning "200 OK" response codes. Moreover, it speaks for Google Reader use as a vibrant censorship circumvention culture. This study appears to render visible censorship circumvention at a large scale, or at least shows that blocked websites are still online. Of the webs checked for filtering, the crowd-sourced sites as well as the Likekhor listing are the most blocked, raising the question not only of the substance of those spaces (we treat Balatarin's below), but also of the convenience of the platforms as URL lists for monitoring. While many sites are blocked and still responsive, of interest here are other signs of health. Are they fresh? If the sites are blocked yet responsive and fresh, there is a strong indication of the ineffectiveness of censorship (to date).

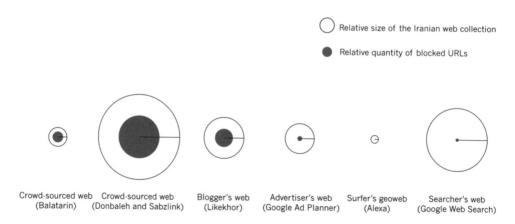

○ Relative size of the Iranian web collection

● Relative quantity of blocked URLs

Crowd-sourced web   Crowd-sourced web   Blogger's web   Advertiser's web   Surfer's geoweb   Searcher's web
  (Balatarin)   (Donbaleh and Sabzlink)   (Likekhor)   (Google Ad Planner)   (Alexa)   (Google Web Search)

Figure 6.5
Censorship on the Iranian web, as measured through the share of "403 Forbidden" HTTP response codes, August 2011. Data collected by the Censorship Explorer tool by the Digital Methods Initiative (DMI), Amsterdam. (cc) Digital Methods Initiative, Amsterdam, 2011.

The Iranian Web and Freshness

Having identified the spaces of particular interest (crowd-sourced as well as bloggers' webs), and having found that they are highly responsive as well as heavily blocked, the next question to be pursued is whether censorship kills content. Or, despite having their sites censored, do the bloggers keep on blogging, and does the crowd keep posting, and rating? Is there an expectation that the readers can routinely circumvent censorship, and thus that the content can continue to be recommended, commented on, etc.? Apart from the responsiveness test (which found nearly all of the websites online), it is necessary to know whether they are active. Is the content on the websites fresh? It is important to point out that a subset of the webs is under study here—the blocked sites in the crowd-sourced and the bloggers' webs. To determine how fresh these sites are, first each host (in each list) is run through the Google feed API to check whether each site has a feed (e.g., RSS or atom). If it does, it is parsed with the Python Universal Feed Parser library and the date of the latest post is extracted.[41] Overall, 63 percent (5,147 of the 8,222) of the three webs have feeds. Of the blocked sites in these webs, 71 percent (2,986 of the 4,189) have feeds. For Balatarin, 79 percent of blocked sites have feeds (504 of 639 blocked hosts), for Donbaleh/Sabzlink 68 percent (1,630 of 2,413), and for Likekhor 75 percent (852 of 1,137). These are the sites to be checked for freshness.

What constitutes a fresh site? One may turn to blog search engines for advice about freshness and staleness. In an FAQ about blog quality guidelines, Technorati states that they "only index 30 days' content, so anything older than that will not appear on Technorati."[42] Similarly, Blogpulse, a search engine and analytics system for blogs, takes 30 days as a measure of fresh content: "A blog's rank is based on a moving average of its citation counts over the past 30 days."[43] Thus, freshness here means having at least one post published via a feed in the last month, counted from the moment the site was last checked for blockage. Would there be an expectation that these sites are fresh? To draw the findings into stark relief, it is of interest to note that a well-known survey conducted by Technorati in 2008 found that about 7 million of the 133 million blogs it follows had been updated in the past four months. The *New York Times* wrote that the finding implied that "95 percent of blogs [were] essentially abandoned, left to lie fallow on the Web, where they become public remnants of a dream—or at least an ambition—unfulfilled."[44] In the survey of Iran, by contrast, 65 percent of the sites overall are fresh. In the crowd-sourcing platform Balatarin, 78 percent of the blocked hosts that have a feed (395 of 504 hosts) are fresh, and in the crowd-sourcing web organized by Donbaleh and Sabzlink 56 percent of the blocked hosts with a feed (915 of 1,630 hosts) are fresh. For the Likekhor list, 61 percent—or 525 hosts—have a post date within a month of when they were tested and found blocked. The results confirm the general indication that censorship hardly kills content on the Iranian web under study. On the contrary, the most severely censored Iranian webs are both responsive and rather fresh.

The Iranian Web: Voice and Expression

A substantive portion of the research project, touched upon in the introduction, concerns employing the web to gain indications of conditions on the ground. Indeed, it is another health check, for it measures the strength of voice and degrees of expression in hard times. Has voice been suppressed and expression become more dulled online over the past few years? How would one measure this? This particular piece of research builds on the work on the Iranian blogosphere by John Kelly and Bruce Etling.[45] Prior to the 2009 elections, and the uprising known as the green movement, they argued that the Iranian blogosphere organizes voice in a particular way:

> Given the repressive media environment in Iran today, blogs represent the most open public communications platform for political discourse. The peer-to-peer architecture of the blogosphere is more resistant to capture or control by the state than the older, hub and spoke architecture of the mass media model, and if Yochai Benkler's theory about the networked public sphere is correct in relation to blogs, then the most salient political and social issues for Iranians will find expression and some manner of synthesis in the Iranian blogosphere. Future research could address whether or not this is true.[46]

I would like to inquire into "expression" by employing data from arguably the most significant Iranian website of the past four years, Balatarin. As discussed above, Balatarin is considered here to be a set of URLs collected through a particular device culture. One of its salient features is the organization of the database that has been built up over time. Among other data held, Balatarin has the date that each URL was posted on its site since 2006. For the project, Balatarin's database was scraped in order to obtain the top URLs (from all topic categories) that appeared on the crowd-sourced platform, and the dates of their appearances. Subsequently, the pages that were linked to from within the Balatarin posts were downloaded, so as to be able to query them for a series of words, effectively making the work desktop research (searching for words). Our word list is comprised of what in Persian are called "smelly" words, or language that would be considered critical and out of order these days.[47] I have devised a scheme of term types that would allow the research project to judge the effects of the suppression over time on voice and expression. 539 words were compiled, including terms, phrases, and names of individuals. For the analysis, 235 of them were used, leaving aside phrases as well as many individuals' names, with certain exceptions such as Neda and Mousavi (see figure 6.6). The list was subdivided into three categories (where a word may belong to multiple categories): fiery, side-taking, as well as coded. By fiery language is meant language which would be (nearly intentionally) incendiary.

If used, it would lead to the censoring of a blog or website. Side-taking language refers to terms that show (obvious) affiliation or alignment. The analysis of side-taking language gives an indication of the increasing partisanship of Balatarin (and the URLs its users recommend), but also lets us gain a sense of which language continues to be expressed and which not, as more and more websites are blocked by the state. Has that situation changed in the sense that more care is now taken in word choice? By coded or unspoken language, we specifically focus on language that is employed so as to not be blocked or raise ire. All of the words on the three lists have been chosen for their significance as forms of expression regarding some of "the most salient political and social issues for Iranians," as Kelly and Elting phrased it.[48] The differentiation among types of words (fiery, side-taking, and coded) was made so as to gain a sense of behavioral changes, for example the rise of coded language together with the decline of the use of fiery words. Also, would oppositional voices grow weary or move underground (and use fewer side-taking words)? Would the use of coded words become more prevalent as censorship (and harsher) activities expand?

The study is phrased as one concerning the organization of voice. Of particular interest is what is termed the strength, clarity, and volume of that voice (described above as continued use of words over time, the choice of fiery and side-taking words over coded ones, and the sheer numbers of websites containing the words, respectively). Generally speaking, it was found that the use of the malodorous words did not decline but rather held steady and actually increased over the three summers of the study (2009–2011). As with fiery language, the use of side-taking language grew in volume over these years. Instead of self-censorship (of the fiery language) and a greater use of coded words, or the quieting of side-taking, the voices grew louder, using all word types more and more frequently. (The words are held constant; generally new smelly words are not added as they become *en vogue*.) The finding is all the more remarkable for the fact that there has been a concomitant rise in the blocking of the sites where the language is published. As sites were blocked, they were not dulled but rather enlivened.

In the summer of 2009, around the date of the elections, as expected there was a significant rise in the use of fiery and side-taking (as well as coded) language after the elections on June 12. In subsequent years, when one might have expected a decline as energies flagged and suppression spread, there was, as noted, only a rise in usage. The use of words termed fiery in the websites linked from Balatarin rose from 139,781 in June and July 2009 to 167,735 in June and July 2010 to 252,986 in June and July 2011. There is not only an absolute but relative increase. No general chilling effect was observed for the other critical language used on websites that rose to the top on Balatarin. The use of side-taking language increased from 365,602 occurrences in June and July 2009 to 444,592 in June and July 2010 to 620,883 in June and July 2011. The use of coded language rose from 69,911 in June and July 2009 to 73,589 in June

Fiery Language 2011

Statistics from 2011-06-01 till 2011-08-01

139	distinct words recognized
249546	the sum of word occurences (each word is only counted once per post)
89948	non-deleted and scraped posts
51412	posts with at least one fiery word
54169	posts with a blocked host
34252	posts with a blocked host and at least one fiery word

Color depicts the percentage of blocked hosts containing a particular word.

0% - 20%
20% - 40%
40% - 60%
60% - 80%
80% - 100%

The tag cloud represents the percentage of posted links a particular word appears in.

حقوق بشر (18.48)   موسوی (17.18)   کروبی (16.72) بالاترین

(15.89) زندانیان سیاسی (11.42)   اعتصاب (10.85)   بیانیه (10.71) تجاوز

(10.68) تظاهرات (10.4)   اوین (10.02)   مبارزه (10.01)   معترضان (7.71) دیکتاتور

(7.63) راهپیمایی (7.27)   مجاهدین (5.9)   شکنجه (5.75)   وزارت اطلاعات (5.27)   وطن (4.58) اعتصاب غذا

(4.55) کودتا (4.43)   راه سبز امید (4.26)   کهریزک (3.55)   تقلب (3.28)   اتحاد (3.22)   بند ۳۵۰ اوین (2.93) قتل عام

(2.9) مرگ بر (2.84)   بهایی (2.71)   رادیو فردا (2.64)   بی‌بی‌سی (2.47)   فروپاشی (2.08)   ۲۲ خرداد (2.05) مزدوران

(2.01) آزادگی (1.98)   نامه سرگشاده (1.09)   سکولار (1.03)   مجاهدین خلق (0.98)   اطلاعات سپاه (0.9) شیخ شجاع

(1.24) هرانا (1.22)   کوی دانشگاه (0.82)   آزادیخواه (0.76)   دهه شصت (0.7)   تاج زاده (0.67) سلول انفرادی

(0.86) رهبران سبز (0.64)   دگرباش (0.63)   خاوران (0.59)   شراب (0.57)   ندا آقا سلطان (0.57)   صانع (0.56) خفقان

(0.55) فیلترشکن (0.51)   شعار نویسی (0.5)   فعالیت سیاسی (0.49)   ولایت مطلقه (0.44)   زید آبادی (0.43) رهانا

(0.41) ریشه ها (0.38)   ۲ خرداد (0.38)   عاشورای ۸۸ (0.37)   مانیفست (0.37)   نافرمانی مدنی (0.34)   ان (0.34) بازجو

(0.33) مشروب (0.31)   صانع ژاله (0.29)   شورای راه سبز (0.27)   زندان وکیل آباد مشهد (0.26)   آتئیست (0.22) کودتاچیان

(0.22) مخالف رژیم (0.2)   سید ضیا نبوی (0.2)   بند ۲۰۹ زندان اوین (0.2)   ساندیس خور (0.19)   خر (0.16) کشتار جمعی

(0.16) نداها (0.14)   اسکناس نویسی (0.14)   تظاهرات مردمی (0.13)   تمامیت خواه (0.13)   روز کارگر (0.12) انقلاب مخملی

(0.12) دگراندیش (0.11)   دیکتاتور به پایان سلام کن (0.11)   الله اکبر شبانه (0.11)   جین شارپ (0.11) زندان قرچک

(0.1) رای من کجاست (0.09)   مقاومت مدنی (0.07)   جمهوری ولایت فقیه (0.07)   مستبدانه (0.07) جدایی دین از سیاست

(0.06) جنگ گرگها (0.06)   بازی وبلاگی (0.05)   همجنس گرا (0.05)   اعلامیه سبز (0.05)   بند ۲ الف (0.05) دعوت به

راهپیمایی (0.04)   لائیک (0.04)   آخوندک (0.04)   نیشکر هفت تپه (0.04)   انحصارطلب (0.03)   بنه نظام (0.03) اصل ۲۷

(0.03) مبارزان آزادی (0.03)   اگنوستیک (0.03)   تظاهرات سراسری (0.02)   علی شیره ای (0.02) حسین بازجو

(0.02) امپراطوری دروغ (0.02)   دموکراسی (0.02)   اصحاب قدرت (0.01)   نظام پوسیده (0.01) اعدامهای دسته جمعی

(0.01) اصانلو (0.01)   دین حکومتی (0.01)   پرونده سیاسی (0.01)   نظام منحوس (0.01) نهاد ارتجاعی ولایت فقیه

(0.01)   حسین شیره ای (0)   خاموشی سبز (0)   نظام اوباش سالار زندان ورامین (0)

(0) مبارزه بی خشونت (0)   اخبار ۲۵ بهمن (0)   بی خشونت (0)   رسانه‌های سبز (0)

Figure 6.6

The "redacted web" in Iran. The use of Persian fiery language on web pages linked from Balatarin. com, June-July 2011, with English translation. The darker the color, the higher the percentage of blocked hosts containing the word. (cc) Digital Methods Initiative, Amsterdam, 2011.

human rights (18.48) Mousavi (17.18) Karubi
(16.72) Balatarin (15.89) political prisoners (11.42) strike
(10.85) statement (10.71) rape (10.68) demonstration (10.4) Evin
(10.02) struggle (10.01) protesters (7.71) dictator (7.63) march (7.27) mujahedin (5.9) torture
(5.75) intelligence minister (5.27) homeland (4.58) hunger strike (4.55) coup (4.43) the green path of hope
(4.26) Kahrizak (3.55) fraud (3.28) alliance (3.22) section 350 of Evin Prison (2.93) genocide (2.9) down
with (2.84) Bahai (2.71) Radio Farda (2.64) BBC (2.47) collapse (2.08) Khordad 22nd (2.05) mercenaries
(2.01) Azadegi (1.98) VOA (1.88) women's rights (1.77) totalitarian (1.64) civil society (1.36) political
activists (1.24) HRANA (1.22) open letter (1.09) secular (1.03) People's Mujahedin of Iran (MKO)
(0.98) Sepah's intelligence service (0.9) the brave sheikh (0.86) Tehran universitary dormitary (0.82) liberal
(0.76) 80's (0.7) protesters (0.68) Taj Zadeh (0.67) solitary (0.65) green leaders (0.64) LGBT
(0.63) Khavaran (0.59) wine (0.57) Neda Agha Soltan (0.57) Sane' (0.56) suffocations (0.55) proxy - anti
filter (0.51) writing slogan (0.5) political activity (0.49) absolute ruler (0.44) Zeidabadi (0.43) Rahana
(0.41) Risheha (0.38) Khordad 2nd (0.38) Aushura 88 (0.37) manifesto (0.37) civil disobedience
(0.34) A.N (0.34) interrogator (0.33) liquor (0.31) Sane' Zhaleh (0.29) the green way council (0.27) Vakil
Abad Prison (0.26) atheist (0.22) coup providers (0.22) opposition (0.2) Seyed Zia Nabavi (0.2) section 209
of Evin Prison (0.2) juice drinker (0.19) Kh.R [G.R] (0.16) mass destruction (0.16) Nedas (0.14) writing on
paper money (writing slogans on paper money) (0.14) people demonstration (0.14) totalitarian (0.13) Labor Day
(0.12) color revolution OR velvet revolution (0.12) open minded (0.11) say hello to the end dictator
(0.11) nightly Allah O Akbar (0.11) Gene Sharp (0.11) Gharchak Prison (0.1) Where is my vote?
(0.09) civilized resistance (0.07) republic of Supreme Leader (0.07) arbitrary (0.07) separation of religion and
politics (0.06) the wolves' war (0.06) blogging rallies (0.05) homosexual (0.05) green declaration
(0.05) section 2 A (0.05) inviting people to demonstration (0.04) secular (0.04) mantis (0.04) Haft Tapeh
Sugarcane (0.04) monopolist (0.03) body of the system (0.03) the 27th article of the Iranian constition
(0.03) freedom fighters (0.03) agnostic (0.03) nationwide demonstration (0.02) addicted Ali
(0.02) interrogator Hossein (0.02) the lie empire (0.02) democracy (0.02) the people in power (0.01) rotten
regime (0.01) mass executions (0.01) Mansour Osanloo OR Osanloo (0.01) official governmental religion
(0.01) political file (0.01) sinister regime (0.01) The reactionary velayat-faqih institution (0.01)
Varamin Prison (0) addicted Hossein (0) Green Silence (0) uncouth regime
(0) nonviolent struggle (0) news of Bahman 25th (0) nonviolence (movements) (0) green
media (0)

Figure 6.6
(continued)

and July 2010 to 103,013 in June and July 2011. At least for the web (and the voice) that Balatarin organizes, this is not a general indication of self-censorship. On the contrary, the words that interest the censors (judging by the percentage of the same sites that have received their attention) are in full view. There is also further indication of a hardy audience for the language, and perhaps routine censorship circumvention, if we assume that much of the readership for it is also in Iran.

The use of critical language has increased, and the sites where the terms appear these days are widely blocked, showing a high rate of censorship activity and perhaps a concentration of monitoring of Balatarin. Specific trends in censoring sites that contain such language are not reported, for the censorship data are from the most recent period (summer 2011) only. Nevertheless the overall findings are rather clear.

It is a responsive web, blocked yet blogging, likely with an active readership not only outside but also inside Iran. It would be worthwhile to collect the URLs as they pass through Balatarin (as well as Likekhor), and check for filtering simultaneously. If sites are already blocked when recommended, we have another strong indication of a culture of Internet censorship circumvention, in that there is an expectation that one is able to route around the blockage and access the sites.

Conclusion: National Web Health Index

The research reported in this chapter is first and foremost a methodological plea for capturing and analyzing the diversity of national web spaces, or webs. Rather than predefining national websites, and thereby national webs, according to a principled approach of formal properties (for instance, all websites with ccTLD .ir, all websites in Persian with Iran-related content, or websites with authors inside Iran)—an approach that is often difficult to operationalize or automate—I propose to make use of what is termed "device cultures," and in particular the Iranian web spaces they provide: the bloggers' web, the advertisers', the searchers', the crowd's, and the surfers'. Device cultures more specifically are defined as the interaction between user and engine, the data that are routinely collected, how they are analyzed, and ultimately the URL recommendations that result. National webs are demarcated through devices that "go local"; they have location or language added as a value that sifts URLs that are of relevance to Iranians and Persian-speakers (in this case). In an examination of the data sets, it was found that the majority of the collected hosts from the various Iranian webs are .com websites, not .ir, a finding that expands the scope of national domain characterization studies, and introduces a method of data collection for broader national web studies.

Second, in building on as well as contributing to national web characterization studies, I have proposed a rationale: a national web health index. It is conceptualized as a series of metrics, of which responsiveness, page age, and filtering or blockage, in particular, are employed in this study. (Language detection and top-level domain analysis also were performed, largely as it turned out to show what would be missed if one were to take a formalist approach to Iranian web demarcation and choose only .ir, or Persian-language websites.) The contribution of this work to national web characterization studies is twofold. The first is conceptual, in that national web characterization metrics are repurposed as indices of national web health. Are websites responding? Are pages fresh? Are links broken? Is the code valid? Are file formats proprietary? A form of country profiling comes into view. The second is generalizable for countries that face state censorship, and applicable to our case study of Iran. The results from the responsiveness tests are compared to those of the filtering (or censorship) tests. Are the blocked sites still responsive? The approach led to the finding of a good-sized number of blogs that were blocked yet still responsive. This finding also indicates an audience for the content, both outside Iran but also inside, and likely a widespread censorship circumvention culture in a particular space: the predominantly Persian-language blogosphere authored by Likekhor and Google Reader which in tandem serve as an important filter for Iranian blogs. Although heavily censored, the Iranian blogosphere as listed by Likekhor remains vibrant. This censored but active space is similar to the crowd-sourced web, organized by Balatarin. Blocked yet posting, Balatarin's recommended websites also suggest a similar finding as the one for the blogosphere: the existence of an active audience for blocked websites. Further substantive analysis found that the Balatarin web (as a collection of URLs highly rated and thus rising to the top of the platform) remains clamorous, perhaps even more so after the presidential elections of June 2009 and the initial rise of the green movement. While roundly blocked, the websites comprising that Iranian web are employing critical language that is fiery, side-taking, as well as coded (at least according to the three language category types we summoned for the analysis). It is a web that appears to be neither widely practicing self-censorship nor cowed and drained of spirit.

Third, I would like to mention certain implications of national web studies as country profiling, both as it affects current and future policies with respect to the web (and its study) and for the use of web indicators for social study more generally. As alluded to regarding the early work on Iraq and the state of its web during the Iraq War in 2007, national web health study provides an additional set of measures regarding the current state of a country's universities, ministries, and other institutions. Where is the activity, and where is the neglect? It also may serve as a source of comparative study, and ultimately as a spur to addressing the ill health of one or more webs. Thus it is an approach to the study of the web that could have salutary consequences for portions of it.

7 Social Media and Postdemographics

Postdemographics?

Research into social networking sites considers such issues as presenting oneself and managing one's status online, the different "social classes" of users of MySpace and Facebook, and the relationship between real-life friends and "friended" friends.[1] Another body of work, often from software-making arenas, concerns how to make use of the copious amounts of data contained in online profiles, especially interests and tastes. I would like to dub the latter work "postdemographics." Postdemographics could be thought of as the study of the data in social networking platforms, and, in particular, how profiling is, or may be, performed. Of particular interest here are the potential results of tools built on top of profiling platforms, including two described below. What kinds of findings may be made from mashing up the data, or what may be termed metaprofiling? Elfriendo.com, for example, is an application that profiles a set of friends. It allows one to compare the tastes of one set of friends to those of another, using MySpace data. Which TV shows are most referenced by those who have friended Barack Obama? How do they differ from those shows as well as books, music, and movies from John McCain's "friends" online? (This small case study was performed prior to the U.S. presidential elections in November 2008.) The second example of postdemographic work described here is the Leaky Garden Project (leakygarden.net), which furnishes a list of online services a particular user has subscribed to. One "profiles" an individual (username) from the accounts taken out in Web 2.0 applications. Subsequently one sees the amount and also the details of the username's activity per platform, if, that is, the user's traces have been indexed by the major search engine Google. These are "leaks" in the so-called walled gardens, a term I return to.

Conceptually, postdemographics is intended to stand in contrast to the use of demographics to organize groups, markets, and voters in a sociological sense. It also marks a theoretical shift from the "biopolitical" use of demographics (to govern bodies) to an "info-political" use (to steer or recommend certain information to certain people).[2] The term "postdemographics" also invites new methods for the study of social networks, in which the interest has shifted from the traditional demographics of race, ethnicity, age, income, and educational level—or derivations thereof such as class—to tastes, interests, favorites, groups, accepted invitations, installed apps, and other information that comprises an online profile and its accompanying baggage. As with Elfriendo and the Leaky Garden Project, the question concerns which approaches and methods may be brought to bear in order to create new derivations from profile information, apart from niches and other more specific products of behavioral marketing?[3]

The term "postdemographics" is preferred over "postdemography," as it recognizes the popular sense of a "demographic" as a segment or niche that may be targeted or polled. Crucially, the notion attempts to capture the difference between how "demographers" and, say, "profilers" collect as well as use data. Demographers normally would analyze official records (births, deaths, marriages) and survey populations, with census taking being the best-known of such undertakings. Profilers, contrariwise, have users input data themselves in platforms that create and maintain social relations. They capture and make use of information from users of online platforms.

Another means of distinguishing between the two types of thought and practice might start from the idea of "digital natives," those growing up with online environments and foreign to everyday life prior to the Internet, especially to the use of earlier manual systems like a library card catalog.[4] A traditional demographic way of thinking might study digital natives as a category, taking a generational view of how they differ from earlier cohorts. A postdemographic project would be less interested in new digital divides (digital natives versus nonnatives) and the narratives that emerge around them (e.g., moral panics) than in how profilers recommend information, cultural products, events, or other people ("friends") to users, owing to common tastes, locations, travel destinations, and more. There is no end to what *could* be recommended, if the data are rich and stored.

Social Networking Sites as Object of Postdemographic Study

"We define social networking websites here as sites where users can create a profile and connect that profile to other profiles for the purposes of making an explicit personal network."[5] Thus begins the study of American teenage use of such sites as MySpace and Facebook, conducted for the Pew Internet and American Life Project. 91% of the respondents use the sites to "manage friendships"; less than a quarter use the sites to "flirt." What is less well known is what "nonusers" do with social network sites (with occasional exceptions such as how spammers leverage MySpace).[6]

Nonusers are those who do not manage friendships or flirt, but still visit the sites and read the profiles. They also may be interested in the data sets, and in automated means of capturing them, such as making use of the APIs, or screen-scraping the pages. With "postdemographics," the proposal is to make a contribution to nonusers' studies—those profilers and researchers who both collect as well as harvest (or scrape) social networking sites' data for further analysis or software-making, such as mashups.[7]

How could one characterize the difference between the databases of online platforms and the old (and new) databases that profile people to "sort" them?[8] Database philosophers were once deeply concerned about mandatory fields and field character limits—the number of letters and numbers that would fit on each line in the electronic or hard-copy form. The paucity of fields and the limited space available for an entry would impoverish the self, just as bureaucracy transformed individuals into numbers.[9] People could not describe themselves fittingly in a few fields and characters.

Other critiques of early database profiling practices pointed out that the "anomaly" was the most significant output of analysis. Certain people (in the sense of data constructs) would stand out from the rest, owing to their lack of statistical normalcy. In a cultural theory sense, the database became the site to derive the other.

With newer online platforms, there are now longer character limits, more fields, and far greater agency to author oneself, or as one scholar aptly put it, "to type oneself into being."[10] "Other," that last heading available on the form, standing for difference, or taxonomic indeterminacy, has been replaced, generally speaking, by "more." For example, the user is invited to "write note," a freestyle field that provides opportunities for further self-definition and self-presentation.

Now that the database is reaching out, providing you with more space to be yourself, questions may be posed. What does your form-filling say about you? Do you fill in the defaults only? Do you have many empty fields? What do your interests, and those of your friends, tell the profiler?

From a postdemographics perspective, the profile, together with the entities in orbit around it, lies at the core of research. Profilers are interested in what to do with all the "interests" and "favorites."

You Are Media

What surrounds the profile? Generally it has been observed that the web, or at least a part of it, has new glue, or "plasma" in the Latourian sense.[11] Where once hyperlinks tied sites together, now the social networking sphere is viewed as less a hypertext than a hyperobject space. From this perspective, the web is more social than informational. The network has profiles as its nodes, with links between friends as well as social objects, not to mention "social" third-party applications and socially derived recommendations as well as adverts.[12] An initial question is how sociality is organized.

For one's profile, the user is invited to fill in certain personal information and list favorites. The earlier fields for age, gender, and location are still present; yet profiles invite the postdemographic, with requests for media listings, favorite movies, music, TV shows, books, etc. The platform also asks for and stores media files, such as pictures, clips, and tunes.

Once the profile has been completed (for the time being), the social linking begins. One "friends" (a new verb), shares, joins groups, and accepts invitations for events.

Sociality breeds more of it. The more social you are, the more prominent your presence. That is, your own activity boosts you on other (friends') pages, be it a tweet, wall writing, or comment, which may appear as running entries on other (friends') pages (Facebook). The platforms continually encourage more activity, inviting commentary on everything posted, and recommending more friends to you (who are friends of friends). With all the ties being made, and all the activity being logged, the opportunities for analysis, especially by social network researchers and profilers, appear to be boundless.

There are of course constraints. Certain of these concern the issues involved in harvesting the data and making derivations. Which social networking sites are scrapable, and to what extent? When, and under which conditions, is it acceptable to harvest data? Apart from data collection, at issue is also data use. The depersonalization of the data would be helpful in particular ethical discussions of social network site analysis, however much celebrated cases have shown "why 'anonymous' data sometimes isn't."[13] There are norms for data use, the most basic of which is user consent. When signing up, the user makes an agreement with the platform, and there are terms of use for both parties, as well as a service privacy policy. Of crucial importance, however, is the blurring of who is the primary agent of ensuring privacy. Arguably, on social networking sites the user is assuming more and more responsibility for privacy in the settings chosen. While the services have thought through the default settings, the user (in 2010 and 2011) chooses the visibility settings on Facebook, for example, so that each action taken can be seen by friends only, friends of friends, or everyone. Privacy is customizable in the sense that one's actions or certain ones of others may be made visible to specific people. There is also the minimum-exposure setting that makes actions visible "only to me," which one would expect would remove oneself from profiling.

How do social networking sites make available their data for profilers? Under the developers' menu item at Facebook, for example, one logs in and views the fields available in the API (or application programming interface). Sample scripts are provided, as in "get friends of user number x," where x is yourself. Thus the available scripts generally follow the privacy culture, in the sense that the user decides what the profiler can see. It becomes more interesting to the profiler when many users allow access, by clicking "I agree" on a third-party application.

Another set of profiling practices are not interested in personal data per se, but rather in tastes and especially taste relationships. One may place many profiling activities in the category of depersonalized data analysis, including Amazon's seminal recommendation system, where it is not highly relevant which person also bought a particular book, but rather that people have done so. Supermarket loyalty cards and the databases storing purchase histories similarly employ depersonalized information analysis, where of interest is the quantity of particular items purchased as well as the purchasing relationships (which chips with which soft drink). Popular products are subsequently boosted. Certain combinations may be shelved together.

Postdemographic Machines

While they do not describe themselves as such, of course the most significant postdemographic machines are the social networking platforms themselves, collecting user tastes and showing them to others, be they other friends, everyday "people watchers," or profilers. Here, however, I would like to describe briefly two pieces of software built on top of machines, in the postdemographic analytical spirit, and the kinds of research practices that result.

Elfriendo.com makes use of the profiles on the social networking platform MySpace. At Elfriendo.com, enter a single interest and the tool creates a new profile on the basis of the profiles of people expressing that single interest. One may also compare the compatibility of interests, i.e., whether one or more interests, tunes, movies, TV shows, books, and heroes are compatible with other ones. Is Christianity compatible with Islam, in the sense that people with the respective interests listen to the same music? Elfriendo answers those sorts of questions by analyzing sets of friends' profiles, and comparing interests across them. Thus a movie, TV show, etc. has an aggregate profile, made up of other interests. (For example, Eminem, the rapper, appeared in both the Christianity and Islam aggregate profiles in early February 2009.)

One also may perform a semblance of postdemographic research with the tool, gaining an appreciation of relational taste analysis with a social networking site more generally.[14]

It is instructive to state that MySpace is more permissive and less of a walled garden than Facebook (at least it was when we were conducting our project in 2008 and 2009), in that it allows the profiler to view a user's friends (and his/her friends' profiles) without having friended anybody. Thus, one views all of Barack Obama's friends, and their profiles; if one queries Elfriendo for Barack Obama as well as John McCain, the profiles of their respective sets of friends are analyzed. The software counts the items listed by the friends under interests, music, movies, TV shows, books, and heroes. What does this relational taste-counting practice yield? The results provide distinctive pictures of the supporters of the two presidential candidates campaigning in 2008. The compatibility level between the interests of the friends of the two candidates is generally low: the two groups share few interests. (The tastes of the candidates' friends are not compatible for movies, music, books, and heroes, though for TV shows the compatibility is 16%. See figure 7.1.) There seem to be particular media profiles for each set of candidate's friends, with those of Obama watching the *Daily Show*, for example, while those of McCain watch *Family Guy*, *Top Chef*, and *America's Next Top Model*. Both sets of friends watch *Lost*. Here one may begin a practice of inferring political preference from TV shows and other "favorite" media.

Figure 7.1
Output of Elfriendo.com: the compatibility of the interests of the friends of two user accounts. The interests of Barack Obama's and John McCain's MySpace friends compared, September 10, 2008. Elfriendo.com. © Govcom.org Foundation, Amsterdam, 2008.

The Leaky Garden Project

"Social networks require a degree of exclusion to work properly."[15] While commonly associated with certain social network sites, the term "walled garden" also refers to a business practice, notably in the software and hardware industries, in which one firm's formats are incompatible with another's, thereby keeping the consumer "locked in."[16] Mobile phone rechargers come to mind: Nokia's does not fit a Motorola phone, and vice versa. One of the arguments in favor of such lock-in is that dedicated hardware ensures the proper functioning of the technology. AT&T, with its historical slogan of "one company, one system, universal service," made this argument repeatedly, in efforts to disallow "foreign" or third-party products and services to run on the phone system, until the MCI lawsuit, and subsequent antitrust work, finally unwound the Ma Bell monopoly in the 1970s and 1980s. With social networking sites, the notion of a walled garden cannot be applied as effortlessly. Such sites, especially Facebook, encourage third-party applications in the new media style, realizing that not only users' content but also their applications increase the value as well as levels of participation. This is the classic argument concerning the inversion of the "value chain" in online games as well as in the entire Web 2.0 industry, summed up in the idea that the more who use it, and contribute to it, the better and more valuable it becomes.[17] (Figure 7.2 renders the flows between leading 2.0 services Facebook, Flickr, and Twitter, recalling the now famous graphic by Bruce Clay that shows the dependencies between search engines in a kind of data ecosystem approach.)[18]

Just how walled, then, are these gardens? Apart from examining the data flows between applications, the question may be approached by examining whether and to what extent each is indexed by search engines. In order to do so, leakygarden.net sits atop a machine that checks the availability of a particular username across a growing list of Web 2.0 applications. Usernamecheck.com is a useful service. When considering a new username, you may wish to know whether and where it is taken across the broader landscape of platforms. In our study usernamecheck.com is repurposed, in the first instance made into a profiling machine: one can type in a username and check which services a person uses. Here the project researchers observed that people generally seem to have two usernames, an alias as well as the real name (first and last name) as one word. Thus one may need to perform two queries for a fuller picture. Subsequently, leakygarden.net looks up references to the username. Does Google return pages from that username on a particular platform? In all, the Leaky Garden Project shows which "walled gardens" leak, and which are watertight (see figure 7.3).

Walled Garden Data Flows

Characterizing the types of Web 2.0 data flows between three applications: Facebook, Twitter and Flickr.

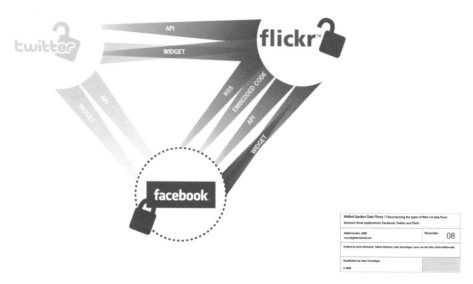

Figure 7.2

Artist's rendition of walled garden data flows. (cc) Digital Methods Initiative, Amsterdam, 2008.

Conclusion: What Would Nielsen Do?

Two methods dominate old-media-style "audience" research, the handwritten diary of a TV viewer or radio listener and the automated meter registering how long a TV or radio channel is on, for a given household or household member. The diary technique is still in use, with the Nielsen company sending out a survey pack to its randomly selected families four times per year to record viewing habits during the so-called "sweeps weeks." Each person surveyed provides demographics and a list of the shows they watch. Advertising is subsequently targeted to a TV show's demographic, with soap operas being the classic case of ads tied to a type of show. Because of survey effects (i.e., people changing their viewing habits owing to their need to keep a diary and fit a profile), an automated technique may be preferred.[19] In the United States, such recording devices were first employed for radio listeners, with the introduction in the 1940s of the Nielsen audimeter, which registered which frequency a radio was tuned to and for how long.[20] The results were useful for advertis-

Figure 7.3
Output of Leakygarden.net: username service subscription profile of silvertje (Anne Helmond), including the "leaks," or the amount of silvertje references per service, indexed by Google. © Govcom.org Foundation and the Digital Methods Initiative, Amsterdam, 2008.

ers, and remain so. Of the initial study performed with the audimeter in 1942, *Time* wrote: "When the star of one of radio's most popular nighttime shows said "Good night," listening dropped sharply. The sponsor's closing commercial was heard by only a fraction of the program's audience."[21] Nielsen's automated television ratings began in the 1950s, and were taken to the next level with the black box known as the Storage Instantaneous Audimeter, which captured TV viewing of each set in the household, sending data back to headquarters daily through a phone line. "People meters" have been employed since the 1980s, with each member of the household having his/her own button on the remote control. Behind the button, in the database, are the user's age and gender, and the meter on top of the television is tagged with a location.

TV shows are rated through a point system, with one point defined as one percent of all households watching. Advertising rates are subsequently expressed in cost per point. A show has an expected rating (based on history) as well as an actual rating. Of interest to the advertisers is the "post-buy" calculation of actual audience reach, that is, whether their advert actually had the expected audience types and numbers. Was the advert a good buy?

Top 50 Popular Brands in Hyves

Research Question_Are Hyves users brand-homogenous? The anxiety
about visible data on social networking sites such as Hyves comes
from the 'public display of the informal.' Hyves.nl 'cleanses' the
user-collective by presenting a top 50 list of popular brands that
makes Hyves users seem 'decent.' Behind the scenes, profile data may
tell different stories.
Findings_In the research protocol all brands were scraped by brand_id
(with 103,239 distinct brands). We found that the majority of users are
single-fan brands & 'no logo' Hyvers (59,105).

H&M   G-star   Coca Cola   Nike

Mc Donalds   Björn Borg   Hyves   Hotmail

Ben & Jerry's   Samsung   Puma   Diesel   Replay

Esprit   Only   Zwitsal   All Stars   Adidas   Vero Moda

Dolce & Gabbana   Mexx   Dove   iPod   Albert Heijn   Ikea   Red Bull

Nokia   Bacardi   Tommy Hilfiger   Heineken   Hunkemoller   G-sus   Nivea

Converse   Douglas   Hugo Boss   L'Oreal   Zara   Gucci   Burberry

Chanel   K-swiss   O'Neill   DKNY   Le Coq Sportif

Apple   ICI Paris   Playstation   Ralph Lauren

Source_hyves.nl/brands
Method_Take top 50 and scale and cloud by value (descending)
Tools_Tag Cloud Generator
Date_6 August 2007

Product_of the Digital Methods Initiative,
dmi.mediastudies.nl. Analysis_by Erik
Borra, Marijn de Vries Hoogerwerff and
Sabine Niederer. Design_by Anne
Helmond.

CC_BY:NC:SA

Figure 7.4
Top 50 brands of Hyvers (users of the Dutch social networking site hyves.nl), August 2007. (cc)
Digital Methods Initiative, Amsterdam, 2007.

Should postdemographics emulate the Nielsen machines and metrics? Are there
postdemographic equivalents? Indeed, one may transfer the counting method from
TV audience research to social networking sites, using the available interest fields
as well as basic demographic data (gender, age, and location). Thus one may tally
references to a particular interest across an entire social networking platform, as
colleagues and I did for the Hyves platform in the Netherlands in 2007 (see figure
7.4). (No demographic data were used in the example.) Among the types of favorites at Hyves are brands, and Hyvers, as the users are called, fill in that field, albeit
often without the care and diligence that would be demanded of a Nielsen family
member.

Examples of Hyvers' "noncooperative" filling of the brands field:

My Style is My Brand
ben geen merkentype
Houd er niet van ge(brand)merkt te worden
ik ben niet zo van de merken
I don't spend much time thinking about brands

Daar doe ik dus ff lekker niet aan mee he
Ik merk het
geen zin in aanvinken[22]

How to tidy the data and make ratings? What would Nielsen do? One could strive to transfer the audience research technique to the new medium. Perhaps particular Hyvers would agree to become Nielsen social networkers and provide meticulous up-to-date profiles. The fields would be monitored by Nielsen for changes in interests and tastes, and ratings could be provided with a point system, with fans being the equivalents of viewers.

As unlikely as the proposal may sound, it points up the larger question of whether and when to apply standard methods of study to the new medium. It also raises the question of the distinctive uses to be put to postdemographics.

8 Wikipedia as Cultural Reference

Introduction: National or Neutral Points of View?

In *The Long Tail*, an account of popularity on the web, Chris Anderson argues that "Wikipedia is arguably the best encyclopedia in the world: bigger, more up-to-date, and in many cases deeper than even Britannica."[1] With about 20 million articles, Wikipedia is sizable and also highly visible on the web. Of crucial importance for its significance is the appearance of its articles at the top of Google's search engine results, which prompted the head of *Encyclopaedia Britannica* to call Google and Wikipedia's relationship "symbiotic."[2] The overall popularity of the project is also often discussed in terms of how it empowers its users as "editors" and of its collaborative, rewarding culture that fosters continued engagement.[3]

Established in 2001, Wikipedia's English-language version was joined that same year by its first non-English ones, including Dutch.[4] To date there are approximately 270 language editions (or subdomains of wikipedia.org, such as nl.wikipedia.org for Dutch), each sharing Wikipedia's three core principles: neutral point of view (NPOV), verifiability, and no original research. NPOV means that articles are to be written to "[represent] fairly, proportionately, and as far as possible without bias, all significant views that have been published by reliable sources."[5] The verifiability principle requires all articles to be anchored by reliable sources outside of Wikipedia, often with outlinks to those sources. Independently of what editors write, readers, it is said, should be able to check the material, and, if they find errors, themselves become editors and correct them.[6] The third principle is no original research; Wikipedia is to be a source of existing, "recognized knowledge."[7] The principles are meant to have a cumulative effect over time. Wikipedia points out that as more users contribute, the content should become more reliable and neutral. The goal is for the contributors to reach consensus, "a decision that takes account of all the legitimate concerns raised."[8] Wikipedia's core principles are also guidelines for achieving that consensus.[9]

This chapter is a comparative study of select Wikipedia articles that concern the Srebrenica massacre of July 1995.[10] The articles (dated December 20, 2010) are in languages spoken by significant parties to the events in Srebrenica: Dutch, Bosnian, and Serbian. The Dutchbat (Dutch battalion) contingent under the United Nations Protection Force (UNPROFOR) was protecting the U.N. safe area of Srebrenica in Bosnia and Herzegovina, over 8,000 Bosniaks (Bosnian Muslims) were killed, and the Bosnian Serb army of the Republika Srpska (VRS) were the perpetrators. The study also analyzes the English, Croatian, and Serbo-Croatian articles on the events, which complicates the opposition between national and neutral points of view. The English-language article has multiple points of view, with voices continually contesting accounts of events. The Croatian article is similar to the Bosnian (both of which were translated originally from the English), while the Serbo-Croatian, representing what was the unifying language in former Yugoslavia, appears to assume that role again by representing as well as softening both the Bosnian and the Serbian points of view. When it was reopened for editing in 2005 (having been locked earlier that year because of disuse), the Serbo-Croatian Wikipedia generally was meant to be liberal and antinationalist in outlook. (There is no Montenegrin article. Montenegrins have requested their own language edition, but it has been rejected four times by Wikipedia's language committee.)[11] In conclusion I discuss the rationale and approach to studying Wikipedia as cultural reference, including the compatibility (rather than the opposition) between neutral and distinctive points of view.

For the contentious articles in existence for at least five years, it was found that they could be said to express rather less neutral than specific Bosnian, Dutch, Serbian, and other umbrella points of view. In the case of the Srebrenica massacre, the Bosnian, Dutch, and Serbian articles' respective viewpoints can be attributed to specific sets of editors contributing in their own language version, and to the references they employ. Editors of the various language versions participate in the English version, which results in an inclusive and continually contested article often referred to (in the Serbian) as western. The Serbo-Croatian strives to be antinationalist and apolitical, employing a variety of means to unify the Bosnian and Serbian points of view. In general, the analysis provides footing for studying Wikipedia's language versions as cultural references.

The approach taken in the comparative study is relatively straightforward. The comparisons across language versions of Wikipedia are based on a form of web content analysis that focuses on basic elements that comprise an article: its title, authors (or editors), table of contents, certain content details, images, and references.[12] Three further elements are added that make the analysis more medium-specific (or webby): the location of the anonymous editors (based on IP address), readings of the talk pages that are behind the articles, and the flagging of templates, or banners, alerting users to specific problems with an article such as an alleged violation of neutral point of view. Other similarly specific elements that are also of interest in the study of Wikipedia articles are left out, such as the activity of software robots (bots), which in this case are highly active editors both across an entire language version of Wikipedia as well as of a single article.[13] Finally, Damir Pozderac, a power editor, was consulted; he is one of the few editors who has worked across language versions and not banned from editing Wikipedia. He created the translated Bosnian, Croatian, and Serbian articles, with special changes to the article title and content details for each. Dado, as his username reads, eventually ceased taking part in the discussions and editing the articles, he said, because of the bickering in the talk pages between Bosnians and Serbs.[14] In the analysis Dado acts less as an informant than as one making claims that can be checked in the discussion pages. Indeed, the discussion behind the language versions shows dissensus among article editors and throws into stark relief the call for separate Serbian, Bosnian, and Croatian Wikipedias, as opposed to a single Serbo-Croatian one, as detailed below.

Wikipedia's core principles of neutral point of view, verifiability, and no original research, when applied in a collaborative, consensus-building process, are meant to result in a quality article. They also may result in a dispute, with a locked article and voluminous discussion, or perhaps a fork, when one article is split into two.[15] Even those disputes and divisions are supposed to achieve some sense of closure with time, even if that closure means a permanently locked article or the suspension of anonymous edits, as is the case with the Bosnian article, which has achieved featured article status. During times of article conflict, as well as relative calm after lockdown, editors may turn to coordination and other nonediting activities such as procedure writing, user coordination, and maintenance.[16] Scholars have described Wikipedia as a well-functioning bureaucracy.[17]

Either through writing articles or creating rules and procedures, it is the work of editors that in time is meant to lead to the accretion of quality. As Jimmy Wales, the founder of Wikipedia, put it, during his appeals for financial support of the project in 2009 and 2010, "one person writes something, somebody improves it a little, and it keeps getting better, over time. If you find it useful today, imagine how much we can achieve together in 5, 10, 20 years."[18] The articles explored here were more than five years old at the time of analysis, with the Dutch article being the oldest, or most mature, at over six years old (creation date July 9, 2004), and the Serbo-Croatian the youngest at over five years old (creation date August 30, 2005) (see table 8.1). It was found that the articles are edited at times when new evidence becomes available and claims made; they are also edited around anniversaries of the events of July 1995. The articles diverge either dramatically (as in the article titles) or in crucial detail (victim counts), to take two of the most immediate examples of distinctiveness. Ultimately our analysis makes the case for the normalcy of cultural difference across the "same" Wikipedia article, at least for politically charged articles, as other authors and projects have also found. Manypedia, the online interactive tool, is based on the premise that the same articles across Wikipedia language versions are ripe for comparison. It loads

Table 8.1
Select Wikipedia Language Versions with Creation Dates, and Srebrenica Articles with Creation Dates

Wikipedia	Wikipedia creation date	Srebrenica article name as of December 20, 2010	Srebrenica article creation date
English	January 15, 2001	Srebrenica Massacre	July 13, 2004
Dutch	June 19, 2001	Fall of Srebrenica	April 4, 2002
Serbo-Croatian	circa February 2002	Srebrenica Massacre	September 30, 2005
Bosnian	December 12, 2002	Srebrencia Genocide	July 22, 2005
Serbian	February 16, 2003	Srebrenica Massacre	August 16, 2005
Croatian	February 16, 2003	Srebrencia Genocide	August 16, 2005

the same article from two Wikipedia language versions side by side so as to check the compatibility and spot the differences, for example in the articles on Jerusalem in the Hebrew and Arabic Wikipedias. These are examples of what the project dubs LPOVs, or linguistic points of view.[19] The approach taken in our study differs in the sense that it rests more on web content analysis than on automated concept compatibility analysis.

Researching the Quality and Accuracy of Wikipedia

Debates concerning the quality of Wikipedia generally and of certain types of articles in particular have drawn the attention of scholars, often seeking to test this quality. If anyone can edit, as is said, then anyone can insert errors and vandalize the content, even if the robots that help to maintain Wikipedia are vigilant (a point often neglected in much of the early Wikipedia research).[20] Scholars have probed the quality control mechanisms, born of collaboration, bureaucracy, as well as software and bot maintenance in Wikipedia, largely in terms of accuracy and bias. In the now famous side-by-side test, with a blind review of articles by experts, Wikipedia fared well against the venerable *Encyclopaedia Britannica*, however much the results of the study were vigorously contested by *Britannica* itself.[21] It is worthwhile to note that the selection of the articles in the comparison test of the English-language Wikipedia with *Encyclopaedia Britannica* was made on the basis of *Nature* news reporters' general familiarity with the subject matters, as opposed to topicality, recentness, editing activity, or other characteristics that are likely to be the source of a quality article, as discussed below. Other scholars, in library and information science, expanded and repeated side-by-side tests by choosing articles to be reviewed at random, or in special subject matters. A comparison between a number of biographies in the English-language Wikipedia with those in the *American National Biography Online* and *Encarta* found Wikipedia to be less accurate but larger in scope.[22] On historical subject matters Wikipedia's accuracy was put to the test anew against that of *Encyclopaedia Britannica* as well as the *Dictionary of American History* and *American National Biography Online*, where it was again found to be less accurate, and also the source of glaring errors.[23] Other scholars pointed out that accuracy is likely to vary, given the comprehensiveness of Wikipedia's subject matters on the one hand and the articles' versioning (or varying states of completeness) on the other.[24] Indeed, another randomly selected set of articles from a broad sweep of subject matters was found to be reasonably accurate, and its "reasonable accuracy is sufficient to support initial forays into 'serious research'."[25] As the authors point out, Wikipedia's articles are unfinished, but certain collections of them (featured articles) at given times have been considered worthy of print publication.[26] In all, the scholarship employing side-by-side tests has found that Wikipedia is not as accurate overall as standard reference books, yet has an unmatched scope; featured (and other good) articles are an acceptable place for beginning one's enquiries.

Another approach to studying Wikipedia's accuracy has been to insert errors and monitor what transpires, a research practice coming on the heels of celebrated cases of gross inaccuracy, including John Seigenthaler's, whose piece in the newspaper *USA Today* in November 2005 recounted his attempts to track down the Wikipedia "biographer" who wrote falsely of his role in John F. Kennedy's assassination.[27] One scholar, Alex Halavais, inserted errors so as to learn more about the vigilance and correction culture of Wikipedians, later disavowing the practice as destructive.[28] The speed at which errors are corrected is of interest, as Halavais as well as Jon Udell found, with Udell reporting the findings in a well-known screencast documentary of the revision history of the "Heavy metal umlaut" article in the English-language Wikipedia, a subject of chapter 3.[29] As mentioned, in the early work that tested accuracy through error insertion, scant attention was paid to the bots that monitor changes or to triggering software that informs editors of changes or identifies suspicious edits through association and pattern recognition. In some sense these accuracy tests are also tests of the bot vigilance, so to speak, and the capacity of Wikipedia as a technical system to spot and react to untoward behavior. Another researcher, in a similar test of accuracy through error insertion, attempted to outwit such automated monitoring practices by entering mistakes into articles only three at a time (as opposed to Halavais's thirteen), with each group of insertions originating from a different IP address.[30] The researcher also removed the fibs, as he called them, after 48 hours to mitigate their destructive effects. It was found that approximately half of the inaccuracies had been corrected. Such work has prompted other approaches to understanding accuracy as well as quality. In one case, expert reviews of a series of articles were compared to nonexperts' of the same articles; it was found that the experts had more favorable views of the articles.[31] As in previous studies, the researcher also reported a number of errors in the articles.

I would also like to discuss briefly the sources of quality in Wikipedia articles. Quality has been studied in relation to the bureaucracy's control mechanisms, editor coordination, actual editing, and types of subject matters.[32] One scholar evaluated the quality of articles on the basis of the number of edits and the number of contributors; he suggests that the quality of the articles increases with the subject's appearance in the press, and writes that Wikipedia represents a decent "working draft of history."[33] A study of German Wikipedia articles drew similar conclusions; the higher the interest and relevance of a subject, the greater the quality of the article.[34] There is a relationship between topicality on the one hand and editing activity on the other. Having examined (in 2007) all 50 million edits to the 1.5 million articles in the English-language Wikipedia, the authors concluded that the number of "edits correspond on average to an increase in article quality," with a featured article taken to be a quality article.[35] Editing cultures also matter, especially in articles with work by power editors, responsible for the largest part of the content. Quality is more likely to be achieved when a small group of editors coordinate their substantive activity, as opposed to similar numbers without coordination, or larger numbers of editors.[36] Further evidence suggests salutary effects of power editor activity on the quality of the articles. Edits by "Wikipedians," as the power editors responsible for the majority of the content are also called, endure, compared to those by non-Wikipedians.[37] The power editors are also more normative, justifying their long-lasting edits in discussions according to the Wikipedia principles. Indeed, power editors tend to adhere strictly to Wikipedia standards, and also appear to be responsible for the promotion and enforcement of them.[38] There are other approaches to the study of editing. In a media ecology framework, the term stigmergy has been applied to Wikipedia work, comparing its flow to the indirect coordination of ants.[39] As with ant coordination, a minimal amount of information (cues in the form of templates and other notices) passes from Wikipedian to Wikipedian, enabling the work.[40]

Cross-Cultural Comparison in Wikipedia Research

While there is a body of literature on the culture and mechanisms behind Wikipedia article accuracy and quality generally, somewhat less attention has been paid to the question of perspective in the articles. The bias of Wikipedia has been studied by ranking articles through techniques such as PageRank, revealing that the top articles are on western subject matters or related to American events.[41] Other work has drawn similar conclusions with finer-grained analyses, including a comparative analysis. The hypothesis that Wikipedia language versions "distort" by emphasizing the local over the universal was studied in greater detail through a comparison of entries on famous Poles and Americans in the Polish- and English-language Wikipedias.[42] The English-language articles were found to contain more information (for example) about the personal lives of famous Poles than the Polish articles did about famous Americans. Indeed, the English-language Wikipedia, which the researchers call a kind of global version of the online encyclopedia, "appear[s] to reflect the cultural values and history of the United States."[43] One recommendation the study makes is not to translate the English-language articles as seminal entries in other language versions, but rather to allow the articles to grow on their own. Indeed, research into the featured articles in Arabic, English, and Korean found that 40% of the Korean and over 50% of the Arabic have no matching articles in the English-language version.[44] It also was found, contrary to earlier findings, that the number of editors and number of edits by registered users did not correlate with featured article status, suggesting distinctive cultural quality mechanisms.

Wikipedia itself has projects on "systematic bias," which report on the frequency of appearance of a country name in Wikipedia, the various lengths of language versions, the characteristics of the average Wikipedian, the tendency of recentism in the articles written, etc.[45] In this area of inquiry, scholars have come to the conclusion that the articles should not be understood as "value-free information source[s]."[46]

Our study may be situated in the emerging literature on cross-cultural comparison, or cross-language-version comparison of the "same" articles, though in this case the titles of the articles differ slightly (which in itself marks the different views on the controversy).[47] The main contribution lies in the approach to comparative article analysis, providing a means to operationalize generally the question of Wikipedia as cultural reference. Before discussing the Srebrenica articles in detail, it may be worth considering the general question of how people choose which articles to create and to edit (what researchers refer to as self-selection of topics by editors), especially in the case of articles on controversial or sensitive topics. For subject matters that are not highly charged, self-selection is often considered beneficial, not only for the affinities editors may have with their subject matters and with each other, but because it saves time.[48] For topics that are matters of dispute, self-selection may have other effects, such as edit wars and article locks.[49] In this case, many of the most active editors of the English-language article on the Srebrenica massacre have been subsequently blocked for not adhering to Wikipedia rules, raising the general question of the willfulness of editors of controversial subject matters. With respect to templates on the articles, the Bosnian is a featured article that does not allow anonymous edits (as mentioned), and the Serbian has both its accuracy and its neutral point of view (NPOV) disputed. The Dutch, Serbo-Croatian, English, and Croatian articles contain no article templates, which suggests that there are currently no major issues with them. They also are not featured.

Mindful of the potential effects of controversial subject matter on collaborative authorship, the research takes up the similarity or difference of accounts of an event across a series of language versions. Do the five-year-old articles on the same subject settle into narratives that are similar or rather distinctive across language versions? What kinds of versions of events emerge when the articles have grown on their own (so to speak), or have been translated from the English or another language? If the articles have distinctively different contents, are Wikipedians authoring points of view? How may Wikipedia articles be considered cultural references?

Articles may be unique to particular language versions; articles may have grown on their own, while others were seeded (and transplanted) from the English or another language. Indeed, as reported above, Wikipedia language versions have provided opportunity for studying cultural specificity. Here I would like to build upon such work through a comparison of the articles on the Srebrenica massacre of July 1995 across six language versions: Dutch, English, Bosnian, Croatian, Serbian, and Serbo-Croatian. The rationale for the existence of Wikipedia versions in Bosnian, Croatian, and Serbian is illustrated by the incident around the locking and unlocking of their former Yugoslavian umbrella language version, Serbo-Croatian. In May 2005 Pokrajac, active in the English, Bosnian, Serbian, and Croatian Wikipedias, persuaded the Wikipedia language committee to unlock the Serbo-Croatian version, which had been in existence since February 2002 and had been locked by Andre Engels owing to lack of editing in February 2005: "So, this Wikipedia (if you open it) will be absolutely NPOV, liberal and antinationalist. Many liberal and antinationalist people said that they are talking Serbo-Croatian despite Balkan war(s)."[50] In the accompanying discussion, Caesarion acknowledges that the Serbo-Croatian is mutually intelligible by the successor languages, and adds: "But the wounds of the nineties Balkan wars are all too fresh to . . . let Serbs, Croats and Bosniaks cooperate on one Wikipedia. We must use separate Wikipedias just to keep the whole project peaceful."[51] Thus the treatment here of points of view as national derives from the discussion about the closing and reopening of the Serbo-Croatian Wikipedia, and the related founding of the Bosnian, Croatian, and Serbian ones, which are considered solutions to the burden of collaboration after the Balkan wars. At least for the western Balkans (meaning the former Yugoslavia, not including Slovenia, and Albania) there are national Wikipedias (and the unifying Serbo-Croatian version, which is larger than the Bosnian, half the size of the Croatian, and one-third of the Serbian). (See table 8.2.)

Wikipedia Articles Compared: The Fall of Srebrenica, the Srebrenica Massacre, and the Srebrenica Genocide

Of the language versions under study, the Dutch article about the events in Srebrenica was the first to be created, on April 4, 2002, just before the publication of the comprehensive report by the Netherlands Institute for War Documentation, an institution founded in 1945 to document and study the Second World War, and given the mandate by the Dutch government in 1996 to study the fall of the U.N. safe area of

Table 8.2

Characteristics of Select Balkan Wikipedia Language Versions, September 2011, According to Wikipedia's Statistics

Rank by Article Count	Wikipedia	Articles	Edits	Users	Active Users
28	Serbian	143,855	4,644,728	85,181	633
38	Croatian	99,039	3,074,575	75,094	640
55	Serbo-Croatian	43,063	806,294	31,446	155
70	Bosnian	31,401	1,570,125	39,643	184

Source: List of Wikipedias, 2011.

Srebrenica.[52] The Wikipedia article was started by a former Dutchbat soldier, M. van Koert, and was entitled simply "Srebrenica." In the talk page, Van Koert writes that he created the article so as to clarify how Srebrenica fell. He describes how the Dutchbat soldiers had been the object of scorn until the Institute for War Documentation exonerated them.[53] The finding, he relates, helps Dutchbatters, as the soldiers in the contingent call themselves, move on with their lives. Shortly thereafter the name of the article was changed to the "Drama of Srebrenica," which is also the title of classroom materials for middle-school-age students produced by the World War II-era Camp Westerbork Memorial Center, where the story of a Dutchbat soldier is interwoven with those of a number of Bosnian Muslims in Srebrenica.[54] In September 2004 it was changed to the "Fall of Srebrenica," the military term also used in the Institute for War Documentation's report of 2002. That title eventually stuck. The change took place after a series of discussions about the neutrality of the word "drama" and the fact that the English-language Wikipedia calls its article the "Srebrenica massacre." The question of the title was reopened in 2007, when at least four Dutch Wikipedians (Känsterle, André Engels, Oscar, and Art Unbound) thought that employing "massacre" would be the equivalent to a point of view, and one Wikipedian felt that "drama" would be hurtful to the survivor families, also known as the Mothers of Srebrenica. While the consensus remained squarely with the "Fall of Srebrenica," one user in July 2010, Reportages3, tried to change it to "massacre," arguing that "fall" is a "political euphemism, only used in NL, for obvious reasons."[55] The discussion went on about whether "massacre" is a Dutch word, with Reportages3 pointing out that it is in the unabridged *Van Dale* dictionary ("dikke *Van Dale*"), whereas other editors found the word to be too obscure, and its ready alternative ("slachting," or slaughter, butchering) to be value-laden. Hettie, Dutch power editor, seemed to settle the debate by arguing that a title with "massacre" would not cover the contents of the article. Most recently in August 2011, user Bacchus summed up the word choice in the title: "A good reason why 'fall' should be used in the NL Wikipedia is that the fall as such (and the role of UNPROFOR) are much more interesting from a Dutch perspective."[56] Thus there has been a series of successful defenses of the term as it stands. The other tension to date in the discussion was prompted when a user (Amela Malkic) brought up the graffiti the Dutch soldiers left behind at the camp in Potočari, where they were stationed. In the scrawls Bosnian girls were said to be malodorous, toothless, and mustached.

The creation of the English, Bosnian, Croatian, Serbian, and Serbo-Croatian Wikipedia articles on Srebrenica followed two to three years after the Dutch. The English-language article was begun in July 2004 as a near duplication of a detailed online piece, "Srebrenica massacre."[57] The title has persisted, despite much ensuing discussion about employing the term "genocide" instead, certainly on the basis of the 2004 ruling by the International Criminal Tribunal for the former Yugoslavia (ICTY), which Dado, the power editor, calls "a landmark ruling that put to rest any doubts about the legal character of the massacre. . . . [T]he Appeals Chamber of the International Criminal Tribunal for Former Yugoslavia unanimously ruled that it was an act of genocide."[58] After the 2007 ruling by the International Court of Justice (ICJ), which found in the case of *Bosnia and Herzegovina v. Serbia and Montenegro* that Serbia did not do all it could to prevent the Srebrenica genocide (and also had not cooperated with the court in transferring indicted suspects), to certain Wikipedia editors the article title no longer was current. GriffinSB writes: "The point of calling it massacre is outdated and should be updated to genocide."[59] It was not changed. Attempting to retitle the English article to "genocide" in December of 2010, Bosonian entered into discussion with power editors (Opbeith, Jonathanmills), who prefer "Srebrenica massacre" over "Srebrenica genocide" because it is more recognizable.[60] Recognition was tested by comparing the Google result counts for each term. The editors have been confronted by the issue repeatedly. For example, Emir Arven would not accept the term "massacre" and on July 10, 2005 (one day before the Srebrenica memorial day) created another article in the English Wikipedia entitled "Srebrenica genocide"; it has been redirected to "Srebrenica massacre."[61]

The Bosnian, Croatian, Serbian, and Serbo-Croatian articles have common origins. In 2005 a group of Bosnian Wikipedia editors translated the "Srebrenica massacre" article in the English-language Wikipedia into Bosnian, or B/C/S as the Bosnian/Croatian/Serbian language(s) are called, since "Serbo-Croatian" is now considered the language of former Yugoslavia, and also somewhat nostalgic.[62] The idea was suggested by Millosh, a Serbian editor who also participated in reaching consensus in the translation of the English article, and who is a power editor in the Serbian (with the B/C/S spelling of Miloš). Three other power editors of the English-language version (Emir Kotromanić, HarunB, and Dado) set to work on the Bosnian (or B/C/S) translation with the purpose of also pasting it into the Croatian and Serbian Wikipedias (see table 8.3). In the event, the term "massacre" was changed in the titles to "genocide" ("Genocid u Srebrenici").

Table 8.3
Interlanguage Srebrenica Article Editors

	English	Bosnian	Serbian	Croatian	Serbo-Croatian	Dutch
Dado	■	■	■	■		
Emir Arven*	■	■	■			
Asim Led**	■	■	■			
Mladifilozof		■	■			
Pyramid			■	■		
Nikola Smolenski	■		■	■		
Halbkreis	■		■	■		
Bormalagurski	■		■	■		
Pokrajac			■	■	■	

Editors active on more than one Wikipedia edition of the Srebrenica article, where active is defined as three or more edits.

* Emir Arven contributes under the name Emir Kotromanić in the Bosnian Wikipedia.

** Asim Led contributes under the name HarunB in the Bosnian Wikipedia.

The Bosnian version added detail that was not in the English-language version, including the initial finding of mass graves, the 10th memorial day of the Srebrenica massacre (and its speakers at the event), the notorious Scorpions video, the Scorpions being a Serbian paramilitary or police unit, which contains footage of their executions of young Bosnian males in July 1995. It also changed the general framing of the events to a Serbian attack and ethnic cleansing of the Bosnians. The English-language piece mentions that the number of killings is disputed by some nations, whereas the Bosnian version states that the figure is disputed by the Serbs. Also the external link to the report by the Srebrenica Research Group, and their report critical of the ICTY and ICJ findings, is dropped in the Bosnian translation.[63] The accounts of the provenance of the forces that took Srebrenica and committed the killings are worthy of mention. While the English-language piece speaks consistently of "Bosnian Serb" forces, the Bosnian (or initial B/C/S articles) intermingles "Bosnian Serb" and "Serb" forces. The rest of the English article is translated rather literally in the Bosnian. After pasting into the Croatian and Serbian Wikipedias, Dado remarks in August 2005, "Let's see how long it will last."[64]

In the Croatian Wikipedia the "genocide" title lasted. Dado says in the Croatian talk page that it is a Bosnian translation of the English article. It is not discussed until June 2007 when Flopy remarks: "Excellent and objective article. May it never be forgotten!"[65] As time passes, the Croatian Wikipedians modify the syntax, editing the article to make it more Croatian in a linguistic sense (which also was Dado's original request). Then in 2007 an anonymous user's off-color remarks lead to the locking of the article for anonymous edits, and Ygrain, the main contributor to the Croatian article, thereupon sets the template to "work in progress," reediting the piece by himself and making the account more local, in a sense. He edits the larger storyline, putting the creation of the U.N. safe area in April 1993 into the context of the fighting between Bosnian Serb and Bosnian forces, and in particular the territorial gains by Naser Orić, Bosnian army military commander (serving from 1992 to 1995), which included the swatch of land in the Republika Srpska including Bosniak and Serbian villages as well as the town of Srebrenica. By early 1993 Bosnian Serb forces under Ratko Mladić had reversed the gains and surrounded Srebrenica, calling on Orić's Bosnian forces in April to admit defeat and evacuate or face attack. Days later the safe area was created by U.N. mandate. The subsequent description of the killings is still detailed and left untouched. Here it is of interest to note that the Croatian, like the Bosnian article, employs the term "plan" and elaborates on the mass executions in a detailed and matter-of-fact manner, in keeping with the definition of genocide as a planned mass murder.

In contrast to the Croatian, the Serbian article did not last long, for it was "immediately attacked as propaganda," according to Dado.[66] Within hours of its posting, power editor Obradović Goran changed the title to "Masakr u Srebrenici," or Srebrenica massacre. Miloš also put up the edit warring template, explaining in the discussion page that the article's point of view is western. The immediate change of the title in the Serbian Wikipedia is discussed in the Bosnian discussion page by Bosnian as well as Serbo-Croatian article editors. Emir Arven (aka Emir Kotromanić), a power editor in both the English-language and Bosnian articles, opens the discussion by saying that this title change is the best evidence yet of Serbian genocide denial, to which Pokrajac responds that the English-language Wikipedia also refers to the event as a massacre, pointing out, too, that the Bosnian and Croatian are in fact the only Wikipedia editions that refer to the events as genocide.[67] The English Wikipedia is the "real reference," as he puts it.[68] A couple of months later, in September, Pokrajac edits the fledgling Serbo-Croatian article on the subject, removing the copy-pasted Bosnian article, calling it the "Events in Srebrenica of July 1995," and providing three links, two to the Srebrencia genocide articles (Bosnian and Croatian) and one to the Srebrenica massacre article (Serbian).

Over at the Serbian Wikipedia, exchanges were taking place about the title change. Svetlana Miljkovic, who has been working on the identification of mass graves, argues that Srebrenica is a case of genocide, to which Obradović Goran responds:

"[T]he arguments you apply do not make it a case of genocide. . . . The taking over of Srebrenica was a correct decision and moral imperative. The Orićs [Bosnian army under Naser Orić] went through [Serb] villages and didn't leave anything alive; they took everything. . . . Someone needed to stop their oppression. Now, the question of what happened after the taking over of Srebrenica is a different one."[69]

Miloš, echoing the sentiments of Pokrajac from the Bosnian talk page, points out that of the twenty-one Wikipedia language versions with Srebrenica articles, only the Bosnian and the Croatian have the word "genocide" in the title, though he adds that he cannot decipher the Arabic and Hebrew article titles. In the discussion page one encounters the recognition that what happened after the Bosnian Serb military operation Krivaja '95 was perhaps genocide. In the article, however, the aim is to describe the military operation, at least at this point in time. It may be worthwhile to point out that in March 2010 the parliament of Serbia apologized for the "Srebrenica massacre," without reference to the term "genocide"; this drew no immediate discussion in the Serbian talk page.

The Serbo-Croatian article underwent a series of title changes from its creation in September 2005, though the precise course of events is difficult to reconstruct from the talk histories of the three articles: "Events in Srebrenica of July 2005" (which is a typo and should read "July 1995"), "Genocide in Srebrenica," and "Massacre in Srebrenica."[70] Suffice it to say that the term "event" was thought to be too palpably neutral (one discussant put forward the proposed title "Crimes of Srebrenica"). The term "genocide" was thought to be too political, though a preferred term in Bosnia and Herzegovina, especially by the Bosniaks, to paraphrase the edit made by OC Ripper on January 4, 2007. At the outset the Serbo-Croatian was called a unifying version, a view deriving initially from the argumentation used to unlock the Serbo-Croatian Wikipedia (mentioned above) and the discussion of how to entitle the article there. Defending the initial word choice, Pokrajac writes, "The word 'event' is used precisely to avoid politicization, because the different parties have not reached consensus on how to characterize this event. If you find a better synonym that does not lean to either side (which is very important, at least in Wikipedia), feel free to nominate it."[71] Another user, David, writes that titling the article "Events" will prompt what the author seeks to avoid. Id, arguing against unoffensive language, writes that he or she "knows no value-free synonym for 'genocide' in Serbo-Croatian (or any other language)."[72] In July 2007 (around the time of the anniversary), the Bosnian article was pasted into the Serbo-Croatian, and OC Ripper, the article's power editor, changed the title to "Massacre," beginning an editing process that ultimately would soften the tone of the article. He removed most of the pictures, except for the few shared by the Serbian, Croatian, and Bosnian articles, as discussed below. Perhaps OC Ripper's overall outlook on the function of the Serbo-Croatian Wikipedia is relevant here. He observes on his user page that certain of the same articles are better and worse across the entire Bosnian, Croatian, and Serbian Wikipedias. "The Serbo-Croatian Wikipedia would be the perfect way to fill up those gaps, for it could serve as a universal matrix for the hr [Croatian], bs [Bosnian] and sr [Serbian] Wikipedias, which could later, with far less difficulty, be adapted to local conditions."[73]

Editing the Srebrenica Articles

Apart from the articles' titles, our study compared the discussions about them and the templates they may carry, their table of contents, the introductory paragraphs, and the information boxes. There are discrepancies in the content, especially with regard to three basic points around which accounts of Srebrenica often revolve: the number of victims, the responsibility or blame, and the controversy about the first two points. The editors are also compared, particularly the power editors or top contributors across the language versions, the locations of the anonymous editors (if anonymous editing is allowed), the references made in the articles, and the images that appear in them. One of the purposes of the comparison is to note any migration of editors across the language versions: in fact, it was found that the editors tend to be dedicated to single versions, with the exception of the English-language article (see table 8.3). The lack of cross-editing is one means to account for the distinctiveness of the articles in the respective Wikipedia language versions, especially the Dutch article, which is alone in its lack of interlanguage editors.

Indeed, with the exception of Dado, the power editors of each article do not contribute significantly to other Balkan-language versions (see also table 8.4). Power editors from the Serbian- and Bosnian-language versions, however, do participate in the English-language one. As Dado recounted, the road to consensus in the English article was not easily traveled. Fairview, an English-language Wikipedian, summarized one part of the writing process in 2008 as an "intensive round of edits, arguing, edit warring, interventions, blocked editors, sockpuppets, etc."[74] For the editors of the Bosnian, Serb, Croatian, and Serbo-Croatian Wikipedia articles, the English-language version is both the seminal and often the baseline piece. Judging from the mix of editors of the various versions, it serves as the common article on the subject rather than the Serbo-Croatian, which is edited by mainly one user.

Dado has remarked that editors do not participate in language versions other than their own, so to speak, because "it is too intellectually and emotionally draining to deal with so much conflict, especially when you do it voluntarily. It is a stressful hobby."[75] As noted above, power editors do contribute to each other's discussion pages (to some extent) and thus follow the goings-on of the equivalent article elsewhere, especially the Bosnian and the Serbian (as well as the English).

The Serbo-Croatian article on Srebrenica, like the Bosnian, Croatian, and Serbian, ultimately shares its origins with the English, though by the time the Bosnian piece was introduced into the Serbo-Croatian Wikipedia in July 2007 nearly two years' worth of adjustments to the original translation had been made. The migrations had effects on the content, with certain additions and excisions. The publication of the Serbian article was met with a flurry of activity, and Dado described how the change of setting

Table 8.4

Top Ten Editors of Srebrenica Articles per Wikipedia Language Version, by Number of Edits

English	edits	Bosnian	edits	Croatian	edits
Bosniak*	384	Dado	41	Ygraine	13
Osli73*	377	Emir Kotromanić	33	SieBot	8
Jonathanmills	352	HarunB	18	Dado	7
Fairview	318	EmxBot	13	Roberta_f	5
HanzoHattori*	269	Jasmin A.	10	BodhisattvaBot	4
Dado	210	Pyramid	9	EmxBot	4
Opbeith	169	Mladifilozof	9	SashatoBot	4
Emir Arven*	138	Palapa	8	YurikBot	4
Jitse Niesen	110	SieBot	6	JAnDbot	4
The Dragon of Bosnia*	93	Demicx	6	217.24.19.163 (Belgrade)	4

Serbian	edits	Serbo-Croatian	edits	Dutch	edits
Miloš	38	OC Ripper	56	Hjvannes (aka Hettie)	24
Obradovic Goran	34	80.109.29.186 (Vienna)	8	node_c_2246_a2000_nl	13
AntiDiskriminator *	29	77.78.215.209 (Sarajevo)	6	77.162.77.117 (Utrecht)	10
Bas-Celik	24	SieBot	6	Compro	7
Pyramid	21	JAnDbot	5	Eiland	7
BokicaK	20	MelancholieBot	4	Tdevries	6
Halbkreis	18	Autobot	3	SieBot	6
Jovanvb	18	Xqbot	3	Besednjak	6
DzordM	17	Thijs!bot	3	Johan Lont	5
Sokolac	15	Pokrajac	2	Apdency	5

* Indicates blocked user or user suspected of sockpuppeting through the use of multiple names or anonymous editing. Anonymous editors are indicated by IP address, and the geolocation of that address is reported.

for the piece that was once agreed to in the English-language version had greater effects. Even to its original Serbian editors, the article was no longer acceptable when it appeared in the Serbian Wikipedia. It immediately received the template charging it to be a source of an edit war.

Although power editors largely confine themselves to their respective language versions of the article, this is apparently not the case for the anonymous edits. Anonymous edits are made from different countries of ex-Yugoslavia in each article except the Dutch, where both anonymous edits and power edits are from Dutch IP addresses. Thus, contributing to one another's articles mainly occurs anonymously (see figure 8.1). It should be noted that the Bosnian version has been closed to anonymous edits, indicating that they are a source of vandalism or unacceptable contestation.

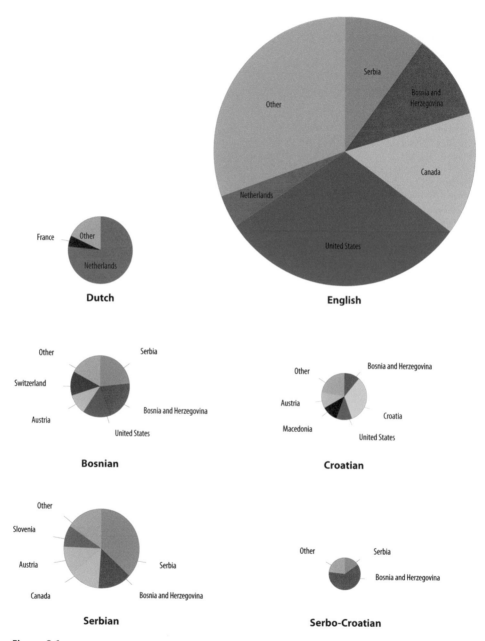

Figure 8.1
Locations of anonymous editors of the Srebrenica articles, as of December 20, 2010. Size of charts relative to number of edits. Analysis tool: Wikipedia Edits Scraper and IP Localizer. (cc) Digital Methods Initiative, Amsterdam, 2011.

Table 8.5

Comparison across Wikipedia Language Versions of the Numbers of Dead in the Srebrenica Articles, December 20, 2010

Wikipedia Language Version	Number of Bosniak Victims
Dutch (Nederlands)	7,000–8,000
English	8,372
Bosnian (Bosanski)	8,000
Croatian (Hrvatski)	8,000
Serbian (Srpski)	6,000–8,000
Serbo-Croatian (Srpsko-Hrvatski)	8,000

Note: The number of Bosniak victims of the Srebrenica killings is taken from the information box found in the English, Bosnian, Serbian, and Serbo-Croatian articles. For the Dutch and Croatian articles (without information boxes), the numbers are from the introduction.

The same holds for the Croatian and Serbian versions, albeit for shorter periods of time.

Where the number of victims, the responsibility or blame, as well as the controversy surrounding those fundamental points (and others) are concerned, there are differences between the language versions. First there is the question of the number of Bosniaks killed in Srebrenica, where the Dutch and Serbian versions have lower estimates than the Bosnian, Croatian, English, and Serbo-Croatian (see table 8.5).

In the discussion pages, there are various standpoints on how to provide further context to the victim count, provided by the editors and the references they choose. The creator of the Dutch article points out that there were 40,000 people living in the Srebrenica enclave and 7,500 killed, leaving 32,500 safely evacuated by "our boys."[76] Gradually the (military) language of the editors is phased out, including the replacement of "we" and "us" with "Dutchbatters" and acronyms with full words (e.g., "OP" becomes [military] "observation post"). From the revision history it is clear that for the victim count the article follows the Dutch official report by the Netherlands Institute for War Documentation in 2002 (7,000 killings), and later the earlier ICTY verdict of 2001 (7,000–8,000 killings). There have been discussions about lowering the figure; Compro put the number between 5,500 and 6,000, citing a newspaper article that 500 victims were still alive (and Compro's previous recollection of 6,000 victims). The conclusion of the discussions is reflected in the introductory paragraph, emphasizing the uncertainty over the number.

The English-language article is meticulous in its count (8,372), and maintains and updates a listing of identified victim numbers on its discussion page. The 8,372 figure, according to the article, derives from the count at the Potočari Memorial Center. The Center for the Srebrenica-Potočari Memorial and Cemetery for the Victims of the 1995

Genocide (as the Memorial Center is officially called) maintains the list (which currently has 8,373 names on it). As one Wikipedian put it, in reference to the slight
difference in victim counts, "For some reason the memorial stone refers to 8372."[77]
The number is higher than the figure given by Martin Frost (8,100) in the online piece
that formed the basis for the original Wikipedia article. 8,106 is the number given by
the International Commission on Missing Persons, which collects blood samples from
relatives of missing persons, and performs DNA analysis on exhumed remains so as
to identify victims.[78] The Federal (Bosnian) Commission on Missing Persons maintains
the victim list, which changed the figure from 8,106 to 8,373 in 2005, according to
the Mothers of Srebrenica and Zepa website, which I come to in the more detailed
discussion of the differences in referencing practices between the articles. It is important to point out that 2005 was the tenth anniversary of the killings, a moment when
the Republika Srpska adjusted its numbers, too.

The Serbian Wikipedia article on the Srebrenica massacre lists 6,000–8,000 victims.
Further context emerges in the discussion, along with another list. Đorđe Stakić, in
October 2006, refers to a list of 3,287 Serbians killed in Srebrenica and surroundings
in 1992–1995, citing a list on the governmental website of the Republika Srpska. Bas-
Celik returns to that list in August 2010 when other contextualizations are discussed,
including the deaths of 11 Serb civilians, though the argument (by Thom977, who
according to his user page speaks Serbian and Dutch) is made that it would be in poor
taste to relativize the deaths of 11 Serbs in a comparison with those of 8,372 Bosnian
Muslims. An anonymous editor with IP address from Serbia (on August 23) observes
that it is also "in poor taste to compare the 8,372 lives in Srebrenica to the 6 million
Jews, 1 million Rwandans and 73,316 children killed in Jasenovac," the World War II
Croatian concentration camp.[79]

The actual victim count discussion is more detailed, for Miloš, a power editor, points
out that Lewis MacKenzie (former commander of UNPROFOR in Sarajevo) put the
figure at 2,000 killed in battle rather than mass murder, while the BBC, CNN, and B92
put the victim count at over 8,000. (The use of MacKenzie as a source at the English-
language Wikipedia article is not accepted, with the argument, by Opbeith, that
MacKenzie's 2005 *Globe and Mail* piece was "an act of genocide denial.")[80] The difference between the Serbian article's victim count and that of the others in question does
not appear to be based on MacKenzie's number, however. Rather, the introduction of
the figure "6,000–8,000" victims to the information box (and to the opening paragraph) by Jakša on July 20, 2010, refers to a documentary broadcast on July 9 by Radio
Television of Serbia (RTS), "Srebrenica Killing Fields," which Jakša felt was researched
better than the Wikipedia article. He says that the article calls for hard facts specific
to the massacre, not further contextualization like the bad blood built up through
centuries of Ottoman rule or events in World War II. In that vein, the 6,000–8,000
range likely refers to the approximate number of bodies exhumed from the mass graves

and the estimated victim count in the other articles (excepting the English-language one). On August 10, 2010, Thom977 attempts to modify the number to 8,372, but it was reverted ten minutes later, and to date has remained 6,000–8,000.

In the discussion Miloš raises the issue of the accuracy of the figures also in relation to a lack of knowledge of the population of Srebrenica at the time, arguing that a census had not been taken prior to the war or since. On this point it is of note that the Bosnian article once contained a long section (now moved to the discussion page archive) in which the population, its demographics, and victim counts are discussed in some detail. Here the article once read that from April to July 1995 some 8,991 were killed, and that the number could be over 10,000. This even higher figure does not last in the Bosnian article. The Bosnian talk page also discusses the number of Serbian deaths, and asks whether anyone would translate the section in the English-language article, entitled "Dispute regarding Serb casualties around Srebrenica," which begins with a quotation from Human Rights Watch about how the nationalist Serbian Radical Party started a media campaign in 2005 to raise awareness about Serb deaths prior to the Srebrenica killings. In July 2005 the official victim count was raised from 1,400 to 3,500 by the government of the Republika Srpska, a figure that the ICTY, among other sources, declares to be greatly overstated, as discussed in the English-language talk page. In the Serbo-Croatian Wikipedia, the number of deaths does not appear to be in dispute, though the matter is framed as uncertain.[81]

Recall the description of the Serbo-Croatian article as a softened version of the Bosnian, and of its power editor, OC Ripper, as having a unifying outlook. As a case in point, the sentence in the Bosnian article about the Scorpions video was shortened, removing the description of the Scorpions as part of the Serbian Interior Ministry. Also, the fine-grained, day-to-day descriptions of the mass executions were removed, replaced with a summary. In terms of the victims, the article says that the chronology of events is still unclear, including the locations of the executions, the number of victims, as well as the means by which they were killed. Another reason why the victim count is uncertain, it is said, has to do with the reburials of victims from August to November 1995 by the government of the Republika Srpska.

On the question of who is to blame, a comparison of the discussion pages as well as the tables of contents shows certain commonalities between the Bosnian, Croatian, and English-language articles as well as unique elements in the Dutch and Serbian articles concerning the nature of the events (see figure 8.2). In the Dutch article the report by the Netherlands Institute for War Documentation (2002) is said not to have drawn hard conclusions about who was to blame, though it made inculpable the Dutchbat contingent which, it is said, was given a poor mandate and was ill-prepared and ill-equipped. The Prime Minister Wim Kok and his cabinet members stepped down on July 22, 2002, after the publication of the report, just after the seventh anniversary of the events. What the Bosnian- and Croatian-language versions have in common

"Srebrenica Massacre," English version, August 6, 2005		"Srebrenica Massacre," English version, December 20, 2010	
1	Background	1	Background
1.1	April 1993: the Security Council declares Srebrenica a "safe area"	1.1	Conflict in eastern Bosnia
		1.1.1	1992 ethnic cleansing campaign
1.2	Early 1995: the situation in the Srebrenica "safe area" deteriorates	1.1.2	Fate of Bosnian Muslim villages
		1.1.3	Struggle for Srebrenica
1.3	Spring 1995: the Bosnian Serbs plan to attack the Srebrenica "safe area"	1.2	"Srebrenica safe area"
		1.2.1	April 1993: the Security Council declares Srebrenica a "safe area"
1.4	6–11 July 1995: the takeover of Srebrenica	1.2.2	Serb refusal to demilitarise around Srebrenica
2	The massacre	1.2.3	Early 1995: the situation in the Srebrenica "safe area" deteriorates
2.1	The crowd at Potočari		
2.1.1	The humanitarian crisis in Potočari: 11–13 July 1995	1.2.4	Possible widespread racism among Dutch peacekeepers
2.1.2	12–13 July: crimes committed in Potočari	1.2.5	4 June and 6–11 July 1995: Serb take-over of Srebrenica
2.2	The column of Bosniak men	2	Massacre
2.3	A plan to execute the Bosnian Muslim men of Srebrenica	2.1	11–13 July 1995: the humanitarian crisis in Potočari
2.4	The mass executions	2.2	12–13 July: crimes committed in Potočari
2.4.1	The morning of 13 July 1995: Jadar River executions	2.3	Separation and murder of Bosniak men in Potočari
2.4.2	The afternoon of 13 July 1995: Cerska Valley executions	2.3.1	Rapes and abuse of civilians
2.4.3	13–14 July 1995: Tišća	2.4	Deportation of women
2.4.4	14 July 1995: Grbavci school detention site and Orahovac execution site	2.5	Column of Bosniak men
		2.5.1	Other groups
2.4.5	14–16 July 1995: Pilica school detention site and Branjevo Military Farm execution site	2.5.2	Tuzla column departs
		2.5.3	Ambush at Kamenica Hill
3	The reburials	2.5.4	Sandići massacre
4	Recent developments	2.5.5	Trek to Mount Udrc
4.1	US resolution 199	2.5.6	Snagovo ambush
5	Revisionism and denial of the massacre	2.5.7	Approaching the frontline
		2.5.8	Breakthrough at Baljkovica
		2.5.9	Baljkovica corridor
		2.5.10	Arrival at Tuzla
		2.5.11	After the closure of the corridor
		2.6	Plan to execute the men of Srebrenica
		2.7	Mass executions
		2.7.1	Morning of 13 July: Jadar River
		2.7.2	Afternoon of 13 July: Cerska Valley
		2.7.3	Late afternoon of 13 July: Kravica
		2.7.4	13–14 July: Tišća
		2.7.5	14 July: Grbavci and Orahovac
		2.7.6	14–15 July: Petkovići
		2.7.7	14–16 July: Branjevo Selo
		2.7.8	14–17 July: Kozluk
		2.7.9	13–18 July: Bratunac-Konjević Polje road

Figure 8.2

Comparison of the tables of contents of the Srebrenica articles, December 20, 2010, also including the table of contents of the English-language article, translated into Bosnian (or B/C/S), August 5, 2005. Similar colors indicate similar contents in these sections of the articles. Analysis by Emina Sendijarevic.

"Srebrenica Massacre," English version, December 20, 2010	
2.7.10	18–19 July: Nezuk-Baljkovica frontline
2.7.11	20–22 July: Meces area
2.8	After the massacre
2.8.1	Wanderers
2.8.2	Reburials in the secondary mass graves
2.9	Greek Volunteers controversy
3	End of the war
4	Post-war developments
4.1	1995 indictment of Radovan Karadžić and Ratko Mladić
4.2	1999 UN Secretary-General's report
4.3	2001 French parliamentary report
4.4	2002 Dutch government report
4.5	2002 First Republika Srpska report
4.6	2003 Srebrenica Genocide Memorial
4.7	2004 Second Republika Srpska report and official apology
4.8	2005 Release of Scorpions massacre video
4.9	2005 US Congress and other resolutions
4.10	2005 Potočari Memorial bomb plot
4.11	2005 UN Secretary-General's message to the 10th anniversary commemoration
4.12	2005 Perpetrators named
4.13	2006 Discoveries of further mass graves
4.14	2006 Suppressed list of perpetrators in positions of authority published
4.15	2006 Dutch Srebrenica medal controversy
4.16	2007 Arrest of Zdravko Tolimir
4.17	2008 Arrest of Radovan Karadzić
4.18	2009 EU Parliament resolution
4.19	2010 Serbia's official apology
4.20	2010 Second Republika Srpska report revision
5	DNA analysis
6	Legal proceedings
6.1	International Criminal Tribunal for the Former Yugoslavia
6.2	International Court of Justice
6.3	National courts
6.3.1	Serbia
6.3.2	Bosnia and Herzegovina 6.3.2 United States
6.3.3	The Netherlands
7	Analyses
7.1	Role of Bosnian forces on the ground
7.2	Dispute regarding Serb casualties around Srebrenica
8	Opposition to the term "genocide"

"Genocida u Srebrenici," Bosnian version, December 20, 2010	
1	Introduction
1.1	April 1993: the Security Council declares Srebrenica a "free zone"
1.2	Early 1995: state of "safe area" of Srebrenica deteriorates
1.3	Spring 1995: Serbs planned attack of the "safe area" of Srebrenica
1.4	Period 6 to 11 July 1995: the takeover of Srebrenica
2	The massacre
2.1	The mass of people in Potočari
2.1.1	12–13 July: crimes committed in Potočari
2.1.2	The separation of Muslim men in Potočari
2.2	The column of Bosniak men
2.3	Plan to execute the Bosniak men from Srebrenica
2.4	The mass executions
2.4.1	13 July 1995 morning: the executions of Jadar
2.4.2	13 July 1995: afternoon: Cerska Valley
2.4.3	13–14 July 1995: Tišća
2.4.4	14 July 1995: place of detention at a school in Grbavci and execution in Orahovac
2.4.5	14–16 July 1995: school detentionsite Pilica execution at Branjevo Selo
3	The reburials
4	Epilogue and recent developments
4.1	Role of Bosniak forces on the ground (conclusions of the United Nations)
4.2	Resolution of the United States no. 199
4.3	The role of Serbia in genocide
5	Revisionism and denial of genocide

Figure 8.2
(continued)

"Genocide u Srebrenici," Croatian version, December 20, 2010	"Masakr u Srebrenici," Serbian version, December 20, 2010
1 Introduction	1 Background
1.1 April 1993: the Security Council declares Srebrenica a "free zone"	2 Operation Krivaja '95. The taking of Srebrenica
	3 Operation Stupcanica '95. Taking Zepa
1.2 Early 1995: state of "safe area" of Srebrenica deteriorates	4 Chronology of massacre
	4.1 Beg** of Bosniaks in Potočari
1.3 Spring 1995: Serbs planned attack of the "safe area" of Srebrenica	4.2 Transport women, children and the elderly
1.4 Period 6 to 11 July 1995: the takeover of Srebrenica	4.3 Separation of Bosniak men
2 The massacre	4.4 The column of refugees and soldiers
2.1 The mass of people in Potočari	4.5 Executions
2.1.1 12–13 July: crimes committed in Potočari	4.6 Primary and secondary mass graves
2.1.2 The separation of Muslim men in Potočari	5 Reports on the massacre in Srebrenica
2.2 The column of Bosniak men	6 Criticism of the official version of events
2.3 Plan to execute the Bosniak men from Srebrenica	7 Controversy
2.4 The mass executions	8 Consequences
2.4.1 13 July 1995 morning: the executions of Jadar	9 Trials
2.4.2 13 July 1995: afternoon: Cerska Valley	9.1 The Hague Tribunal
2.4.3 13–14 July 1995: Tišća	9.2 International Court of Justice
2.4.4 14 July 1995: place of detention at a school in Grbavci and execution in Orahovac	9.3 Trials in Serbia
	10 Reports and resolutions of Serbian institutionsand the Republic of Srpska
2.4.5 14–16 July 1995: school detentionsite Pilica execution at Branjevo Selo	
3 The reburials	
4 Epilogue and recent developments	
5 The role of Serbia	
5.1 The resolution of the United States no. 199	
6 Trials	
7 Revisionism and the denial of genocide	

Figure 8.2
(continued)

(and to an extent the English-language one) is the explicit accusation that Serbs executed a methodical plan, invading the town, separating the men from the women and children, evacuating the women and children, and killing the men. Like the Dutch to some extent, the Serbian piece focuses on the military operation, especially with the headers "Operation Krivaja '95" and "Operation Stupcanica '95," the respective force plans for the taking of Srebrenica and Žepa (another U.N. safe area) by the army of the Republika Srpska. Unlike with the Dutch article, however, heated discussion prompted a change in the wholesale framing of the article. Initially the headers for

"Masakr u Srebrenici," Serbo-Croatian version, December 20, 2010		"De Val van Srebrenica," Dutch version, December 20, 2010	
1	Creating a safe area	1	Background
2	The situation in the safe zone (1993–1995)	2	Battles before the fall of Srebrenica
3	The fall of the Srebrenica enclave	3	The fall of Srebrenica
4	Breakthrough of Muslim men to Tuzla	4	Aftermath
5	Evacuation of women and separation of menfrom Potočari	4.1	Investigation of the circumstances
		4.2	The ones responsible
6	Mass executions	4.3	The NIOD report and its implications
7	The military and political consequences of the massacre	4.4	Charges pressed by survivors
7.1	Apologies by Serbia		
8	Court proceedings		
9	Alternative visions of events, revisionism and conspiracy theories		

Figure 8.2
(continued)

the military operations were links to separate articles of the same names, and subsequently to empty subsections within the article itself. In May to July 2010 (in the run-up to the fifteenth anniversary of the events), a somewhat administrative discussion about headers and information box templates segued into the much larger issue of the overall thrust of the article, whether a military operation (with a Bosnian Serb army victory) or a massacre. For Wikipedia articles there are two distinct information box templates for military conflict and civilian attack, respectively, and AntiDiskriminator would like to replace the current military info-box with the massacre one. After a short round of reverts and heated discussion (initiated by Bas-Celik, who prefers the retention of the military framing and reintroduced the military conflict info-box for the last time at 3 in the morning on July 20), the massacre info-box with the cemetery and victim counts currently holds sway (see figure 8.3). One discussion point raised by CrniBombarder! is worth pointing out. Military conflict articles, with that template, deal with "strictly military" and not "ancillary events," thus prompting the question of whether Operation Krivaja '95 and the Srebrenica massacre should have separate articles rather than be merged.[82]

The scope of the people to blame is also at issue. The Serbian article avoids using the terms Serb and Bosnian Serb forces, preferring instead VRS, or the army of the Republika Srpska. In the Serbian talk page, a discussion on the framing of the introductory parts of the article between Dordezm and Miloš reveals the sentiments on who is to blame for the killings. Dordezm, in response to the questioning of the

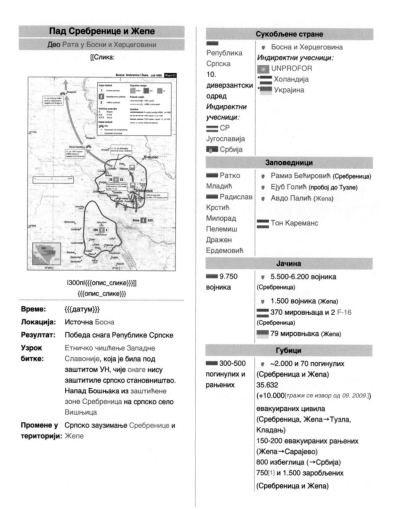

Пад Сребренице и Жепе

Део Рата у Босни и Херцеговини

[[Слика:

I300nl{{{опис_слике}}}]]
{{{опис_слике}}}

Време:	{{{датум}}}
Локација:	Источна Босна
Резултат:	Победа снага Републике Српске
Узрок битке:	Етничко чишћење Западне Славоније, која је била под заштитом УН, чије снаге нису заштитиле српско становништво. Напад Бошњака из заштићене зоне Сребреница на српско село Вишњица
Промене у територији:	Српско заузимање Сребренице и Жепе

Сукобљене стране

Република Српска 10. диверзантски одред Индиректни учесници: CP Југославија Србија	Босна и Херцеговина *Индиректни учесници:* UNPROFOR Холандија Украјина

Заповедници

Ратко Младић Радислав Крстић Милорад Пелемиш Дражен Ердемовић	Рамиз Бећировић (Сребреница) Ејуб Голић (пробој до Тузле) Авдо Палић (Жепа) Тон Кареманс

Јачина

9.750 војника	5.500-6.200 војника (Сребреница) 1.500 војника (Жепа) 370 мировњаца и 2 F-16 (Сребреница) 79 мировњака (Жепа)

Губици

300-500 погинулих и рањених	~2.000 и 70 погинулих (Сребреница и Жепа) 35.632 (+10.000[тражи се извор од 09. 2009.]) евакуираних цивила (Сребреница, Жепа→Тузла, Кладањ) 150-200 евакуираних рањених (Жепа→Сарајево) 800 избеглица (→Србија) 750[1] и 1.500 заробљених (Сребреница и Жепа)

Масакр у Сребреници

Гробље у оквиру Сребреница-Поточари Меморијалног центра

локација	Сребреница, Босна и Херцеговина
датум	11. јул 1995. – 22. јул 1995.
погинуло	8.000+
починиоци	Војска Републике Српске
браниоци	Армија Републике Босне и Херцеговине

Figure 8.3

Info-box edit war, Srebrenica massacre article, Serbian Wikipedia, 2010. Military conflict template (with military map and detail) and civilian attack template, with the details of the Operation Krivaja '95 and the Srebrenica massacre, respectively. Power editors replaced one with the other, the last time being on July 20, 2010, when the military conflict box was inserted by Bas-Celik at 3:03 and the civilian attack box reinserted by AntiDiskriminator four hours later at 7:35. Since then the military conflict information box has not reappeared. Source: sr.wikipedia.org.

validity of the verdicts posed by the ICJ, states that the ICJ's main objective was to find out who committed this genocide:

1) Serbia did not commit the genocide.
2) Serbia did not participate, supplied or supported the genocide.
3) Serbia didn't do everything in its power to prevent the genocide.
4) Serbia is not suspected of genocide . . . the ICJ ordered this crime to be a genocide committed by someone in Bosnia against someone else in Bosnia, and not as a genocide that was committed by someone from Serbia against the Bosnians. OK?[83]

In the Serbo-Croatian talk pages, it is asked why the term "Bosnian Serbian forces" is used. OC Ripper, power editor in the Serbo-Croatian edition, declares that the reason is precision. "'Serbian' would imply that Serbia and the people of Serbia as a whole, are to blame, and that would give this article a POV dimension and material for counterproductive political discussions. The terms Bosnian Serb and Bosnian Serbian are therefore used as adjectives, because it is difficult to use Republika Srpska as an adjective."[84]

The English-language version covers a variety of controversies: "Possible widespread racism among Dutch peacekeepers," the "Greek volunteers controversy" about Greek forces joining the Bosnian Serbs, "Role of Bosnian forces on the ground," and "Dispute regarding Serb causalities around Srebrenica." The section "Opposition to the term genocide" also provides a list by name of those who challenge the designation of the killings as genocide. Arguably the controversy-making goes back to the very beginning of the article with the repeated insertion and removal of the word "alleged," a discussion of which is on the first of the nineteen archived talk pages. As the article grows (and with it the talk pages), it is as if every paragraph becomes a source of dispute. From the outset it is often observed that the Bosnian and Serbian power editors are discussing what should be in the article, and that it is the "western" power editors who decide what is ultimately included, also playing peacekeeper. One (relatively early) example is a contribution to the controversy on the "Role of Bosnian forces on the ground," and in on particular Naser Orić, the Bosnian army commander. Nikola Smolenski and Asim Led (aka HarunB, cocreator of the Bosnian article) are in dispute about the extent to which Orić should be covered in the English article. Finally, power editor Jitse Niesen calms them down: "I understand this is an emotional subject, but can we please try to keep our heads cool? Asim, I doubt it is helpful to indulge in personal attacks (thank you, Asim). Nikola, can you please explain what you mean with your remark about Orić? He is mentioned in the current article, in the fourth paragraph."[85]

The Bosnian and Croatian articles speak of "Revisionism and the denial of genocide." The header "Role of Bosniak forces on the ground" is included in the Bosnian article but is missing in the Croatian. The line in the table of contents called

"Revisionism and denial of genocide" in the Bosnian is called "Criticism of the official versions of events" in the Serbian article. Here it is helpful to refer to Kaster, an editor of the Serbian Wikipedia version, who summarizes what he refers to as the western, popular-media account as having roughly ten points, all of which should be rebutted in a special section called "critique of the general account of events," or "the Serbian version of the truth about Srebrenica":[86]

- the safe haven was demilitarized before the events of July 1995;
- the "safe haven" was at peace and under control of the blue helmets;
- all or the majority of those killed were civilians;
- the number of deaths is more than 8,000;
- the killings were planned beforehand;
- the killings were ordered by Ratko Mladić and Radovan Karadžić;
- the regular police as well as the Yugoslavian army participated in the killings;
- the Serbians as an ethnic group are to blame for what happened;
- foreign influences (Dutchbat) as well as the Muslim side in the events of July were "innocent";
- the Hague tribunal is just and treats all sides equally.[87]

While the edit warring template was put on the article directly after its creation date, the more recent Serbian article version has NPOV and factual inaccuracy templates (in place since August 2009). Nikola summarizes what could be described as a big-picture controversy about the article's POV (point of view). "The version of the course of events that has been forced by the west is taken as the most accurate one, while the local one is taken as a reaction to the former."[88] Indeed, after the placement of the NPOV template, a discussion erupts in the Serbian talk page on the question of how the Serbian article is supposed to represent a neutral point of view while still remaining its own version of the account of events. Here the relationship between the neutral and the Serbian is discussed (historiographically) in terms of the current and future needs of the Serb people. Miloš argues, "I realize [we] need revisionism . . . because it is not easy when five thousand to eight thousand people were killed *in the name of your people*."[89] He also asks whether the article will improve with greater historical distance or hindsight, proposing at one point (in the interim) that the English write the Serbian article, and the Serbian the English-language one. In that vein he also poses a further question about why the Serbian-language encyclopedia needs to be a Serbian encyclopedia any more than the German-language a German one. In the event, the Serbian editors settle on a header (unique to the articles) called "Reports and resolutions of Serbian institutions and the Republika Srpska," which offers additional sources and views so as to make the account less western.

The Serbo-Croatian article uses a combination of terms, "Alternative visions of events, revisionism, and conspiracy theories," whereas the Dutch table of contents does not have a header referring to controversy as such, closing with the section title "Charges by the survivors," referring to the legal proceedings brought by the group referred to as the Mothers of Srebrenica.

Referencing and Providing Images to the Srebrenica Articles

Anyone can edit Wikipedia articles, though there are hurdles to be cleared. In Srebrenica articles editors are encouraged to turn to the talk pages, where edits are discussed or drafted. Editors sometimes ask for further substantiation and referencing; it is at this point that contributors are occasionallly admonished for the introduction of particular sources as well as types of sources. As a case in point (mentioned above), in the English-language article on the Srebrenica massacre, the 2005 *Globe and Mail* piece by former Sarajevo UNPROFOR commander Lewis MacKenzie was not deemed credible, given his alleged Serb sympathies, physical distance from the events in question, and so forth. A reprint of that piece is referenced (twice) in the Serbian article and in none of the other five articles in question. In the English-language version, there are also types of sources considered out of order, notably blogs such as srebrenica-genocide.blogspot.com, which is the (Bosnian) source of the pictures of the graffiti on the walls at the Dutchbat compound in Potočari, raised in the Dutch discussion pages (and elsewhere). Like the MacKenzie piece, it is talked about in most language versions, and referenced only in one—the Bosnian article. In both the MacKenzie and srebrenica-genocide.blogspot cases, the sources are referenced for their recognized knowledge, not in specific sections about revisionism, criticisms of official versions of events, or similar alternative points of view. Thus certain sources are deemed acceptable by the editors of one language version and not by those of another, which leads to the question of which sources are unique (and which are shared) in the articles under study, as well as to the larger issue of the distribution of attribution or spread of references across articles. Are the articles relying on similar or vastly different authorities? Here it may be worthwhile to quote from the Serbian talk page during the NPOV dispute period (approximately one year after the pasting of the B/C/S article, translated from the English, into the Serbian Wikipedia). The question is raised of what "side" references are on. "The only reliable sources are those two. The rest is Bosnian, and controversial to Serbians. What to do?"[90] Also, on which subject matters are the sources the same (both on the document as well as on the level of source name), and on which do they differ? There is also the question of context of use, or how (and where in the article) sources are cited. The approach taken here to the analysis of the referencing follows along the above lines of a comparison of shared and unique sources, including their usage.

Wikipedia articles often have both references (in the form of footnotes) as well as suggestions for further reading. Both the references and suggestions are hyperlinked, which provides the opportunity for harvesting and comparing the links across articles, both on the level of the page (or document) and on that of the host (or general source name). (The links made to other Wikipedia pages in the body of the Srebrenica articles, and in menus, are left out of our analysis because they are not external sources and as such do not serve to substantiate accounts. It is worth noting that in the menu there are links to other language versions of the "same" article, including the German, which, like the Bosnian, is a featured article; the Japanese as well as Norwegian enjoy the status of good articles on the subject.) It is instructive at the outset to point out that the English-language article has the most references by far (308 of the 438 in all articles, or 70% of the total), followed by the Serbian (56), Croatian (38), Bosnian (17), Dutch (12), and Serbo-Croatian (7). Not surprisingly, it has the most unique references (276, or 90% of the unique references of all the language versions). Recall that the power editors of the various articles (with the exception of the Dutch) contribute to the English-language article. Thus in principle it would not be unusual for references to be shared, if one takes into account that the editors potentially bring their references with them to the English-language article, and also take them back to their own version (so to speak). Perhaps the more remarkable finding, however, is that the majority of references in all the articles (with the exception of the Serbo-Croatian) are unique references: Serbian 77% (43/56), Bosnian 59% (10/17), Croatian 87% (33/38), and Dutch 83% (10/12). If one assumes that some reference sharing should occur across articles with the same power editors, one could expect that at least English-language sources would recur. As a set, the six articles have no common page-level outlinks as references or external sources, whether in English or any other language. The only article whose (seven) references appear in at least one other article is the Serbo-Croatian (again, in a sense, unifying the various articles or views). Five of the six share a (page-level) reference to the original war crimes indictment in 1995, and four share a reference to the Mothers of Srebrenica, the group representing the survivors.

Our page-level analysis is accompanied by host comparison, so as to address the issue of articles' referencing translations of the same document, especially from international organizations and governments. The pattern of sourcing specificity becomes less dramatic on a host level, where the English and Dutch articles still have a majority of unique hosts (74% and 64% respectively), while the Serbian, Bosnian, and Croatian now have a minority (34, 31,and 24% respectively) (see figure 8.4). The United Nations (un.org) as source is shared by all six articles, and the Mothers of Srebrenica (srebrenica.ba) and the International Criminal Tribunal for the former Yugoslavia (icty .org) by five of the six. The unique sources (on a host level) are specific to particular communities: three Dutchbat sources are referenced in the Dutch article, one concerning Manja Blok who piloted one of the two Dutch F-16s that bombed VRS positions just prior to the fall of the enclave. Apart from the srebrenica-genocide.blogspot.com source, the website of the 300-family-strong Bosnian-Islamic cultural community of

Oberhausen, Germany, is referenced in the Bosnian article alone. The Serbian article refers to serbiancafe.com (which has not come up in discussion at the English-language Wikipedia) as well as serbianna.com, described by a power editor (Bosniak) in the English-language article as hosting "Serbian writers known for their spread of propaganda and bald faced lies, including ridiculing [the] Srebrenica genocide."[91] Perhaps more to the point, it also hosts the 2011 study "Deconstruction of a Virtual Genocide: An Intelligent Person's Guide to Srebrenica," which as the title perhaps indicates is an alternative account of the events, and also a part of the "Srebrenica Project," which highlights (among other aspects) the Serbian victims of a conflict broader than the events of July 1995.

One of the main reasons for the discrepancy in the number of unique pages and hosts referenced concerns which U.N. documents are cited in each of the articles. Here it may be instructive to look more closely at the differences among the main protagonists' citation patterns, and at the same time take note of which documents cover which events and employ which terms. Comparing references is another means to look behind the accounts given in the articles. Un.org is the only host shared by the Serbian, Bosnian, and Dutch articles, though the individual documents cited differ. The seminal U.N. document is shared across the articles: the 1995 indictment of Ratko Mladić and Radovan Karadžić by the International Criminal Tribunal for the former Yugoslavia, charging them with genocide and crimes against humanity. (The Serbian and Bosnian articles link to it at a un.org site, while the Dutch article links to the icty.org site.) The next major document (chronologically speaking) is the U.N. Secretary General's report to the General Assembly on the "fall of Srebrenica" (1999), referenced in the Dutch article as well as the Serbian, but not in the Bosnian.[92] The subsequent document, the 2001 ICTY judgment against Radislav Krstić, in which the presiding judge (Theodor Meron) ruled that genocide was committed, is referenced by the Serbian and Dutch but not the Bosnian article, whereas the 2004 final verdict against Krstić (after his appeal) is referenced by the Bosnian only. Recall that it was the 2004 ruling that confirmed the crimes committed as "genocide" and prompted Dado, power editor, to put forward the title change in the English-language version from "massacre" to "genocide." Additionally that case, as well as the 2007 ICJ ruling, dated the term "massacre," according to GriffinSB in one of the many debates about the article title in the English-language Wikipedia. There are also references shared by the Bosnian and the Serbian articles, such as srebrenica.ba, the Mothers website. The other Mothers website, the movement of the Mothers from the Srebrenica and Žepa enclaves (srebrenica-zepa.ba), containing a list of 8,106 victims (to July 2005, and now reaching 8,373), is also linked from the Serbian and Bosnian articles. For the issue of the survivors, the Dutch article points to the detailed (multilanguage) dossier kept by the Dutch law firm Van Diepen and Van der Kroef, representing the Mothers in their case against the Dutch state and the United Nations. While the Bosnian and the Serbian

1 2 3 4 5 6

Serbian	Bosnian	Dutch	Croatian	Serbo-Croatian	English
un.org	un.org	un.org	un.org	un.org	un.org
srebrenica.ba	srebrenica.ba	icty.org	srebrenica.ba	srebrenica.ba	srebrenica.ba
icty.org	ic-mp.org	groene.nl	icty.org	srebrenica-zepa.ba	icty.org
bosnia.org.uk	idc.org.ba	vandiepen.com	bosnia.org.uk	srebrenica.nl	bosnia.org.uk
guardian.co.uk	srebrenica-zepa.ba	books.google.nl	guardian.co.uk	vladars.net	guardian.co.uk
ic-mp.org	helsinki.org.yu	dutchbat.luchtmobiel.nl	icj-cij.org		ic-mp.org
icj-cij.org	hlc.org.yu	dutchbat1.com	idc.org.ba		icj-cij.org
iwpr.net	ogrish.com	emperors-clothes.com	iwpr.net		idc.org.ba
news.bbc.co.uk	sense-agency.com	nu.nl	news.bbc.co.uk		iwpr.net
nytimes.com	vladars.net	ochtenden.nl	nytimes.com		news.bbc.co.uk
ohr.int	dzemat-oberhausen.de	volkskrant.nl	ohr.int		nytimes.com
srebrenica-zepa.ba	inzl.unsa.ba		vreme.com		ohr.int
vreme.com	preventgenocide.org		balkaninsight.com		vreme.com
128.121.186.47	srebrenica-genocide.blogspot.com		bim.ba		128.121.186.47
b92.net	zeneucrnom.org		domovina.net		b92.net
helsinki.org.yu			edition.cnn.com		balkaninsight.com
hlc.org.yu			europarl.europa.eu		bim.ba
news.independent.co.uk			independent.co.uk		domovina.net
ogrish.com			newsweek.com		edition.cnn.com
reuters.com			pbs.org		europarl.europa.eu
slobodan-milosevic.org			potocarimc.ba		groene.nl
spiegel.de			thomas.loc.gov		independent.co.uk
srebrenica-report.com			213.222.3.5		news.independent.co.uk
srebrenica.nl			birn.eu.com		newsweek.com
thomas.loc.gov			chrissmith.house.gov		pbs.org
washingtonpost.com			nacional.hr		potocarimc.ba
amnesty.org.uk			opencongress.org		reuters.com
arbeiterfotografie.de			war-memorial.net		sense-agency.com
boursier.com			yihr.org		slobodan-milosevic.org
csees.net					spiegel.de

Figure 8.4

Serbian	English			
glas-javnosti.rs	srebrenica-report.com	documen.tv	jmss.org	telegraph.co.uk
news.serbianunity.net	vandiepen.com	dutchbat3.nl	jurist.law.pitt.edu	time.com
novosti.rs	washingtonpost.com	dx.doi.org	mail-archive.com	timesonline.co.uk
pogledi.co.yu	193.173.80.81	english.aljazeera.net	markdanner.com	tiscali.co.uk
politika.rs	advocacynet.org	epress.lib.uts.edu.au	martinfrost.ws	today.reuters.com
serbianna.com	ap.google.com	eurozine.com	nato.int	todayszaman.com
srbija.gov.rs	archiv.medienhilfe.ch	fabrika.com	news.scotsman.com	trial-ch.org
srpska-mreza.com	archive.serbianunity.net	fas.org	news.smh.com.au	turkishdailynews.com.tr
strategicstudies.org	authorsden.com	france24.com	news.yahoo.com	tuzilastvobih.gov.ba
transnational.org	baacbh.org	gendercide.org	norveska.ba	tuzilastvorz.org.rs
www2.serbiancafe.com	balkanpeace.org	genocid.org	nrc.nl	unhchr.ch
zeit.de	bookrags.com	globalpolicy.org	observer.guardian.co.uk	ushmm.orgveteranen.org
	books.google.com	globalresearch.ca	oslobodjenje.ba	virtual-security.net
	bosniak.org	glypx.com	otvoreno.ba	voanews.com
	bratunac.com	hague.bard.edu	parlement.com	voices.washingtonpost.com
	cbc.ca	haguejusticeportal.net	prestonm.com	war-crimes-genocide-memories.org
	cm.greekhelsinki.gr	hdmagazine.com	projects.washingtonpost.com	web.amnesty.org
	cnn.com	helsinki.org.rs	publicinternationallaw.org	ww4report.com
	cobiss.ba	hri.org	radionetherlands.nl	yale.edu
	columbia.edu	hrw.org	sarajevo-x.com	youtube.com
	commdocs.house.gov	iht.com	scribd.com	zmag.org
	counterpunch.org	iol.co.za	srebrenica-project.com	zoeken.rechtspraak.nl
	crimesofwar.org	islam.co.ba	srebrenica.brightside.nl	
	daccess-dds-ny.un.org	isn.ethz.ch	srebrenica95.com	
	dailymail.co.uk	janinedigiovanni.com	srebrenicagenocide.org	
	dnevniavaz.ba	javno.com	sudbih.gov.ba	

Figure 8.4

Referenced hosts in the Srebrenica articles per Wikipedia language version, colored by frequency and ordered by frequency and by alphabet, December 20, 2010.

articles share the links to the Mothers, the Bosnian and Dutch share no references at all, indicating the distance between the two accounts.

Since it is the most specific, perhaps the selectivity of the Dutch referencing deserves a further (brief) examination, so as to shed further light on the peculiarity of the account there. There are twelve links (and one unlinked reference to the 2002 report by the Netherlands Institute for War Documentation). There is the link to the U.N. document on the "fall of Srebrencia" (which is of course the title of the Dutch article) and the links mentioned above to the Dutch law firm and to three Dutchbat sources (one of which treats the history of a medical evacuation team and their aid of the Bosnians, which could be considered as contrapuntal to Dutchbat's alleged aversion to them). There is a link to a news article on a 2010 discovery that might have the effect of lowering the victim count: some 500 Bosnians listed as victims supposedly were discovered to be alive. Apart from news of a recent court ruling in the Netherlands, finding against the Dutch state for failing to protect Bosnian families employed at the camp (which is the smaller of the two cases brought against the state), the remaining references include two critical (and intellectual) articles from the *Groene Amsterdammer* weekly, "Deconstruction of a Trauma" and "The Netherlands Were Collaborators in Srebrenica," the latter of which is an interview with Janja Bec-Neumann, a genocide studies scholar, who refers to the Dutchbat contingent as "racists and cowards." An accompanying reference to a newspaper article from 1995 serves as counterweight to the idea of the Dutch as collaborators and racists: the so-called Franken's list of the names of about 250 Bosnians compiled by a commanding officer (Major Franken), not a list of those the Dutch forces wanted saved (in collusion with the Bosnian Serbs' plans), but rather an Amnesty International technique, according to the major, warning the Bosnian Serbs that the Bosniaks they were taking away have names. The list, it was said, had been faxed to The Hague (and was to be smuggled out in the major's undergarments).[93]

The analysis of the images follows a similar path, looking at the sheer numbers (62 in total), the shares of them (English with 20, Bosnian 15, Croatian 14, Serbian and Serbo-Croatian 5 each, and Dutch 3), the common ones, and those that are unique. The images are scraped from the articles and placed in columns in the order in which they appear on the pages. (They also may be reordered to show matches and uniques, as in figure 8.5.) The Dutch article contains two maps, the first providing the location of Srebrenica in the Republika Srpska (Bosnia and Herzegovina) near the Serbian border, and the second a military campaign map (made by the CIA) showing the advance of the Drina Corps of the VRS and the flight of the Bosnian army (the ARBiH), ambushed twice in their retreat by the VRS on July 13 and 14. It also has a burial image with green-draped coffins. These images recur in most of the other articles, either as exact matches or in similar form. The Serbian shares two with the Dutch (military campaign map and burial) and three others with the Bosnian, Croatian, and

English (the cemetery at Potočari, a satellite photo of the mass graves at Nova Kasaba, and a picture of Ratko Mladić, the Bosnian-Serb commander of the VRS). The Serbo-Croatian is similar, using the pictures in the Serbian piece but adding the grave of a 13-year-old boy, which recurs across the Bosnian, Croatian, and English articles. The Serbian article has a discussion of that picture in the talk page, where consensus emerges against (or at least not for) using it: "It would give the impression that all or most of the victims of the massacre were children or minors, which is not the case."[94]

The Bosnian article has the most unique images, which unlike those of the English are evidentiary from the days themselves in July 1995. At the outset of the article there are the cemetery and the grave of the 13-year-old, and at the end a picture of a boy about that age kissing a gravestone. Three of its 15 image files are not found in the other articles: Bosnian-Serb tanks in action at Srebrenica, Serbian soldiers separating Bosniak men in Potočari (July 12, 1995), and a still from the Scorpions video recording of the execution of four boys and two young men from Srebrenica—all rather grainy and generally of lesser quality than the rest of the images in all the articles. The English and the Croatian (together with the Bosnian) contain pictures concerning the evidence-gathering since the events, including the exhumed body blindfolded with hands tied behind back as well as the aerial photography of the mass graves. (The English and the Croatian show pictures of the Commission for Missing Persons' files, a room of shelves with stored and labeled evidence.) The images unique to the English article are of a Dutchbat military vehicle, the Dutchbat headquarters at Potočari, and a visit to a mass grave by a group from the International Association of Genocide Scholars (IAGS), an image used in the Bosnian and Croatian articles but without the scholars. Generally it could be said (from the images present) that the Bosnian article presents more evidence concerning the events themselves, including the deaths of boys of nonfighting age, whereas others (largely the Croatian and the English) are more inclined to emphasize the investigation. The Dutch and the Serbian images are more of a military nature, with maps and burials, with the Serbian (not the Dutch) also emphasizing mass graves and the memorial to the victims.

Conclusion

The contribution of this study lies in the development of an approach that could be called cultural research with Wikipedia. In short, it undertakes comparative analysis of articles on the same subject matter across language versions, proposing to study Wikipedia not so much for its accuracy as a reference work, or its biases, but as cultural reference in itself. This means, in the first instance, examining which features of an article are shared with other language versions and which are unique to one version. At first glance such an approach to Wikipedia might appear counterintuitive, given its principles and its collaborative, consensus-building environment. One may imagine

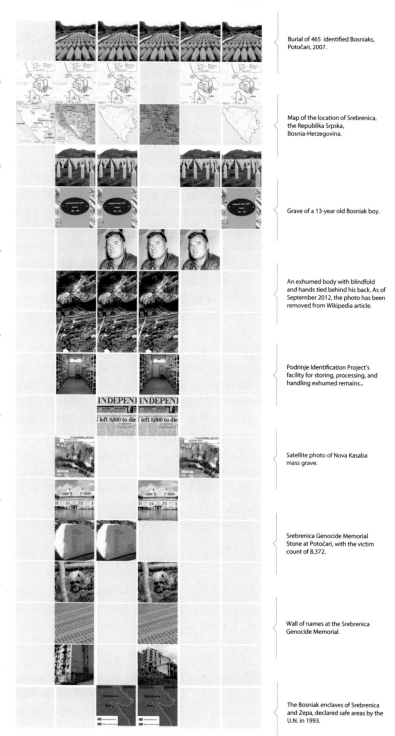

DUTCH	ENGLISH	BOSNIAN	CROATIAN	SERBIAN	SERBO-CROATIAN

Burial of 465 identified Bosniaks, Potočari, 2007.

Map of the Srebrenica military operations, made by the U.S. Central Intelligence Agency, with green arrow showing the route of the Bosnian forces.

Map of the location of Srebrenica, the Republika Srpska, Bosnia-Herzegovina.

Srebrenica-Potočari Memorial and Cemetery, Bosnia-Herzegovina.

Grave of a 13-year old Bosniak boy.

Ratko Mladic.

An exhumed body with blindfold and hands tied behind his back. As of September 2012, the photo has been removed from Wikipedia article.

Exhumed grave of victims, 2007.

Podrinje Identification Project's facility for storing, processing, and handling exhumed remains..

"UN left 8,000 to die in Bosnia." Headline in The Independent, October 30, 1995.

Satellite photo of Nova Kasaba mass grave.

International Criminal Tribunal for the Former Yugoslavia, Den Haag, the Netherlands.

Srebrenica Genocide Memorial Stone at Potočari, with the victim count of 8,372.

Skull exhumed outside of Potočari, July 2007.

Wall of names at the Srebrenica Genocide Memorial.

War-damaged buildings in Srebrenica.

The Bosniak enclaves of Srebrenica and Zepa, declared safe areas by the U.N. in 1993.

DUTCH   ENGLISH   BOSNIAN   CROATIAN   SERBIAN   SERBO-
                                                          CROATIAN

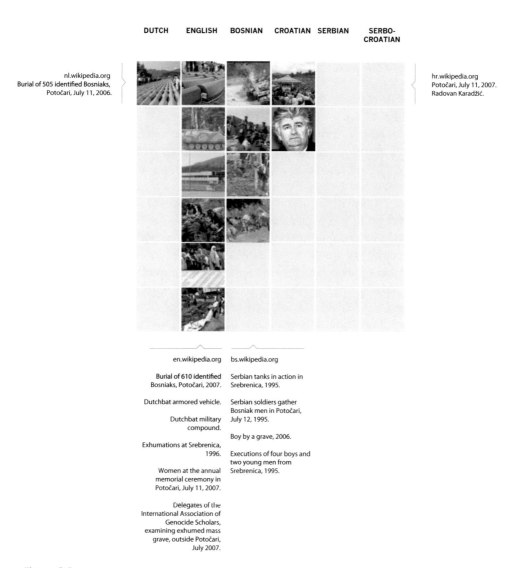

nl.wikipedia.org
Burial of 505 identified Bosniaks,
Potočari, July 11, 2006.

hr.wikipedia.org
Potočari, July 11, 2007.
Radovan Karadžić.

en.wikipedia.org   bs.wikipedia.org

Burial of 610 identified   Serbian tanks in action in
Bosniaks, Potočari, 2007.   Srebrenica, 1995.

Dutchbat armored vehicle.   Serbian soldiers gather
                               Bosniak men in Potočari,
Dutchbat military   July 12, 1995.
compound.
                               Boy by a grave, 2006.
Exhumations at Srebrenica,
1996.   Executions of four boys and
                               two young men from
Women at the annual   Srebrenica, 1995.
memorial ceremony in
Potočari, July 11, 2007.

Delegates of the
International Association of
Genocide Scholars,
examining exhumed mass
grave, outside Potočari,
July 2007.

Figure 8.5

Images in the Srebrenica articles, December 20, 2010, listed by Wikipedia language version and ordered by similarity. (cc) Digital Methods Initiative, Amsterdam, 2012.

that the principle of neutral point of view upon which it is founded, and the bureaucracy in place to further it, would make Wikipedia articles universal, or at least increasingly similar, across language versions. It was found that such a presumption does not hold.

One source of universality, or similarity, is translation: articles would be the same or similar if translated from one language version to another. Thus there may be parent versions of articles with offspring, such as those on the Srebrenica massacre (Serbian) or Srebrenica genocide (Bosnian and Croatian), which originated as translations from the English-language article. (The English-language article itself originates from another online piece written by Martin Frost.) Indeed, any number of Wikipedia articles may start as translations, the product of copy-paste, or otherwise seeded, like the 30,000 articles on U.S. counties and cities created by RamBot from census data and the CIA World Fact Book, beginning in October 2002 with Autaugaville, Alabama. Whatever their origin, the question put forward here is whether they become more particularistic or more universal as they are refined. As mentioned above, comparative research into Wikipedia language versions found that the entries on famous Poles in the English-language Wikipedia chronicled their personal lives far more than the "same" articles in the Polish-language Wikipedia. The plea for cultural specificity—for homegrown articles in one's own Wikipedia language version, and for transplanted articles to be allowed to grow organically in the local language[95]—could be read at the same time as a critique of (American-content) values embedded in an encyclopedia. As also has been found, there are large numbers of articles that appear in one language version and not in others, including the Arabic, Korean, and English (the largest).[96]

In the case of the Srebrenica articles, even the names of the articles reflect important distinctions, depending on whether (as a Serbian editor phrased it) the fall of Srebrenica and its aftermath (massacre, genocide) are considered a single event. The English, Bosnian, and Croatian articles (following the ICTY and ICJ rulings) take the planned killings of a group of Bosniaks (based on their identity) as part and parcel of the conquest of the town, hence constituting one event: genocide. For the Dutch article, however, the fall of the town is the primary subject matter. As a power editor pointed out, a title like "Srebrenica massacre" does not cover the contents of the article and would be misleading. Here the cultural specificity of the parsing of the events in Srebrenica of July 1995 becomes a compelling object of study.

The Srebrenica articles belong to a particular class of controversial subject matters whose editors may have particular qualities. The benefits of topic self-selection by editors (editorial passion and knowledge) may not adhere as well to controversial articles, where versions of events are emotionally contested, as the Wikipedia English-language power editors put it to their Bosnian and Serbian counterparts in the discussion pages. As was found, contributors are not only attracted to such articles (for reasons of setting the record straight and others) but also leave them, after arguing and performing other Wikipedia bureaucratic work, including investigating other editors' "socking" (referring to the practice of changing names so as to leave behind one's previous editing and discussion page reputation). Emir Arven, for one, has had nearly a dozen names, according to the sockpuppet investigations. In fact, five of the top ten power editors of the English-language article on the Srebrenica massacre have been blocked indefinitely or suspected of socking by using multiple user names. After one or more usernames are blocked, one may return as an anonymous editor—and see that IP address blocked as well. Here is further context to the remarks made by Dado, the seeder of the Bosnian, Croatian, and Serbian articles, who found consensus-building frustrating and exhausting.

Our comparative analysis of (controversial and sometimes hard-fought) articles across language versions uses a kind of web content analysis that takes seriously the units of analysis Wikipedia has to offer, including ones that are specific to the medium. By this is meant the features of wiki software, with its built-in revision history; media-wiki's wiki, with its talk pages and its retention of the IP addresses of anonymous editors; and Wikipedia's bureaucracy, with its templates and its locking and unlocking pages (for example). (It would be convenient for the researcher to have IP addresses of the registered editors as well, so as to be able to automate a geolocation analysis of all the editors of the articles.) The analysis compares the article titles, templates, tables of contents, particular content details, talk pages, editors' names and locations, references, and images. It was found that most articles seldom shares titles, tables of contents, editors, references, and images. They are also distinctive in their contents, beginning with the scope covered in the articles. Should an article on the events in Srebrenica in July of 1995 emphasize the prehistory, say 1992–1995 (as the Serbian and Croatian editors have remarked), the taking of Srebrenica or its fall (the Dutch), or the planned taking of the town and slaughter of the Bosniak men (the Bosnian, Croatian, and English)? The choice of scope would affect not only the title but also the type of information box chosen, a discussion about encyclopedic administration which paved the way for a decision (in the Serbian) to accept the massacre frame over that of military conflict.

The various victim counts are a special case in our study, not only showing differences in themselves but often relying on sources that are not shared. The report by the Netherlands Institute for War Documentation (2002) has a lower victim count than the Federal (Bosnian) Commission on Missing Persons. The government of the Republika Srpska has a higher Serb victim count than other institutions. Relying on one's national authority leads to discrepancies across articles. There are also contrarian or skeptical sources, and space is made for them in special sections at the conclusion of the article, under titles such as "Revisionism" or the "Serb account."

One of the more sensitive questions concerns whether the victims were of fighting age, and thus how to construe the killings. The Bosnian article, through its choice of images, places emphasis on boys too young to fight, for example showing the grave of a 13-year-old. Other articles share war crime imagery, with the picture of an exhumed body blindfolded with hands tied behind the back. These images are not in the Serbian or the Dutch Wikipedia articles, which have fewer pictures generally, though they share with other articles the geographic and military maps as well as the picture of the cemetery and the caskets with green drapings. The map of the location of Srebrenica and the picture of graves are shared across all articles.

In a sense, the neutral point of view and the related guidelines should not be taken as incompatible with the distinctive accounts across the Wikipedia language versions. The power editors in the Bosnian, Serbian, Dutch, and Serbo-Croatian Wikipedias are continually altering their articles to keep acceptable pieces that still fit with Wikipedia's three core principles and the accompanying guidelines as to how to achieve them. Some language versions have more difficulty in defending their specific content and sources against vandalism and other accounts of events, e.g., western ones.

In the English-language edition it becomes apparent that many of the power editors are willful, defending their versions, their sources, and their accounts, often to such a degree that they are blocked temporarily or indefinitely from contributing. Some of these editors subsequently return to their own version, where they continue to edit. With the exception of the English and the Serbo-Croatian, the editors of different language Wikipedias are consciously creating both their own account as well as a "negotiated" account of events with the other versions. While it would be difficult to term any a universal article, there are what may instead be called umbrella articles, one variety of which is created through the work of many, another through the work of few. There is a highly contested one with many interlanguage editors (the English) and a softened, rather unifying one with very few editors (the Serbo-Croatian).

9   After Cyberspace: Big Data, Small Data

This chapter examines the web's status as source of data, big and small.[1] The overall argument is to take the Internet far more seriously than we have in the past, specifically in terms of what it has to offer for social and cultural research.

The first step is to dispense with the idea of cyberspace and the virtual as primary points of departure for Internet-related research, or rather to reposition those terms to reflect the conceptual opportunities they currently offer. Cyberspace, with its origins in science fiction literature and its legacy in cybercultural studies, most recently has become a specific realm of inquiry in Internet security studies, with the U.S. military, for example, creating a "Cyber Command" in 2009, and in the same year the U.S. Air Force phrasing its mission as "fly, fight and win in air, space and cyberspace."[2] Similarly, "the virtual," a term with a rich theoretical history, refers less to the Internet generally than to virtual worlds such as Second Life and game environments such as World of Warcraft.[3] Studies of the virtual, as in those specific types of online worlds and environments, would thus become a subset of Internet-related research just as cyberspace studies also now refers to niche areas: cyberwar together with cyberespionage and cybercrime.[4]

Second, we may wish to reconsider the treatment of the web as a site for the study of amateur production practices and user-generated content, in a rerun of the "online quality" debates. Arguably the Internet has seen recurrences of such debates, the first in the 1990s on the value of information online, where the web was widely seen as a rumor mill and a breeding ground for conspiracy theory.[5] In the mid-2000s, the second such debate referred to the quality of content, with the web now seen as a free amateur content space threatening the paid professional.[6] I would like to argue that the web continues to pose problems for the analysis of content in that it disappoints those in search of traditional markers of quality and an underlying interpretive apparatus.[7] Especially with the decline of surfing and of hypertext as literary theory underpinning a surfer's space, the web has lost some of its early hermeneutic productivity.[8] The web nowadays invites a stance more like that of popular culture and television researchers some decades ago regarding their relatively new object of study—that one can read and diagnose cultural concerns from the medium, beginning with the study of *TV Guide* and what is on (and what is not). Thus a British historian in the late 1930s (quoted by Asa Briggs) described the BBC's magazine *The Listener* as "a guide to the multiple and changing interests and activities of the age."[9] The question, however, becomes the means and techniques by which to do so. As I have argued, "digital methods" provides means distinct from other contemporary approaches to the study of digital materials, such as cultural analytics and culturomics, which both make use of the digitized over the natively digital.[10] The approach put forward here also may be distinguished from dominant points of departure to date in the computational social sciences and digital humanities, where there is an urge to work with large data sets and to create accompanying infrastructures for them.[11] Throughout the book I have sought to consider the productivity of modest tools and small web data, too. Here I approach data, no matter the size, from the angle of digital methods.

Third, and most extensively, the argument recognizes that the Internet has reputational issues for researchers accustomed to thinking of it as cyberspace and virtual realm, as domain of rumors and self-publication, as well as, most recently, a site of messy data. The quality-of-information debate that was followed by the quality-of-(amateur)-content debate has become the quality-of-data debate. Initial concerns had to do with incomplete web archives, as discussed in chapter 3. Additionally, multiple dates on webpages and search engine indexing were unable to provide accurate results for date range queries; longitudinal analysis, a marker of quality research, was thought to be doomed.[12] Questions now arise about the robustness of so-called user-generated data such as social bookmarks, tags, comments, likes, and shares.[13] It is unstructured. How could it all possibly be cleaned?

The Web as Data

New web data sources are increasingly becoming available, yet they suffer from an overall reputational problem, in the long line of such problems online. The concerns about web data still stem from their historical association with a free-for-all "cyberspace" and an epistemology based on a do-it-yourself medium of self-publication, with an absence of editors performing quality control. Indeed, traditionally the web has been thought of as a source of *doxa*, or opinion yet to be substantiated. The substantiation of opinion "floating around on the Internet" would require leaving the medium, for instance, by making a phone call, obtaining an eyewitness account, etc. Thus web accounts could not stand alone as sources; they also could not serve as the crucial second source, confirming a claim, in a journalistic sense. Web claims required grounding offline.

Above I mentioned how the web initially arrived on the scene as infrastructure awaiting content. In a sense, it was a space of data only—command, communication, and traffic data—with the content (traditionally speaking) under preparation. "Under construction" sites or pages may be regarded as sources of nostalgia these days, like other aesthetics of the 1990s such as starry blue nights as website backdrops, the animated gif, or "random site" links which invite surfers to navigate to unknown territories and jump-cut to another hyperspace, themes I touched on earlier.[14] The "I'm Feeling Lucky" button on Google is such a hyperspace jump cut, and the names of the browsers (Netscape Navigator, Internet Explorer, and Safari) suggest the user as adventurer. This was our cyberspace web, the precursor to what is now becoming historicized in business circles as Web 1.0 (info-web) and Web 2.0 (social web), and which I strove to elaborate as a history of the web as hyperspace, cyberspace, space of shapes (sphere, network), and grounded or locative space.

In any case, in the new history of Web 1.0 followed by Web 2.0, the web is seen as a succession of two stable software versions. Each version has had particular quality debates associated with it. Whether associated with fandom, porn, and aliens, with imposters, conspiracy, and self-publishers (in the first version), or with amateur production practices, user-generated content, and lolcats (in the second), the Internet has not offered sources of great standing.

To view the web as data set for social and cultural research is to be confronted with a variety of issues about messy data. The webometrician Mike Thelwall summarized the challenges of employing the web for research:

One [issue] is the messiness of web data and the need for data cleansing heuristics. The uncontrolled web creates numerous problems in the interpretation of results. . . . Indeed, a sceptical researcher could claim the obstacles . . . are so great that all web analyses lack value. [O]ne response to this . . . is to demonstrate that web data correlate significantly with some non-web data in order to prove that the web data are not wholly random.[15]

Here the general reputation problem about quality online is transformed, initially, into the question of how to clean up the data, since there is a lack of uniformity in how users fill in forms, fields, boxes, and other text entry spaces. In a sense the (unedited) web is viewed as one large "free text" space. There are misspellings. There are too few conventions. Different tags are used for the same content, with no clever means of disambiguating contents of such mass and scale. This state of affairs makes many researchers simply renounce the web as source, unless data sets come whole (all transactions in Second Life) and one studies online culture only (amateur production practices and user-generated content). Finally, if web data are to be used, Thelwall argues that one must introduce offline data for comparative purposes; web data should be correlated with nonweb data.

To the issues above, I would like to add a remark made by David Lazer, in a key text on the computational turn in the social sciences: "Perhaps the thorniest challenges exist on the data side, with respect to access and privacy."[16] Web data are tainted for their ultimate capacity to identify persons who do not consent or expect to be identified. Indeed, anonymization of the identifiable people in the data may fail, as in the well-known AOL data release when a list of anonymized users' search queries became a puzzle for investigative journalists, who used it to piece together users' identities. The lessons learned from the data release have had further consequences for the tidiness of web data. Certain web data now come degraded by design.

Tidying the Mess Online

The sundry issues surrounding web data, or at least the three Thelwall introduces (messiness, wholeness, and offline grounding of data) and the additional one from Lazer (anonymization), are being worked upon, though each "solution" reintroduces the complication that to date they have been addressed rather well by Google and other big data corporations. It is likely to exacerbate what one could call Google envy, that is, the capacity of search engine companies and social networking sites to collect data that approximates both the type and the scale social scientists would like to generate themselves, though without the even finer-grained texture that researchers may prefer (e.g., more demographic and ideological information).[17] As if answering the calls of Thelwall and Lazer, Google Labs in 2011 made available server-side software that assists in cleaning data (Google Refine) and software that correlates online data with offline data (Google Correlate).[18] In chapter 1, I discussed the notion of scooping as it has been used in the sociology of science (as well as in journalism), in which one's object of study comes to the conclusion the researcher had been working on and publishes it first. The object of study thereby puts the researcher in the unexpected and sometimes unenviable position of having to confirm the object's prior art; Google has addressed the criticism that is being made of web data, and has gone even further by inviting researchers to work with engine log data, in ways that differ both in form and in format from the AOL data release. In doing so, the company follows the new media platform spirit I referred to earlier (make not the tool, but the toolmaker), and as such provides the underlying apparatus that enabled the making of the Google Flu Trends project, discussed earlier. With Correlate, Google also may have initiated precisely what the computational social scientists and webometricians have called for: a large-scale data infrastructure of web data (query logs) that one may use to compare with nonweb data (an offline baseline).

Digitized Data and Natively Digital Data

In the discussion of digital data and their properties compared to others, information scientist Christine Borgman lists classic types of data as observational data, computational data, experimental data, and records, and describes why they are considered of quality.[19] Good data are collected "as cleanly as possible and as early as possible in [their] life cycle"; they are captured regularly, and preferably over long periods of time.[20] Certain web data, especially search engine logs, would fail miserably according to these criteria. Certain digitzed data sets would meet the criteria, however. As cases in point, I would like to touch on two relatively novel undertakings in digital humanities in order to make clear the current reliance on digitized data, which pass the above tests, and the challenges of natively digital data, which do not.

One program of cultural research relying on digitized data, cultural analytics, proposes to consider "culture as data [to] be mined and visualized."[21] Indeed, new media theorist Lev Manovich and colleagues have performed longitudinal analyses of the changing properties of all of the front covers of *Time*, *Science*, and *Popular Science*, as well as all Mark Rothko paintings. To the digitized artwork they apply computer vision techniques "to generate numerical descriptions of their structure and content" such as levels of grayscale, brightness, hue, saturation, and forms.[22] Another recent research undertaking along these lines, albeit larger, is called culturomics, a field of study of recent coinage that pursues a "quantitative analysis of culture" using as its initial corpora Google Books, whose scanned collection is described as 4% of all books ever published.[23] The founders of culturomics discuss the impossibility of actually reading the works they are now able to analyze through elaborate search. Generally speaking, culturomics shares with digital methods a "search as research" program, and examines the context and frequency of word use over time and across world cultures. There are intriguing lexicographical findings (American English is gradually taking over from British spelling of the same words) as well as broader cultural trends, such as an increasing proclivity to forget the past, or at least to refer to specific years in the past far less frequently. Celebrity is also becoming shorter-lived, in the sense that more and more celebrities are being referred to less and less as time goes by.[24]

Can one view the web as more than an infrastructural platform for the storage of digitized data sets, yet also deploy insights from the study of digitized materials related above? That is, can the web furnish its own data sets, and eventually become a privileged place from which to read and diagnose cultural and social change? In this regard, social theorist Noortje Marres has turned on its head the debate surrounding the reputation problem of the web (and the messiness of its data) by arguing that "web services incorporate social science methods like textual analysis, social network analysis, and geospatial analysis, arguably ordering data for . . . research."[25] In other words, it is the method incorporated into the web services that is worthy of study for its ability to make sense of web data. May the web deliver structured data after all? In this way of thinking, web services—search engines, collaboratively authored wikis, and social networking platforms—become the data filterers, cleaning and ordering the data for end use as well as perhaps for research.

I would like to concentrate on search engine log data, for they require negotiated access, large-scale infrastructure, as well as skill in being able to handle big data. Often it is thought that data are collected by devices such as search engines in an unobtrusive manner. That is, for search engines and arguably also for collaboratively authored wikis and user-populated platforms such as social networking sites, the web may be considered a site in which to make unobtrusive measurements, i.e., those less affected by the effects of other methodological apparatuses.[26] While the data may be collected without a clear and present methodological apparatus in front of the user, or the presence of an ethnographer casually listening in, any use of the data must be viewed against the backdrop of the scandal surrounding the data release in 2006 by AOL. AOL Research, the AOL scientific unit, made available some 650,000 users' engine queries over a three-month period for researchers, with lists of queries per numbered user and other data, such as URL clicked.[27] The *New York Times* was able to "de-anonymize" one of the users by looking at the list of queries and performing relatively straightforward detective work, identifying user 4417749 as Thelma Arnold, a 62-year-old resident of Lilburn, Georgia.[28] She had searched for people with her last name, Arnold, and services in her home town, Lilburn. All the search data that AOL made available to the scientific community during the SIGIR information retrieval conference in Seattle was taken offline a few days after the release.[29] The data were described by computer scientist Jon Kleinberg as tainted, for "the number of things [they reveal] about individual people seems much too much."[30] Released in a manner considered "naïve," the data also were organized in a way that arguably invited detective work and de-anonymization.[31] From a research point of view, the log data were formatted to facilitate a particular style of research, namely inquiry into search engine user behavior and ultimately the improvement of personalized search (see table 9.1).

In particular, the AOL data fields that were provided suggest engine effectiveness research with relatively straightforward questions. Do engine users click the top results

Table 9.1
Fields and Field Descriptions of the AOL Search Engine User Data Set, 500k User Session Collection

AnonID—an anonymous user ID number
Query—the query issued by the user, case-shifted with most punctuation removed
QueryTime—the time at which the query was submitted for search
ItemRank—if the user clicked on a search result, the rank of the item on which they clicked is listed
ClickURL—if the user clicked on a search result, the domain portion of the URL in the clicked result is listed

Source: Greg Sadetsky's mirror of AOL's 500k User Session Collection Data and Readme Text, 2006, http://www.gregsadetsky.com/aol-data/U500k_README.txt.

returned to them? This information is available in the ItemRank field. More nuanced is the question, Do users find what they are looking for?[32] If users click on the top result for a query (ItemRank), and there is only one query in their session (QueryTime), the user will have found what he or she is looking for, and the engine presumably would be doing its job the best. Long sessions, repeatedly reformulated queries, and URLs clicked that appear on the second or third results page (11–30 ItemRank) would prompt questions about the effectiveness of the search engine. One useful line of inquiry might be an investigation into the characteristics of such queries.

In reaction to peculiar query-builders, researchers could seek to build elements into the algorithm that would help engines return results to such users (see table 9.2). For example, users may pose engines actual questions. They may make remarks to engines. They may converse with them, or even confess to them. One such user is the subject of the "true and heartbreaking (search) history" of AOL search user 711391, the subject of the video art project *I Love Alaska* that is named after a query.[33] Indeed 711391's query style is precisely the type that the AOL researchers envisaged when they wrote the Read Me text inviting the scientific community to work with "real query log data

Table 9.2
AOL Search User 711391 Queries, 2006

cannot sleep with snoring husband . . . god will fulfill your hearts desires . . . online friendships can be very special . . . people are not always how they seem over the internet . . . gay churches in houston tx . . . who is crystal bernard romantically linked with . . . is crystal bernard bisexual . . . men need encouragement . . . how many online romances lead to sex . . . how many online romances lead to sex in person . . . the bible says be kind to one another . . . i cant stand dr. phil or his wife . . . is george clooney gay . . . how can i be a good example to an unsaved friend . . . farting preacher . . . who's the hottest porn star . . . devotions for women . . . hillary swanke nude . . . best nude scenes of 1999 . . . how to take your body measurements . . . jake gyllenhaal is hot . . . bleached pubes . . . oprah gained weight lately . . . star jones hubby is a flaming homosexual . . . how to make a good first impression . . . accepting your body . . . why do i weigh so much though i am in shape . . . the lord's table bible study . . . how can i tell if spouse is spying on me while i'm online . . . tempted to have an affair . . . extra maritial affairs are not the answer . . . staying calm while meeting an online friend . . . guilt cheating spouses feel . . . bryce howard nude . . . what the bible says about worry . . . female pirate costumes . . . symptoms of bladder infection . . . god will show you future events . . . symptoms of herpes of the tongue . . . i don't want my ex back . . . why do christian men cheat . . . don't contact an ex if you want to get over them . . . christian men that feel guilty about cheating on their wives . . . if you are upset can it cause bad dreams . . . and after you have suffered a little while god will make you stronger than ever . . . kelly ripa is so annoying . . . how to forgive yourself . . . how to recover from internet affairs . . . denise richards is a bitch . . . reason for constant bad dreams . . . having an affair is a waste of time . . . how to make a man want you . . .

Source: "User 711391," *Smith Magazine*, August 10, 2006, http://www.smithmag.net/2006/08/10/user-711391/.

that is based on real users."[34] The data were to be employed for work on personalization as well as "query reformulation," whereby the engine turns the user's query into
one it can better handle.[35] For our purposes here, what is of interest is how the data
were formatted: lists of queries per numbered individual. Indeed, the data set of many
individual users may fill in the idea of engine logs' furnishing a "database of inten-
tions," as John Battelle put it, with respect to the new "databody" brought into being
by one's search history.[36] According to the logs, AOL search engine users are victims
of despicable acts, for they have searched for remedies to them. Or they may be plotting revenge and planning behavior from the sensitive to the heinous.[37] In their
complaint to the Federal Trade Commission about the data release and what it revealed
about users who did not expect to have their queries made public, and perhaps become
personally identifiable, the Electronic Frontier Foundation writes:

> The disclosure . . . made public extremely sensitive search queries such as "how to tell your family
> you're a victim of incest," "surgical help for depression," "how to kill your wife," "men that use
> emotional and physical abandonment to control their partner," "suicide by natural gas," "how
> to make someone hurt for the pain they caused someone else," "revenge for a cheating spouse,"
> "will I be extradited from ny to fl on a dui charge," and "my baby's father physically abuses me."[38]

Many of the (subsequent) commentaries on the search log data focused on the
privacy breaches as well as on the opportunities for law enforcement, and such attention led search engine companies to grow more wary of the use of search logs for
academic research purposes.[39] A main lesson drawn from the AOL search log data
release is the improbability of anonymization of search engine users.[40] Identifying each
user by a number and a list of queries does not mask identities, but rather invites
detective work.

Two further consequences of the AOL search log release are of relevance to social
researchers employing web data. The first is that search engine companies subsequently made pledges to protect user privacy through data anonymization and data
destruction directives, downgrading the data they collected and also making it shorter-
lived—violating two of the criteria of "good data" as discussed above, and one of the
reasons why the web data would fail the test of quality.[41] Proper names may be
replaced with random characters, so as to comply with data retention laws. In the
event, Google decided to anonymize their engine users (in the logs) by removing the
last few digits of the searcher's IP address, while Microsoft decided to scrub the IP
addresses entirely.[42] The IP address, however, is also a geolocation marker of the user,
and this is the second consequence of the AOL search log release. Instead of focusing
on the individual user (anonymized by applying a number to each or by scrubbing
all or part of the IP address), log research may direct its sights onto what we call the
places of queries. From what locations are users searching for particular terms, such
as a candidate in an upcoming election? Could the location of such collective query

behavior be made relevant to research? Thus a social research outlook, as I have argued in this book, might transform not only how web data are studied but how they are made available. It would be of less interest to have a list of queries by an individual user than a list of queries from a place.[43]

The major breakthrough in this respect has been the Google Flu Trends project, which found that it can "track influenza-like illness in a population . . . accurately [estimating] the current level of weekly influenza activity in each region of the United States."[44] Google Flu Trends thus shifted the attention away from the individual user's privacy, and away from search effectiveness or personalized search research more generally as the main work to be undertaken with search log data. Instead, queries become a means for detecting trends, which has been a by-product of search engines for some time, with such services as Google Trends listing the most popular searches at a given time (and place). With the addition of the data of place (via zip code for registered users of a toolbar or other service, or via IP address), the outlook changes, and the interests may shift from zeitgeist and a marketing mentality to flu and social research.

IP address scrubbing, as mentioned above, is a means of anonymizing users; in the Google case only unauthenticated users (those not logged in) had their IP addresses rubbed out. Authenticated users, on the other hand, agree to allow search companies to retain their data for the purposes of improving search. Research opportunities present themselves. As a case in point, a set of Yahoo! Research's search engine log data, from Yahoo!'s registered users, largely mirrors the demographics of the U.S. population.[45] Thus one could study the distribution of specific cultural and social preferences, employing three variables: query terms (including volume), query locations (zip codes), and the date stamps of the queries.[46]

Here the interest extends to social and political search. One could imagine an array of query log research projects, such as the time and place of the use of hate speech or extremist language, for which one could strive to ground the findings made from archived websites about the hardening of Dutch culture (described in the first chapter) through additional web data (query logs). Here one grounds (or at least triangulates) web findings with web findings. One also could query for candidates in the run-up to an election, and candidates coupled with social issues. One of the crucial challenges is to inquire into the web's ability (through analysis of search engine query data) to provide the place and time as well as intensity of cultural preference and political expression, compared to other means of finding the same. Research focusing on the places, times, and intensities of queries has the social research methodological imagination I wish to describe (as opposed to the online detective's or the personalized search engine builder's), for one is formulating questions concerning attitudes and preference as opposed to ones that may ultimately reveal personally identifiable data.[47] Such research undertakings may involve "big" web data, albeit with a digital methods outlook.

Notes

Introduction

1. Ginsberg et al., 2008.

2. Severson, 2009.

3. Rogers, 2009.

4. Nyirubugara, 2011.

5. Lewis et al., 2008; Neff, 2011; Tumasjan et al., 2010; Gayo-Avello et al., 2011.

6. Black, 2007: 1.

7. Following conventions employed at Google, search engine queries are set in brackets in this discussion, such as [9/11]. If quotation marks have been used in a query (to return only exact matches), the query is recorded that way: ["climate change"]. Leaving out the quotation marks in a query returns equivalents or synonyms: for example, the query [cell phone] also returns results for mobile phone.

8. Pariser, 2011.

9. Feuz et al., 2011.

10. Vaidhyanathan, 2011.

11. The media art project Elfriendo.com appeared in *Mister Motley*. See Toma, 2008.

12. The URLs for the (discontinued) Myspace search services, and their brief explanations, are as follows. http://searchservice.myspace.com/index.cfm?fuseaction=searchandsearchtarget=tpeo pleandsearchType=networkandsearchBoxID=Profileandinteresttype=Gandcountry=andsearchBy =FirstandSubmit=Findandf_first_name=andf_search_criteria=; http://searchservice.myspace.com/ index.cfm?fuseaction=searchandsearchtarget=tpeopleandsearchType=networkandsearchBoxID=P rofileandinteresttype=Muandcountry=andsearchBy=FirstandSubmit=Findandf_first_name=andf _search_criteria=; http://searchservice.myspace.com/index.cfm?fuseaction=searchandsearchtarge t=tpeopleandsearchType=networkandsearchBoxID=Profileandinteresttype=Mandcountry=and searchBy=FirstandSubmit=Findandf_first_name=andf_search_criteria=; and http://searchservice

.myspace.com/index.cfm?fuseaction=searchandsearchtarget=tpeopleandsearchType=networkand searchBoxID=Profileandinteresttype=Bandcountry=andsearchBy=FirstandSubmit=Findandf_first _name=andf_search_criteria=. Interesttype= Here, G, Mu, M, and B are general interests, music, movies, and books, and f_search_criteria= could be filled in with the specific interest sought.

13. The term "native" is employed in a computing sense. An application is native when it has been written for a particular system.

14. Zimmer, 2010a.

Chapter 1

1. Barlow, 1996; Benedikt, 1991; Dibbell, 1998; Rheingold, 1991; Rheingold; 1993; Shaviro, 2008; Stone, 1995; Turkle, 1995.

2. Jones, 1999.

3. Hine, 2000.

4. Miller and Slater, 2000.

5. Woolgar, 2002.

6. Jenkins, 2006; Keen, 2007; Bruns, 2008.

7. Manovich, 2007.

8. Contractor, 2009.

9. Lazer et al., 2009.

10. Manovich, 2008.

11. Vaidhyanathan, 2011.

12. Jeanneney, 2007; Vaidhyanathan, 2007.

13. Jensen, 1998.

14. Rogers, 2003; Centers for Disease Control and Prevention, 2011.

15. Castells, 1996; Goldsmith and Wu, 2006.

16. Marres and Rogers, 2008.

17. Dohmen, 2007.

18. Lynch, 1997.

19. Slee, 2009.

20. McLuhan, 1964.

21. Williams, 1974.

22. Hayles, 2004.

23. Galloway, 2004.

24. Fuller, 2003.

25. Manovich, 2008.

26. Bolter and Grusin, 1999.

27. Rogers, 2004.

28. Introna and Nissenbaum, 2000.

29. Landow, 1994; Watts, 1999; Park and Thewall, 2003.

30. Elmer, 2001.

31. Krebs, 2002.

32. Cf. Beaulieu, 2005.

33. Marres and Rogers, 2000; Rogers, 2002.

34. The Issue Crawler software, with particular allied tools, has been developed specifically to perform such hyperlink analysis. Websites are crawled and links are gathered and stored. The crawler-analytical modules are adaptations from scientometrics (colink analysis) and social networking analysis (snowball). Once a network is located with the Issue Crawler, individual actors may be profiled using the actor profiler tool. The actor profiler shows, in a graphic, the inlinks and outlinks of the top ten network actors. The other technique for actor profiling relies on a scraper that would capture all outlinks from a site, and a scraper of a search engine, the Yahoo! inlink ripper, which provides a list of the links made to a website.

35. Deibert et al., 2007.

36. Krug, 2000; Dunne, 2005.

37. Foot and Schneider, 2006.

38. Screen-capturing software has been employed previously for the analysis of Wikipedia pages, showing the evolution of entries and thus how Wikipedians build knowledge.

39. Spink and Jansen, 2004.

40. The notice appears on the credits page of the Issue Dramaturg, https:// dramaturg.issuecrawler .net/.

41. Rogers, 2004.

42. Mills, 1971: 212; Rogers and Marres, 2002.

43. Foot and Schneider, 2002; Schneider and Foot, 2002.

44. Chun, 2006.

45. Marvin, 2004.

46. Boyle, 1997.

47. Shirky, 2005.

48. Galloway, 2004.

49. Boyd and Ellison, 2007.

50. Giles, 2005.

51. Swartz, 2006.

52. Van Dijck, 2009.

53. Chesney, 2006; Read, 2006; Magnus, 2008.

54. Niederer and Van Dijck, 2010.

55. The end of cyberspace also has not been helpful for projects relying on the classic Internet feature of the anonymous user. For example, organizations and governments ban employees from editing Wikipedia at work, as the edits may be traced to locations and made into subjects of scandal.

Chapter 2

1. Goldsmith and Wu, 2006.

2. Miller and Slater, 2000.

3. Dodge, 2000.

4. November et al., 2010.

5. Mueller, 2002.

6. The Issue Crawler (https://www.issuecrawler.net) is server-side web network location software. Input URLs into the Issue Crawler, and the software crawls the URLs, captures page/site outlinks, performs colink analysis, and outputs the results in lists as well as visualizations. The software was conceived in the mid-1990s at the Department of Science and Technology Dynamics, University of Amsterdam, and funded by the Soros Foundation. It has a forerunner in the Netlocator, also known as the De-pluralising Engine, built in Maastricht during the Jan van Eyck Design and Media Research Fellowship, 1999–2000.

7. Lialina, 2005.

8. Kehoe et al., 1999.

9. Park and Thelwall, 2003.

10. Beaulieu, 2005.

11. Rogers, 2002.

12. Sunstein, 2001.

13. Altena, 1999.

14. Berners-Lee, 1999; Nelson, 1999.

15. Watts, 1999.

16. Marres, 2000.

17. Bush, 1945; Nelson, 1965; Landow, 1994.

18. Brin and Page, 1998.

19. Elmer, 2001.

20. Introna and Nissenbaum, 2000; Rogers, 2004; Van Couvering, 2004.

21. Wouters et al., 2004.

22. Jones, 1999.

23. Nicholas et al., 2005.

24. Garrido and Halavais, 2003; Thelwall, 2004.

25. Dodge, 2000.

26. Introna and Nissenbaum, 2000.

27. Rheingold, 1994.

28. Barbrook and Cameron, 1996.

29. Dean, 2003.

30. Quick, 2002.

31. *Reno v. ACLU*, 1997.

32. Sack, 2002; Kahn and Kellner, 2004; Turner, 2006.

33. Foot and Schneider, 2002; Schneider and Foot, 2004; Schneider and Foot, 2005.

34. Tatum, 2005.

35. Links in the comment space are downgraded owing to the preponderance of so-called spam-dexing, or bots leaving links to websites so as to boost artificially those websites' rankings in search engines.

36. Lawrence and Giles, 1999.

37. Jeanneney, 2007.

38. Govcom.org, 2005.

39. Journal du Net, 2007.

40. Rogers, 2003.

41. Krebs, 2002; Hobbs, 2003; Bureau d'études, 2003.

42. Rennie, 2002.

43. Marres, 2005.

44. Dean, 2002.

45. Keck and Sikkink, 1998; Riles, 2001.

46. Rucht, 1999.

47. Rheingold, 2002.

48. Rogers, 2007.

49. Baran, 1962; Arquilla and Ronfeldt, 1993; Ronfeldt and Arquilla, 2001.

50. Latour, 2010.

51. Van der Velden, 2004.

52. Verkade, 2007.

53. Boyd, 2007.

Chapter 3

1. Examples taken from author's collection of web awards from the 1990s. The awards are dis-cussed in terms of "reliability graphics" and a particular web epistemological practice in Rogers, 2000.

2. However historically dominant, the U.S. web awards culture has been joined by other national ones; for the Danish public-sector context (with a discussion of the Swedish as well as Norwe-gian), see Sørum et al., 2009.

3. Bercic, 2005.

4. Glassel, 1998; Ellis and Vasconcelos, 1999.

5. There are exceptions to the overall decline of URL list-making. Whitelists for child's play and blacklists for the purposes of Internet censorship, or content filtering, are actively maintained, as are those compiled to combat spam.

6. Weltevrede, 2009.

7. Experiments with the Tracker Tracker software, a Digital Methods Initiative tool that builds upon Ghostery and detects ad programs, social plug-ins, analytics, widgets, trackers, and other fingerprints, have found traces of such technologies in archived websites.

8. At the Piet Zwart Institute in Rotterdam, Andrea Fiore developed a means to capture and analyze third-party cookies.

9. Spigel, 1992.

10. Brügger, 2005.

11. Latour and Woolgar, 1986; Knorr Cetina, 1999; Walker, 2005.

12. Kahle, 1997; Lyman and Kahle, 1998. One could make the distinction between the Internet Archive (as repository) and the "current" interface on it (the navigation).

13. Shirky, 2005; Lewis, 2007; Carr, 2008.

14. Galloway, 2004; Sterling, 2010.

15. Schneider et al., 2003.

16. Internet Archive, 2008.

17. Howell, 2006.

18. Rogers, 2007.

19. Rumsey, 2002; Carnevale and Aronsky, 2007.

20. Dullaart, 2009

21. Gehl, 2010; Van Dijck, 2009. Sumoto.iki depopulated the following of content: Delicious, Digg, Last.fm, Technorati, YouTube, Myspace, 43Things, Twitter, Facebook and Netvibes.

22. Moulier-Boutang, 2008.

23. Ryan et al., 2003; Benkler and Shaw, 2010.

24. Krippendorff, 2004; Krippendorff and Bock, 2008.

25. Udell, 2005a.

26. Udell, 2005b.

27. Google, 2008.

28. Govcom.org, 2008.

29. Dohmen, 2007.

30. On April 19, 2011 no scholarly references were returned in Google Book Search, Google Scholar, or Google Web Search. Apart from that of Kirsten Foot, Steven Schneider, and colleagues, some notable research that has made use of the Internet Archive includes Ryan et al., 2003; Brock, 2005; and Hackett and Parmanto, 2005.

31. Thelwall and Vaughan, 2004.

32. Dougherty et al., 2010. For an earlier effort, see Arms et al., 2006.

33. Passion and eclecticism are also on display in the same collection of websites. Apart from those on military as well as African-American history, two of the 23 single sites saved are those of the Hungarian national bank and the coins and currencies collection at Notre Dame University.

34. Pinsent et al., 2008: 19.

35. Foot and Schneider, 2002.

36. Foot et al., 2003; Foot and Schneider, 2004; Wu and Heok, 2006.

37. Derrida, 1996; Veronin, 2002.

38. Foot and Schneider, 2002: 225.

39. Schneider and Foot, 2002; Foot et al., 2003; Schneider and Foot, 2004; Foot, 2006; Foot and Schneider, 2006.

40. Kuhn, 1962.

41. Esther Weltevrede's personal correspondence with Caroline van Wijk, National Library of the Netherlands, May 27, 2009. The quantity of Dutch websites to be archived is rising.

42. Weltevrede, 2009.

43. There is also language-specific crawling. See Somboonviwat et al., 2006.

44. Pinsent et al., 2008.

45. The critique I refer to is a presentation given about Dutch national web archiving on the occasion of the retirement of Eric Ketelaar, the Professor of Archive Science at the University of Amsterdam, in May 2009. It was entitled "998 websites," which was the number of Dutch websites archived to date by the National Library of the Netherlands. An accompanying slide showed this math: 998 / 3364922 = 0.000296 of .nl websites archived to date. To be posed is the question of what has happened to the spirit of website collecting exhibited by the Internet Archive fifteen years earlier?

46. Ubois, 2002; Kimpton and Ubois, 2006; Masanès, 2006.

47. Stevenson, 2009.

48. Rhodes, 2002; Estep and Gelfand, 2003.

49. Ben-David, 2012; Brügger, 2011; Weltevrede and Helmond, 2012.

50. By value I refer to placement of a site among others vying for prominence in the sense of a hyperlink economy. See Rogers, 2002.

Chapter 4

1. Salkever, 2003; Battelle, 2003.

2. Vaidhyanathan, 2007.

3. Van der Vlies, 2008.

4. Vaidhyanathan, 2007.

5. Elmer, 2004; Lyon, 2007.

6. Rogers, 2008.

7. Turow, 2006.

8. Weinberger, 2002; Fuller, 2005.

9. Jensen, 1998

10. Introna and Nissenbaum, 2000; Van Couvering, 2004; Metahaven, 2008.

11. Borges, 1993.

12. Rogers, 2004.

13. Metahaven, 2008.

14. Pasquinelli, 2009.

15. At the time of writing, Yahoo! results are delivered by Microsoft's Bing search engine.

16. Sherman, 2004.

17. Powezek, 2006.

18. Battelle, 2005.

19. Spool, 2006.

20. Norman, 2004.

21. Berger, 1999.

22. Galloway, 2004.

23. Van Ess, 2005.

24. Yahoo!, 2008.

25. Shirky, 2005.

26. Keen, 2007.

27. Sullivan, 2007.

28. Cutts, 2006.

Chapter 5

1. In November 2011 clicking on the directory at google.com (under even more) returned a 404 "file not found" error.

2. Open Directory Project, "about dmoz," http://www.dmoz.org/docs/en/about.html (accessed May 27, 2011).

3. As an aside, spam would occur in yellow pages and business directories using the alphabetical, info-egalitarian model when businesses would name themselves 123 Billiards, or similar, thereby moving to the top of the list of pool halls, for example.

4. Shirky, 2008.

5. Lawrence and Giles, 1998; Lawrence and Giles, 1999; Zimmer, 2010b.

6. Dodge and Kitchin, 2000.

7. Roth, 2009.

8. Levy, 2011; Miller, 2011; Torrence, 2011.

9. Lanier, 2010.

10. Segal, 2011: BU1.

11. Rogers, 2002.

12. Preliminary work on the use of search engine results for research has been performed in the context of MACOSPOL, Mapping Controversies on Science for Politics, the EU 7th Framework project led by Bruno Latour, mappingcontroversies.net. See the projects.

13. Brin and Page, 1998: 116.

14. Van Couvering, 2007.

15. *The World According to Google* project is by Esther Weltevrede and Erik Borra, Digital Methods Initiative, Amsterdam. The human rights query work is described in Weltevrede's forthcoming PhD thesis, University of Amsterdam.

16. Wiggins, 2001.

17. Grimmelman, 2008/2009. The query for [Jew] in google.com returned jewwatch.com in the top five on May 31, 2011.

18. Anti-Defamation League, 2004.

19. Brin, 2004.

20. Anti-Defamation League, 2004.

21. Google, 2011b.

22. Enge, 2007.

23. Rogers et al., 2009.

24. Here I am referring to similar work on the social life of issues and the life cycles of controversies as (in some cases) "a sequence that goes from cold reciprocal indifference, to hot quarrel, to warm consensus" (Venturini, 2010: 271).

25. Shmoogle is by Tsila Hassine.

26. The tool developed to distill URLs out of text and code is called the Harvester, and is online with other digital methods tools at digitalmethods.net.

27. See, e.g., Lippmann, 1927: 58.

28. Lippmann, 1927: 120–121.

29. The notion of a pure PageRank becomes problematic when engines would not calculate "overall" measures of relatedness, but only those between a particular object and a particular user, based for example on the user's immediate network such as with Facebook's EdgeRank. See Kincaid, 2010.

30. Leskovec et al., 2009.

31. Introna and Nissenbaum, 2000.

Chapter 6

1. This chapter was written with Esther Weltevrede, Sabine Niederer, and Erik Borra.

2. Kehoe et al., 1999; Baeza-Yates et al., 2007.

3. Feuz et al., 2011.

4. Pariser, 2011.

5. The data for this study are online at the project website, http://mappingiranonline.digital methods.net/.

6. According to the International Telecommunication Union, 13% of the Iranian population uses the Internet and 21% of Iranian households have Internet access (2011). The marketing research reports an urban concentration of users, with "the vast majority [being] young, mostly 15 to 40" years of age (NetBina, 2010: 10). Figures on the Iranian diaspora are not available.

7. Rhoads and Fassihi, 2011.

8. Deibert and Rohozinski, 2010.

9. Goldsmith and Wu, 2006; Schmidt, 2009.

10. Schmidt, 2009; Whetstone, 2010.

11. Drummond, 2010a; Drummond, 2010b.

12. Higson, 1989; Anderson, 1991; Miller and Slater, 2000; Ginsburg et al., 2002.

13. Kelly and Etling, 2008; Etling et al., 2010.

14. Glanz and Markoff, 2011; Roberts et al., 2011.

15. Arvidson and Lettenström, 1998; Arms et al., 2001; Abiteboul et al., 2002; Koerbin, 2004.

16. PADI, n.d.; Lasfargues et al., 2008.

17. Weltevrede, 2009.

18. Zarrinbakhsh, 2011.

19. Khiabany and Sreberny, 2007: 565.

20. Deuze, 2007; Bruns, 2008.

21. Howe, 2006; Moulier-Boutang, 2008.

22. Rogers, 2002.

23. Google.com's web search was chosen for its dominance in Iran among users of search engines. Search engine market shares in Iran as of 2010 are as follows: Google 90.78%, Yahoo! 4.97%, Bing 3.64%, Ask Jeeves 0.46%, AOL 0.07% (MVF Global, 2010). Another marketing research firm lists 2011 market shares in Iran as Google 87.15%, Yahoo! 7.27%, Bing 4.16%, Ask Jeeves 0.70%, AOL 0.12%, and Lycos 0.01% (Net Applications, 2011). According to Alexa in October 2011, Google.com is the most visited site in Iran, followed by Yahoo.com. We employed site queries in google.com for the top-level (site:.ir) as well as the second-level domains (e.g., site:.co.ir) and concatenated the results. The query technique did not allow for the redirecting to a local-domain Google. Because cookies had not been retained, it also did not allow for the personalization of the results.

24. In order to compare the different platforms, we chose to compare hosts instead of full URLs. That is, for Balatarin, we harvested all the URLs listed on the 150 pages of "hot" links, resulting in 1,102 unique hosts.

25. Iran Media Program, 2010.

26. Gerlitz and Helmond, 2011.

27. Baeza-Yates et al., 2007: 1.

28. Amir-Ebrahimi, 2008.

29. The language autodetection functionality is provided by alchemyAPI, which for academic researchers allows 30,000 queries per day. The tool is at http://www.alchemyapi.com/api/lang/ (accessed 14 July 2011).

30. The research team manually checked the results which returned sites as English or unknown, and corrected any errors. We have not explored further why dual-language sites are considered as one particular language by alchemyAPI. We also would consider using Google Translate as a language detector. The "unknown" tags in the cloud indicate that neither the language detection

tool nor the researcher was able to determine the language, for in most cases the site was no longer online.

31. Additionally, the Iranian webs show various degrees of language distribution, with Alexa being the least diverse with six languages and Google Web Search the most with 36 languages.

32. The http status codes are explained on the dedicated Wikipedia entry http://en.Wikipedia .org/wiki/List_of_HTTP_status_codes (accessed 14 July 2011).

33. URL redirection is explained on the dedicated Wikipedia entry http://en.Wikipedia.org/wiki/ URL_redirection (accessed 14 July 2011).

34. Yossef et al., 2004.

35. Thompson, 2006.

36. Open Net Initiative, 2009; Google, 2011a.

37. In early 2012, when an Iranian proxy returns "403 Forbidden" for a particular site, one is presented with an iframe loading http://10.10.34.34/?type=Invalid%20Site&policy=MainPolicy which 30 seconds later redirects to http://peyvandha.ir, the site run by Ministry of Culture and Islamic Guidance. The former is only accessible from within Iran, and the latter contains a directory of recommended or approved sites, a list of reasons for banning a site, and a form to report a website thought to be in violation of Iran's computer crimes law. While in this study the researchers used response codes as strong indicators of blocked sites, we also conducted additional tests concerning the relationship between the "403 Forbidden" response and the presence of the block-page URL. For blocked sites common to at least three lists (our test sample), we found that a 403 would be accompanied by a blocked page. It also may be noted that http://peyvandha.ir ranks in the top 5 of Alexa's (surfers') geoweb. As blocked sites redirect there, the site's high ranking provides a relative measure of the amount of traffic to blocked sites from within Iran.

38. Murdoch and Anderson, 2008.

39. Villeneuve, 2006.

40. Wright et al., 2011: 5.

41. The Universal Feed Parser downloads structured data feeds of many kinds, including RSS, Atom, and CDF. It extracts post attributes, such as title, author, description, timestamp, and link.

42. Technorati, 2011.

43. Blogpulse, 2011.

44. Quenqua, 2009.

45. Kelly and Etling, 2008.

46. Kelly and Etling, 2008: 24.

47. The Persian term for "smelly" language referred to here is بودار. The word list was created through a collaboration by nearly 20 Iranian bloggers whose blogs have been blocked by the

state over the past three years. When their blogs were blocked, they began to compile a list of "smelly" words, such as "open letter," "manifesto," "opposition party," and "political prisoner." To check the sensitivity (or, in our terms, fieriness) of the words, they would query each in google. com (http://google.com/search?q=smelly_word). If google.com was not blocked and the query result was, then the term was considered censored (and indeed sensitive). Note that a blocked query result containing the fiery keyword was not a criterion for inclusion on the word list, but rather an indication employed by the bloggers. It should be noted too that the words on the list are generally politically sensitive terms rather than routinely blacklisted keywords related to alcohol, sex, etc., however much the latter have been the object of study in larger inquiries into Internet censorship in Iran (Open Net Initiative, 2005, 2009). The choice of politically sensitive terms fits with our aim, which is not so much the general study of Internet censorship in Iran but rather the robustness of Iranian online expression of salient political and social issues.

48. Kelly and Etling, 2008: 24.

Chapter 7

1. Boyd and Ellison, 2007.

2. Foucault, 1998; Rogers, 2004.

3. Turow, 2006.

4. Prensky, 2001.

5. Lenhart and Madden, 2007.

6. Zinman and Donath, 2007.

7. Nonusers refers to profilers. Of course, profilers also may be users of the platforms, and most probably are, for one's sense of what may be mined, and how it may be analyzed or mashed up, would come from use, with at least a minimal level of activity.

8. Gandy, 1993.

9. Poster, 1991.

10. Sunden, 2003.

11. Latour, 2005.

12. Knorr Cetina, 2001; Engeström, 2005.

13. Schneier, 2007.

14. One gains only "a sense" of how analysis may be performed, and the kinds of findings that may be made, because Elfriendo captures only the top 100 profiles, thus providing only an indication, as opposed to a grounded finding from a proper sampling procedure.

15. Shirky, 2003.

16. Arthur, 1989.

17. Shirky, 2008.

18. Clay, n.d.

19. Stabile, 1995.

20. McLuhan, 1951.

21. Time, 1943.

22. *My Style is My Brand; I'm not the brands type; I don't like to be branded; I'm not into brands; I don't spend much time thinking about brands; I'm not participating in this; I'll manage without; I don't feel like checking boxes.* Translations by author.

Chapter 8

1. C. Anderson, 2006: 70.

2. Carr, 2009; Vaidhyanathan, 2011.

3. Baker, 2008; Reagle, 2010.

4. Wikipedia, 2011c.

5. Wikipedia, 2011d.

6. Wikipedia, 2012d.

7. Wikipedia, 2012b.

8. Wikipedia, 2012a.

9. Wikipedia, 2011e.

10. The term "Srebrenica massacre" is employed in the English-language Wikipedia. The term is preferred by the Wikipedians there because it is considered the most recognizable in English, given that it returns, as per Wikipedia practice in term selection, more Google results than other available terms, such as "Srebrenica genocide." The terms used in the other language versions are discussed later in this chapter. Rather than choose one term, we employ the terms used by each Wikipedia language version when discussing that version.

11. Wikimedia, 2011a.

12. McMillan, 2000; Herring, 2010.

13. Geiger, 2011.

14. Personal communication, September 27, 2011. Damir Pozderac is also a power editor of the entry on Hamdija Pozderac, the late Bosnian communist politician who was President of Bosnia and Herzegovina from 1971 to 1974, according to the Wikipedia entry.

15. Vuong et al., 2008.

16. Kittur et al., 2007.

17. Butler et al., 2008.

18. Wikimedia, 2010.

19. Massa and Scrinzi, 2011.

20. Niederer and Van Dijck, 2010.

21. Giles, 2005; Encyclopaedia Britannica, 2006.

22. Rosenzweig, 2006.

23. Rector, 2008.

24. Halavais and Lackaff, 2008.

25. West and Williamson, 2009: 270.

26. Bertelsmann Lexikon Institut, 2008.

27. Seigenthaler, 2005.

28. Halavais, 2004; Read, 2006.

29. Udell, 2005a.

30. Magnus, 2008.

31. Chesney, 2006.

32. Stvilia et al., 2008.

33. Lih, 2004: 9.

34. Braendle, 2005.

35. Wilkinson and Huberman, 2007: 160.

36. Kittur and Kraut, 2008.

37. Panciera et al., 2009.

38. Stvilia et al., 2008.

39. Guéret, 2010.

40. Den Besten et al., 2010.

41. Bellomi and Bonato, 2005.

42. Kolbitsch and Maurer, 2006; Callahan and Herring, 2011.

43. Callahan and Herring, 2011: 1912.

44. Stvilia et al., 2009.

45. Livingstone, 2010; Wikipedia, 2012c, Wikipedia, 2011f.

46. Royal and Kapila, 2008.

47. Pfeil et al., 2006; Hara et al., 2010.

48. Benkler, 2006.

49. Stvilia et al., 2008.

50. Wikimedia, 2011b.

51. Wikimedia, 2011b.

52. NIOD, 2002.

53. Wikipedia: De vrije encyclopedie, 2011.

54. Van der Veen, 2006. "Srebrenica," with the subtitle "The Dilemmas of Peacekeeping," is included in the fifty units of the so-called canon of Dutch history taught in secondary schools in the Netherlands. See Van Oostrom, 2007.

55. Wikipedia: De vrije encyclopedie, 2011.

56. Wikipedia: De vrije encyclopedie, 2011.

57. Frost, 2006.

58. Wikipedia, 2006b.

59. Wikipedia, 2010b.

60. Wikipedia, 2011b.

61. Emir Arven has been blocked indefinitely from contributing to the English-language Wikipedia after being revealed as a disruptive sockmaster of a series of sockpuppets (Wikipedia, 2011a). Emir Arven reappeared in many guises, one of which is the sockmaster Historičar, with nearly a dozen sockpuppets to his name (Wikipedia, 2009). Emir Arven also was active in the Bosnian article. Of the other power editors of the English-language Srebrenica massacre article, Bosniak, HanzoHattori, and The Dragon of Bosnia have been blocked, and Osli73 has been suspected of socking.

62. Greenberg, 2004; Volčič, 2007.

63. Honig and Both, 1996.

64. Wikipedia. Slobodna enciklopedija, 2009.

65. Wikipedija, 2011b.

66. Personal communication, 8 October 2011.

67. The Korean Wikipedia article also is entitled "Srebrenica genocide."

68. Wikipedia. Slobodna enciklopedija, 2009.

69. Vikipedije, 2011a.

70. Wikipedija, 2006; Wikipedija, 2010.

71. Wikipedija, 2006.

72. Wikipedija, 2006.

73. Wikipedija, 2011a.

74. Wikipedia, 2010b.

75. Personal communication, October 8, 2011.

76. Wikipedia: De vrije encyclopedie, 2011.

77. Wikipedia, 2010c.

78. International Commission on Missing Persons, 2011.

79. Vikipedije, 2011c.

80. Wikipedia, 2010b. The *Globe and Mail* is a Canadian national newspaper based in Toronto.

81. The Serbo-Croatian article has undergone three title changes, and only two of the talk pages associated with the original articles have been retained.

82. Vikipedije, 2011c.

83. Vikipedije, 2011c.

84. Wikipedija, 2010.

85. Wikipedia, 2006a.

86. Vikipedije, 2011b.

87. Vikipedije, 2011b.

88. Vikipedije, 2011b.

89. Vikipedije, 2011b.

90. Vikipedije, 2011b.

91. Wikipedia, 2010a.

92. The same U.N. report of the Secretary-General pursuant to General Assembly resolution 53/35, "The fall of Srebrencia," is referenced in the Dutch article as http://www.un.org/peace/srebrenica.pdf, and in Serbian, Serbo-Croatian, and English as http://www.un.org/docs/journal/asp/ws.asp?m=a/54/549.

93. De Koning, 2000.

94. Vikipedije, 2011c.

95. Callahan and Herring, 2011.

96. Stvilia et al., 2009.

Chapter 9

1. An earlier version of this chapter was written with Erik Borra. The title is a variation on Derek de Solla Price's classic monograph *Little Science, Big Science* (1963), where at issue, among other things, is the relationship between status and authority and the size of data as well as apparatus to handle it.

2. U.S. Air Force, 2009.

3. Shields, 2003; Van Doorn, 2009.

4. Information Warfare Monitor, 2009.

5. Marres and Rogers, 2000.

6. Keen, 2007; Thelwall and Hasler, 2007.

7. Hayles, 2004.

8. Elmer, 2001.

9. Briggs, 1991: 212.

10. Apart from content analysis, another candidate approach would be user studies.

11. Boyd and Crawford, 2011.

12. Hellsten et al., 2006.

13. Thelwall et al., 2005.

14. Espenschied and Lialina, 2009.

15. Thelwall et al., 2005: 81.

16. Lazer et al. 2009: 722.

17. Marres, 2011.

18. Google Refine and Google Correlate were introduced in 2011 by Google Labs.

19. National Science Board, 2005; Borgman, 2007; Borgman, 2009.

20. Borgman, 2009: 44.

21. Franklin and Rodriguez, 2008.

22. Manovich, 2009: 208; Huber et al., 2010.

23. Michel et al., 2011.

24. Michel et al., 2011; Bohannon, 2010.

25. Marres, 2009.

26. Webb et al., 1966; Lewis et al., 2008; Taksa et al., 2008.

27. Pass et al., 2006.

28. Barbaro and Zeller, 2006.

29. Hafner, 2006.

30. N. Anderson, 2006: 1.

31. Poblete et al., 2008.

32. Van Couvering, 2007.

33. Engelberts and Plug, 2008.

34. AOL, 2006; Pass et al., 2006.

35. AOL, 2006.

36. Battelle, 2005; Engelberts and Plug, 2008.

37. Electronic Frontier Foundation, 2006.

38. EFF, 2006: 4–5

39. Electronic Frontier Foundation, 2006.

40. Poblete et al., 2008.

41. Search log data could pass "good data" quality tests if they were not regularly destroyed, and if they were not regularly degraded through the insertion of gobbledygook characters in the place of proper names and parts of speech thought to be personally identifiable.

42. Sullivan, 2008.

43. It is also of interest to have a list of queries that through user clicks ultimately land on particular site types, such as right-of-center or left-of-center political blogs, a technique employed by Erik Borra and Ingmar Weber in the development of Yahoo! Political Insights. See Borra and Weber, 2012; Weber et al., 2012.

44. Ginsberg et al., 2009: 1012.

45. Weber and Castillo, 2010.

46. Taksa et al., 2008; Baeza-Yates et al., 2009; Silvestri, 2010.

47. Ess, 2002; Jones et al., 2007; Dutton and Piper, 2010.

References

Abiteboul, Serge, Grégory Cobena, Julien Masanes, and Gerald Sedrati. 2002. A First Experience in Archiving the French Web. Paper presented at the 6th European Conference on Research and Advanced Technology for Digital Libraries, Rome, Italy, September 16–18.

Altena, Arie. 1999. The Browser Is Dead. *Mediamatic* 9/10:49–56.

Amir-Ebrahimi, Masserat. 2008. Blogging from Qom, behind Walls and Veils. *Comparative Studies of South Asia, Africa and the Middle East* 28 (2):235–249.

Anderson, Benedict. 1991. *Imagined Communities*. London: Verso.

Anderson, Chris. 2006. *The Long Tail*. New York: Hyperion.

Anderson, Nate. 2006. The Ethics of Using AOL Search Data. *Ars Technica*. August, http://arstechnica.com/old/content/2006/08/7578 (accessed June 20, 2011).

Anti-Defamation League. 2004. Google Search Ranking of Hate Sites Not Intentional. ADL web post, April 22, http://www.adl.org/rumors/google_search_rumors.asp (accessed February 12, 2012).

AOL. 2006. 500k User Session Collection. Formerly available from research.aol.com.

Arms, Caroline R., Roger Adkins, Cassy Ammen, and Allene Hayes. 2001. Collecting and Preserving the Web: The Minerva Prototype. *RLG DigiNews* 5 (2).

Arms, William, Selcuk Aya, Pavel Dmitriev, Blazej Kot, Ruth Mitchell, and Lucia Walle. 2006. A Research Library Based on the Historical Collections of the Internet Archive. *D-Lib Magazine* 12 (2).

Arquilla, John, and David Ronfeldt. 1993. Cyberwar Is Coming! *Comparative Strategy* 12 (2):141–165.

Arthur, W. Brian. 1989. Competing Technologies, Increasing Returns and Lock-In by Historical Events. *Economic Journal* 99:106–131.

Arvidson, Allan, and Frans Lettenström. 1998. The Kulturarw Project—The Swedish Royal Web Archive. *Electronic Library* 16 (2):105–108.

Baeza-Yates, Ricardo, Carlos Castillo, and Efthimis N. Efthimiadis. 2007. Characterization of National Web Domains. *Journal ACM Transactions on Internet Technology* 7 (2), Art. 9.

Baeza-Yates, Ricardo, Christian Middleton, and Carlos Castillo. 2009. The Geographical Life of Search. Proceedings of the 2009 IEEE/WIC/ACM International Joint Conference on Web Intelligence and Intelligent Agent Technology—Volume 01 (WI-IAT '09). Washington, DC: IEEE Computer Society, 252–259.

Baker, Nicholson. 2008. The Charms of Wikipedia. *New York Review of Books* 55 (4):6–10.

Baran, Paul. 1962. *On Distributed Communication Networks*. Santa Monica, CA: Rand.

Barbaro, Michael, and Tom Zeller. 2006. A Face Is Exposed for AOL Searcher No. 4417749. *New York Times*, August 9.

Barbrook, Richard, and Andy Cameron. 1996. The Californian Ideology. *Science as Culture* 6 (1):44–72.

Barlow, John P. 1996. A Declaration of the Independence of Cyberspace. Davos, Switzerland, https://projects.eff.org/~barlow/Declaration-Final.html (accessed October 19, 2012).

Bar-Yossef, Ziv, Andrei Broder, Ravi Kumar, and Andrew Tomkins. 2004. Sic Transit Gloria Telae: Towards an Understanding of the Web's Decay. *Proceedings of the 13th Conference on World Wide Web*. New York: ACM.

Battelle, John. 2003. The "Creeping Googlization Meme." John Battelle's Searchblog, December 16, http://battellemedia.com/archives/index.php?p=0145 (accessed October 12, 2012).

Battelle, John. 2005. *The Search: How Google and Its Rivals Rewrote the Rules of Business and Transformed Our Culture*. New York: Portfolio.

Beaulieu, Anne. 2005. Sociable Hyperlinks: An Ethnographic Approach to Connectivity. In *Virtual Methods: Issues in Social Research on the Internet*, ed. Christine Hine, 183–197. Oxford: Berg.

Bellomi, Francesco, and Roberto Bonato. 2005. Network Analysis of Wikipedia. *Proceedings of Wikimania 2005*, Frankfurt.

Ben-David, Anat. 2012. Palestinian Border-Making in Digital Spaces. PhD dissertation, Bar-Ilan University, Ramat Gan, Israel.

Benedikt, Michael. 1991. Cyberspace: Some Proposals. In *Cyberspace: First Steps*, ed. Michael Benedikt, 119–224. Cambridge, MA: MIT Press.

Benkler, Yochai. 2006. *The Wealth of Networks*. New Haven: Yale University Press.

Benkler, Yochai, and Aaron Shaw. 2010. A Tale of Two Blogospheres: Discursive Practices on the Left and Right. Research Publication No. 2010-6, Berkman Center for Internet & Society, Harvard University, April 27.

Bercic, Bostjan. 2005. Protection of Personal Data and Copyrighted Material on the web: The Cases of Google and the Internet Archive. *Information & Communications Technology Law* 14 (1):17–24.

Berger, James. 1999. *After the End*. Minneapolis: University of Minnesota Press.

Berners-Lee, Tim. 1999. *Weaving the Web: The Past, Present and Future of the World Wide Web by Its Inventor*. London: Orion.

Bertelsmann Lexikon Institut. 2008. *Das Wikipedia Lexikon in einem Band*. Gütersloh: Mohn Media.

Black, Richard. 2007. BBC Switches Off Climate Special. *BBC News*, September 5, http://news .bbc.co.uk/2/hi/6979596.stm (accessed May 26, 2011).

Blogpulse. 2011. FAQ: How Do You Determine Blog Rankings? Blogpulse.com, http://web.archive .org/web/20110605200225/http://www.blogpulse.com/about.html (accessed October 19, 2011).

Bohannon, John. 2010. Google Opens Books to New Cultural Studies. *Science* 330 (6011):1600.

Bolter, Jay D., and Richard Grusin. 1999. *Remediation: Understanding New Media*. Cambridge, MA: MIT Press.

Borges, Jorge Luis. 2003. The Garden of Forking Paths. In *The New Media Reader*, ed. Noah Wardrip-Fruin and Nick Montfort, 29–34. Cambridge, MA: MIT Press.

Borgman, Christine. 2007. *Scholarship in the Digital Age*. Cambridge, MA: MIT Press.

Borgman, Christine. 2009. The Digital Future Is Now: A Call to Action for the Humanities. *Digital Humanities Quarterly* 3(4), http://www.digitalhumanities.org/dhq/vol/3/4/000077/000077.html (accessed December 15, 2010).

Borra, Erik, and Ingmar Weber. 2012. Political Insights: Exploring Partisanship in Web Search Queries. *First Monday* 17 (7).

Boyd, Danah. 2007. Viewing American Class Divisions through Facebook and MySpace. *Apophenia Blog Essay*, June 24, http://www.danah.org/papers/essays/ClassDivisions.html (accessed September 10, 2007).

Boyd, Danah, and Kate Crawford. 2011. Six Provocations for Big Data. Paper presented at Oxford Internet Institute's "A Decade in Internet Time: Symposium on the Dynamics of the Internet and Society," September 21.

Boyd, Danah, and Nicole Ellison. 2007. Social Network Sites: Definition, History, and Scholarship. *Journal of Computer-Mediated Communication* 13 (1).

Boyle, James. 1997. Foucault in Cyberspace. *University of Cincinnati Law Review* 66:177–205.

Braendle, Andreas. 2005. Many Cooks Don't Spoil the Broth. *Proceedings of Wikimania 2005: The First International Wikimedia Conference*, Frankfurt.

Briggs, Asa. 1991. *Serious Pursuits: Communications and Education*. Champaign, IL: University of Illinois Press.

Brin, Sergey. 2004. Letter from Google to Abraham H. Foxman, Anti-Defamation League, April 21, http://www.adl.org/internet/google_letter.asp (accessed May 21, 2011).

Brin, Sergey, and Larry Page. 1998. The Anatomy of a Large-scale Hypertextual Web Search Engine. *Computer Networks and ISDN Systems* 30:107–117.

Brock, André. 2005. "A Belief in Humanity Is a Belief in Colored Men": Using Culture to Span the Digital Divide. *Journal of Computer-Mediated Communication* 11 (1).

Brügger, Niels. 2005. *Archiving Websites: General Considerations and Strategies*. Aarhus: Centre for Internet Research.

Brügger, Niels. 2011. Historical Network Analysis of the Web. Paper presented at the 8th Conference on Applications of Social Network Analysis, Zurich, Switzerland, September 14–16.

Bruns, Axel. 2008. *Blogs, Wikipedia, Second Life, and Beyond: From Production to Produsage*. New York: Peter Lang.

Bureau d'études. 2003. Governing by Networks. September, http://utangente.free.fr/2003/governingbynetworks.pdf (accessed September 10, 2007).

Bush, Vannevar. 1945. As We May Think. *Atlantic Monthly* 176 (1) July:101–108.

Butler, Brian, Elisabeth Joyce, and Jacqueline Pike. 2008. Don't Look Now, but We've Created a Bureaucracy: The Nature and Roles of Policies and Rules in Wikipedia. *Proceedings of the SIGCHI Conference on Human Factors in Computing Systems* (CHI 08), 1101–1110. New York: ACM Press.

Callahan, Ewa S., and Susan C. Herring. 2011. Cultural Bias in Wikipedia Content on Famous Persons. *Journal of the American Society for Information Science and Technology* 62 (10):1899–1915.

Carnevale, Randy J., and Dominik Aronsky. 2007. The Life and Death of URLs in Five Biomedical Informatics Journals. *International Journal of Medical Informatics* 76:269–273.

Carr, Nicholas. 2008. Is Google Making Us Stupid? *Atlantic Monthly*, July/August, 56–63.

Carr, Nicholas. 2009. All Hail the Information Triumvirate! Roughtype blog, January 22, http://www.roughtype.com/archives/2009/01/all_hail_the_in.php (accessed December 15, 2010).

Castells, Manuel. 1996. *The Information Age: Economy, Society and Culture—The Rise of the Network Society*. Malden, MA: Blackwell.

Centers for Disease Control and Prevention. 2011. Overview of Influenza Surveillance in the United States. Atlanta, GA, http://www.cdc.gov/flu/weekly/overview.htm (accessed October 18, 2012).

Chesney, Thomas. 2006. An Empirical Examination of Wikipedia's Credibility. *First Monday* 11 (11).

Chun, Wendy. 2006. *Control and Freedom: Power and Paranoia in the Age of Fiber*. Cambridge, MA: MIT Press.

Clay, Bruce. N.d. Search Engine Relationships Chart. Bruceclay.com, http://www.bruceclay.com/eu/searchenginerelationshipchart.htm (accessed October 18, 2012).

Cohen, Noam. 2007. Google Halts "Miserable Failure" Link to President Bush. *New York Times*, January 29.

Contractor, Noshir. 2009. Digital Traces: An Exploratorium for Understanding and Enabling Social Networks. Presentation at the annual meeting of the American Association for the Advancement of Science.

Cutts, Matt. 2006. Indexing Timeline. *Matt Cutts: Gadgets, Google, and SEO*, May 16, http://www.mattcutts.com/blog/indexing-timeline/ (accessed December 22, 2008).

Dean, Jodi. 2002. *Publicity's Secret: How Technoculture Capitalizes on Democracy*. Ithaca, NY: Cornell University Press.

Dean, Jodi. 2003. Why the Web Is Not a Public Sphere. *Constellations* (Oxford) 10 (1):95–112.

Deibert, Ronald J., John Palfrey, Rafal Rohozinski, and Jonathan Zittrain, eds. 2007. *Access Denied: The Practice and Policy of Global Internet Filtering*. Cambridge, MA: MIT Press.

Deibert, Ron, and Rafal Rohozinski. 2010. Cyber Wars. *Index on Censorship* 29 (1):79–90.

De Koning, Petra. 2000. Dutchbat voorzag moordpartij Srebrenica. *NRC Handelsblad*, April 5.

Den Besten, Matthijs L., Loris Gaio, Alessandro Rossi, and Jean-Michel Dalle. 2010. Using Metadata Signals to Support Stigmergy. 2nd International Workshop on Quality in Techno-Social Systems at the Fourth IEEE International Conference on Self-Adaptive and Self-Organizing Systems, Budapest.

Derrida, Jacques. 1996. *Archive Fever: A Freudian Impression*. Trans. Eric Prenowitz. Chicago: University of Chicago Press.

Deuze, Mark. 2007. *Media Work*. Cambridge: Polity.

Dibbell, Julian. 1998. *My Tiny Life: Crime and Passion in a Virtual World*. New York: Henry Holt.

Dodge, Martin. 2000. Mapping the World Wide Web. In *Preferred Placement: Knowledge Politics on the Web*, ed. Richard Rogers, 81–97. Maastricht: Jan van Eyck Editions.

Dodge, Martin, and Rob Kitchin. 2000. *Mapping Cyberspace*. London: Routledge.

Dohmen, Joep. 2007. Opkomst en ondergang van extreemrechtse sites. *NRC Handelsblad*, August 25.

Dougherty, Meghan, Eric Meyer, Christine Madsen, Charles Van den Heuvel, Arthur Thomas, and Sally Wyatt. 2010. Researcher Engagement with Web Archives: State of the Art. London: Joint Information Systems Committee Report (JISC).

Drummond, David. 2010a. A New Approach to China. *The Official Google Blog.* January 12. http://googleblog.blogspot.com/2010/01/new-approach-to-china.html (accessed September 9, 2011).

Drummond, David. 2010b. An Update on China. *The Official Google Blog,* June 28, http://googleblog.blogspot.com/2010/06/update-on-china.html (accessed September 9, 2011).

Dullaart, Constant. 2009. *Readymades.* Utrecht: Impakt.

Dunne, Anthony. 2005. *Hertzian Tales: Electronic Products, Aesthetic Experience, and Critical Design.* Cambridge, MA: MIT Press.

Dutton, William, and Tina Piper. 2010. The Politics of Privacy, Confidentiality, and Ethics: Opening Research Methods. In *World Wide Research: Reshaping the Sciences and Humanities,* ed. William Dutton and Paul Jeffreys, 223–240. Cambridge, MA: MIT Press.

Electronic Frontier Foundation. 2006. FTC Complaint, August 14, http://w2.eff.org/Privacy/AOL/aol_ftc_complaint_final.pdf (accessed March 12, 2011).

Ellis, David, and Ana Vasconcelos. 1999. Ranganathan and the Net: Using Facet Analysis to Search and Organise the World Wide Web. *Aslib Proceedings* 51 (1):3–10.

Elmer, Greg. 2001. Hypertext on the Web: The Beginnings and Ends of Web Path-ology. *Space and Culture* 10:1–14.

Elmer, Greg. 2004. *Profiling Machines.* Cambridge, MA: MIT Press.

Encyclopaedia Britannica. 2006. Fatally Flawed: Refuting the Recent Study on Encyclopedia Accuracy by the Journal *Nature.* Encyclopaedia Britannica, Inc., March, http://corporate.britannica.com/britannica_nature_response.pdf (accessed September 29, 2011).

Enge, Eric. 2007. A Look at Latency in Search Engine Ranking. *Search Engine Watch,* May 30, http://searchenginewatch.com/article/2065359/A-Look-at-Latency-In-Search-Engine-Ranking (accessed June 1, 2011).

Engelberts, Lernert, and Sander Plug. 2008. I Love Alaska. Minimovies series, SubmarineChannel production, in collaboration with VPRO Television., http://www.minimovies.org/documentaires/view/ilovealaska (accessed June 20, 2011).

Engeström, Jyri. 2005. Why Some Social Network Services Work and Others Don't. Or: The Case for Object-Centered Sociality. *Zengestrom.* http://www.zengestrom.com/blog/2005/04/why-some-social-network-services-work-and-others-dont-or-the-case-for-object-centered-sociality.html

Espenschied, Dragan, and Olia Lialina. 2009. *Digital Folklore.* Stuttgart: Merz Academy.

Ess, Charles, and AoIR Ethics Working Committee. 2002. Ethical Decision-Making and Internet Research: Recommendations from the AoIR Ethics Working Committee. Association of Internet Research, http://aoir.org/reports/ethics.pdf (accessed October 18, 2012).

Estep, Erik Sean, and Julia Gelfand. 2003. Weblogs. *Library Hi Tech News* 20 (5): 11–12.

Etling, Bruce, Karina Alexanyan, John Kelly, Robert Faris, John Palfrey, and Urs Gasser. 2010. Public Discourse in the Russian Blogosphere: Mapping RuNet Politics and Mobilization. Berkman Center Research Publication No. 2010–11, http://cyber.law.harvard.edu/sites/cyber.law.harvard .edu/files/Public_Discourse_in_the_Russian_Blogosphere_2010.pdf (accessed September 9, 2011).

Feuz, Martin, Matthew Fuller, and Felix Stalder. 2011. Personal Web Searching in the Age of Semantic Capitalism: Diagnosing the Mechanisms of Personalization. *First Monday* 16 (2).

Foot, Kirsten. 2006. Web Sphere Analysis and Cybercultural Studies. In *Critical Cybercultural Studies*, ed. David Silver and Alexander Massanari, 88–96. New York: New York University Press.

Foot, Kirsten, and Steven Schneider. 2002. Online Action in Campaign 2000: An Exploratory Analysis of the U.S. Political web Sphere. *Journal of Broadcasting and Electronic Media* 46 (2):222–244.

Foot, Kirsten, and Steven Schneider. 2004. *Online Structure for Civic Engagement in the Post-9/11 Web Sphere. Electronic Journal of Communication* 14 (3–4).

Foot, Kirsten, and Steven Schneider. 2006. *Web Campaigning*. Cambridge, MA: MIT Press.

Foot, Kirsten, Steven Schneider, Meghan Dougherty, Michael Xenos, and Elena Larsen. 2003. Analyzing Linking Practices: Candidate Sites in the 2002 US Electoral web. *Journal of Computer-Mediated Communication* 8 (4).

Foot, Kirsten, Barbara Warnick, and Steven Schneider. 2005. Web-Based Memorializing after September 11: Toward a Conceptual Framework. *Journal of Computer-Mediated Communication* 11 (1).

Foucault, Michel. 1998. *The Will to Knowledge*. Vol. 1 of *The History of Sexuality*. London: Penguin.

Franklin, Kevin, and Karen Rodriguez. 2008. The Next Big Thing in Humanities, Arts, and Social Science Computing: Cultural Analysis. *HPCWire*, July 29, http://www.hpcwire.com/hpcwire/ 2008-07-29/the_next_big_thing_in_humanities_arts_and_social_science_computing_cultural _analytics.html (accessed June 20, 2011).

Frost, Martin. 2006. Srebrenica Massacre. Martin Frost's former web site, http://www.martinfrost. ws/htmlfiles/srebrenica_massacre.html (accessed December 16, 2011).

Fuller, Matthew. 2003. *Behind the Blip: Essays on the Culture of Software*. Brooklyn: Autonomedia.

Fuller, Matthew. 2005. *Media Ecologies*. Cambridge, MA: MIT Press.

Galloway, Alexander. 2004. *Protocol: How Control Exists after Decentralization*. Cambridge, MA: MIT Press.

Gandy, Oscar. 1993. *The Panoptic Sort: A Political Economy of Personal Information*. Boulder, CO: Westview Press.

Garrido, Maria, and Alex Halavais. 2003. Mapping Networks of Support for the Zapatista Movement: Applying Social Network Analysis to Study Contemporary Social Movements. In

Cyberactivism: Online Activism in Theory and Practice, ed. Martha McCaughey and Michael Ayers, 165–184. London: Routledge.

Gayo-Avello, Daniel, Panagiotis T. Metaxasy, and Eni Mustafaraj. 2011. Limits of Electoral Predictions Using Twitter. Fifth International AAAI Conference on weblogs and Social Media, Barcelona, July, http://www.aaai.org/ocs/index.php/ICWSM/ICWSM11/paper/view/2862 (accessed October 18, 2012).

Gehl, Robert W. 2010. A Cultural and Political Economy of Web 2.0. PhD disseration, George Mason University, http://digilib.gmu.edu:8080/bitstream/1920/5886/1/gehl_diss_full.pdf.

Geiger, R. Stuart. 2011. The Lives of Bots. In *Critical Point of View: A Wikipedia Reader*, ed. Geert Lovink and Nathaniel Tkacz, 78–93. Amsterdam: Institute of Network Cultures.

Gerlitz, Carolin, and Anne Helmond. 2011. The Like Economy: The Social Web in Transition. Paper presented at the MIT7 Unstable Platforms conference, MIT, Cambridge, MA, May 13–15.

Giles, Jim. 2005. Internet Encyclopedias Go Head to Head. *Nature* 438 (7070):900–1000.

Ginsberg, Jeremy, Matthew H. Mohebbi, Rajan S. Patel, Lynnette Brammer, Mark S. Smolinski, and Larry Brilliant. 2009. Detecting Influenza Epidemics Using Search Engine Query Data. *Nature* 457 (7232):1012–1014.

Ginsburg, Faye D., Lila Abu-Lughod, and Brian Larken. 2002. Introduction. In *Media Worlds: Anthropology on New Terrain*, ed. Faye D. Ginsburg, Lila Abu-Lughod, and Brian Larken, 1–36. Berkeley: University of California Press.

Glanz, James, and John Markoff. 2011. U.S. Underwrites Internet Detour around Censors. *New York Times*, June 12.

Glassel, Aimee. 1998. Was Ranganathan a Yahoo!? *InterNIC News*, March.

Goldsmith, Jack, and Tim Wu. 2006. *Who Controls the Internet? Illusions of a Borderless World*. New York: Oxford.

Google. 2008. Google Timeline. Webpage, http://www.google.com/corporate/timeline/ (accessed February 15, 2012).

Google. 2011a. Google Transparency Report. Webpage, http://www.google.com/transparency report/ (accessed August 25, 2011).

Google. 2011b. Webmaster Guidelines. Webpage, http://support.google.com/webmasters/bin/answer.py?hl=en&answer=35769 (accessed October 19, 2012).

Govcom.org. 1999. *The Rogue and the Rogued: Amongst the web Tacticians*. Movie. Jan van Eyck Design and Media Research Fellowship, Maastricht.

Govcom.org. 2005. *The Places of Issues: The Issuecrawler Back-End Movie*. Movie. In exhibition "Making Things Public: Atmospheres of Democracy," curated by B. Latour and P. Weibel, ZKM, Karlsruhe, Germany.

Govcom.org. 2008. Google and the Politics of Tabs. Movie. Amsterdam: Govcom.org.

Greenberg, Robert D. 2004. *Language and Identity in the Balkans: Serbo-Croatian and Its Disintegration*. Oxford: Oxford University Press.

Grievink, Hendrik-Jan. 2009. Template Culture: Form Follows Format. Flickr photo set, http://www.flickr.com/photos/hendrikjangrievink/sets/72157614340281527/ (accessed March 12, 2011).

Grimmelman, James. 2008/2009. *The Google Dilemma*. New York Law School Law Review 53: 939–950.

Guéret, Christophe. 2010. Nature-Inspired Dissemination of Information in P2P Networks. In *Computational Social Network Analysis*, ed. Ajith Abraham, Aboul Ella Hassanien, and Václav Snášel, 267–290. London: Springer.

Hackett, Stephanie, and Bambang Parmanto. 2005. A Longitudinal Evaluation of Accessibility: Higher Education Web Sites. *Internet Research* 15 (3):281–294.

Hafner, Katie. 2006. Researchers Yearn to Use AOL Logs, but They Hesitate. *New York Times*, August 23.

Halavais, Alexander. 2004. The Isuzu Experiment. *A Thaumaturgical Compendium* blog, August 29. http://alex.halavais.net/the-isuzu-experiment (accessed January 12, 2012).

Halavais, Alexander, and Derek Lackaff. 2008. An Analysis of Topical Coverage of Wikipedia. *Journal of Computer-Mediated Communication* 13 (2):429–440.

Hara, Noriko, Pnina Shachaf, and Khe Foon Hew. 2010. Cross-Cultural Analysis of the Wikipedia Community. *Journal of the American Society for Information Science and Technology* 61 (10):2097–2108.

Hayles, N. Katherine. 2004. Print Is Flat, Code Is Deep: The Importance of Media-Specific Analysis. *Poetics Today* 25 (1):67–90.

Hellsten, Iina, Loet Leydesdorff, and Paul Wouters. 2006. Multiple Presents: How Search Engines Rewrite the Past. *New Media and Society* 8 (6):901–924.

Herring, Susan. 2010. Web Content Analysis: Expanding the Paradigm. In *International Handbook of Internet Research*, ed. Jeremy Hunsinger, Lisbeth Klastrup, and Matthew Allen, 233–249. Dordrecht: Springer.

Higson, Andrew. 1989. The Concept of National Cinema. *Screen* 30 (4):36–47.

Hine, Christine. 2000. *Virtual Ethnography*. London: Sage.

Hine, Christine, ed. 2005. *Virtual Methods: Issues in Social Research on the Internet*. Oxford: Berg.

Hobbs, Robert. 2003. *Mark Lombardi: Global Networks*. New York: Independent Curators International.

Honig, Jan Willem, and Norbert Both. 1996. *Srberenica: Record of a War Crime*. Harmondsworth: Penguin.

Howe, Jeff. 2006. The Rise of Crowdsourcing. *Wired* 14 (6), http://www.wired.com/wired/archive/14.06/crowds.html (accessed September 9, 2011).

Howell, Beryl A. 2006. Proving Web History: How to Use the Internet Archive. *Journal of Internet Law* 9 (8):3–9.

Huber, William, Tara Zepel, and Lev Manovich. 2010. Science and Popular Science magazines, 1872–2007. Blog posting, http://lab.softwarestudies.com/2010/11/science-and-popular-science -magazines.html (accessed June 20, 2011).

Information Warfare Monitor. 2009. *Tracking Ghostnet: Investigating a Cyberespinionage Network*. Ottawa: SecDev Group.

International Commission on Missing Persons. 2011. *Locating and Identifying Missing Persons: A Guide for Families in Bosnia and Herzegovina*. Sarajevo: ICMP.

International Telecommunication Union. 2011. *Measuring the Information Society*. Geneva: ITU.

Internet Archive. 2008. Frequently Asked Questions, The Wayback Machine, http://www.archive .org/about/faqs.php#202 (accessed June 12, 2008).

Introna, Lucas, and Helen Nissenbaum. 2000. Shaping the Web: Why the Politics of Search Engines Matters. *Information Society* 16 (3):1–17.

Iran Media Program. 2010. Balatarin: A Battleground for Defining Freedom of Expression. Blog entry. Annenberg School for Communication, University of Pennsylvania, http://iranmediare search.org/en/blog/13/10/11/23/201 (accessed September 9, 2011).

Jeanneney, Jean-Noel. 2007. *Google and the Myth of Universal Knowledge: A View from Europe*. Chicago: University of Chicago Press.

Jenkins, Henry. 2006. *Convergence Culture: Where Old and New Media Collide*. New York: NYU Press.

Jensen, Jens F. 1998. "Interactivity": Tracking a New Concept in Media and Communication Studies. *Nordicom Review* 19 (1):185–204.

Jones, Rosie, Ravi Kumar, Bo Pang, and Andrew Tomkins. 2007. "I Know What You Did Last Summer"—Query Logs and User Privacy. Proceedings of the sixteenth ACM Conference on Information and Knowledge Management (CIKM '07), 909–914. New York: ACM.

Jones, Steve. 1999. Studying the Net: Intricacies and Issues. In *Doing Internet Research: Critical Issues and Methods for Examining the Net*, ed. Steve Jones, 1–28. London: Sage.

Journal du Net. 2007. France: Google frôle les 90% de parts de marché. http://www.journaldunet .com/ebusiness/rubriques/chiffre-cle-hebdo/070716-chiffres-cles/5.shtml (accessed September 10, 2007).

Kahle, Brewster. 1997. Preserving the Internet. *Scientific American* 276 (3):82–83.

Kahn, Richard, and Douglas Kellner. 2004. Oppositional Politics and the Internet: A Critical/Reconstructive Approach. Unpublished ms., http://www.gseis.ucla.edu/faculty/kellner/essays/oppositionalpoliticstechnology.pdf (accessed September 10, 2007).

Keck, Margaret E., and Kathryn Sikkink. 1998. *Activists beyond Borders: Advocacy Networks in International Politics*. Ithaca, NY: Cornell University Press.

Keen, Andrew. 2007. *The Cult of the Amateur: How Today's Internet Is Killing Our Culture*. London: Nicholas Brealey.

Kehoe, Colleen, James E. Pitkow, Katherine M. Sutton, G. Aggarwal, and J. Rogers. 1999. GVU's Tenth World Wide Web User Survey. Graphics Visualization and Usability Center, College of Computing, Georgia Institute of Technology, Atlanta.

Kelly, John, and Bruce Etling. 2008. Mapping Iran's Online Public: Politics and Culture in the Persian Blogosphere. Research Publication No. 2008–01, Berkman Center, Harvard University, http://cyber.law.harvard.edu/sites/cyber.law.harvard.edu/files/Kelly&Etling_Mapping_Irans_Online_Public_2008.pdf (accessed September 9, 2011).

Khiabany, Gholam, and Annabelle Sreberny. 2007. The Politics of/in Blogging in Iran. *Comparative Studies of South Asia, Africa and the Middle East* 27 (3):563–579.

Kimpton, Michele, and Jeff Ubois. 2006. Year-by-Year: From an Archive of the Internet to an Archive on the Internet. In *Web Archiving*, ed. Julian Masanès, 201–212. Berlin: Springer.

Kincaid, Jason. 2010. EdgeRank: The Secret Sauce That Makes Facebook's News Feed Tick. *TechCrunch*, April 22, http://techcrunch.com/2010/04/22/facebook-edgerank/ (accessed February 24, 2012).

Kittur, Aniket, and Robert E. Kraut. 2008. Harnessing the Wisdom of Crowds in Wikipedia: Quality through Coordination. Proceedings of the 2008 ACM Conference on Computer Supported Cooperative Work (CSCW '08). New York: ACM.

Kittur, Aniket, Bongwon Suh, Bryan A. Pendleton, and Ed H. Chi. 2007. He Says, She Says: Conflict and Coordination in Wikipedia. *Proceedings of the SIGCHI Conference on Human Factors in Computing Systems* (CHI 07), 453–462. New York: ACM Press.

Knorr Cetina, Karin. 1999. *Epistemic Cultures*. Cambridge, MA: Harvard University Press.

Knorr Cetina, Karin. 2001. Objectual Practice. In *The Practice Turn in Contemporary Theory*, ed. Theodor R. Schatzki, Karin Knorr Cetina, and Eike von Savigny, 175–188. London: Routledge.

Koerbin, Paul. 2004. The Pandora Digital Archiving System (PANDAS) and Managing Web Archiving in Australia: A Case Study. Paper presented at the 4th International Web Archiving Workshop, Bath (UK), September 16.

Kolbitsch, Josef, and Hermann Maurer. 2006. The Transformation of the Web: How Emerging Communities Shape the Information we Consume. *Journal of Universal Computer Science* 12 (2):187–213.

Krebs, Valdis. 2002. Mapping Networks of Terrorist Cells. *Connections* 24 (3):43–52.

Krippendorff, Klaus. 2004. *Content Analysis: An Introduction to Its Methodology.* Thousand Oaks, CA: Sage.

Krippendorff, Klaus, and Mary Angela Bock, eds. 2008. *The Content Analysis Reader.* Thousand Oaks, CA: Sage.

Krug, Steve. 2000. *Don't Make Me Think! A Common Sense Approach to Web Usability.* Indianapolis: New Riders.

Kuhn, Thomas. 1962. *The Structure of Scientific Revolutions.* Chicago: University of Chicago Press.

Landow, George. 1994. *Hyper/Text/Theory.* Baltimore: Johns Hopkins University Press.

Lanier, Jaron. 2010. *You Are Not a Gadget: A Manifesto.* New York: Knopf.

Lasfargues, France, Clément Oury, and Bert Wendland. 2008. Legal Deposit of the French Web: Harvesting Strategies for a National Domain. Paper presented at IWAW'08, September 18–19, Aarhus, Denmark, http://iwaw.europarchive.org/08/IWAW2008-Lasfargues.pdf (accessed September 9, 2011).

Latour, Bruno. 2005. *Reassembling the Social: An Introduction to Actor-Network Theory.* Oxford: OUP.

Latour, Bruno. 2010. Networks, Societies, Spheres: Reflections of an Actor-Network Theorist. Keynote speech for the International Seminar on Network Theory: Network Multidimensionality in the Digital Age. Annenberg School for Communication and Journalism, USC, Los Angeles.

Latour, Bruno, and Steve Woolgar. 1986. *Laboratory Life.* Princeton, NJ: Princeton University Press.

Lawrence, Steve, and C. Lee Giles. 1998. Searching the World Wide Web. *Science* 280 (5360):98.

Lawrence, Steve, and C. Lee Giles. 1999. Accessibility of Information on the Web. *Nature* 400 (6740):107–109.

Lazer, David, Alex Pentland, Lada Adamic, Sinan Aral, Albert-László Barabási, Devon Brewer, Nicholas Christakis, et al. 2009. Computational Social Science. *Science* 323 (5915):721–723.

Lenhart, Amanda, and Mary Madden. 2007. Social Networking Websites and Teens. Pew Internet Project Data Memo. Pew Internet and American Life Project.

Leskovec, Jure, Lars Backstrom, and Jon Kleinberg. 2009. Meme-Tracking and the Dynamics of the News Cycle. In *KDD '09 Proceedings of the 15th ACM SIGKDD International Conference on Knowledge Discovery and Data Mining,* 497–505. New York: ACM.

Levy, Steven. 2011. TED 2011: The "Panda" That Hates Farms: A Q&A with Google's Top Search Engineers. *Wired,* March 3, http://www.wired.com/business/2011/03/the-panda-that-hates-farms/all/1 (accessed October 17, 2012).

Lewis, Kevin, Jason Kaufman, Marco Gonzalez, Andreas Wimmer, and Nicholas Christakis. 2008. Tastes, Ties, and Time: A New Social Network Dataset Using Facebook.com. *Social Networks* 30 (4):330–342.

Lewis, Paul. 2007. Wilfing on the Web, the New British Pastime. *Guardian*, April 10, 5.

Lialina, Olia. 2005. The Vernacular Web. Paper presented at "A Decade of Web Design" conference, Amsterdam, January, http://art.teleportacia.org/observation/vernacular/ (accessed September 10, 2007).

Lih, Andrew. 2004. Wikipedia as Participatory Journalism: Reliable Sources? Metrics for Evaluating Collaborative Media as a News Resource. Paper for the 5th International Symposium on Online Journalism, University of Texas at Austin, April 16–17.

Lippmann, Walter. 1927. *The Phantom Public*. New York: MacMillan.

Livingstone, Randall M. 2010. Let's Leave the Bias to the Mainstream Media: A Wikipedia Community Fighting for Information Neutrality. *M/C Journal* 13 (6), http://journal.media-culture.org.au/index.php/mcjournal/article/viewArticle/315 (accessed January 12, 2012).

Lyman, Peter, and Brewster Kahle. 1998. Archiving Digital Cultural Artifacts: Organizing an Agenda for Action. *D-Lib Magazine*, July/August.

Lynch, Michael. 1997. A Sociology of Knowledge Machine. *Ethnographic Studies* 2:16–38.

Lyon, David. 2007. *Surveillance Studies*. London: Polity.

Magnus, P. D. 2008. Early Response to False Claims in Wikipedia. *First Monday* 13 (9).

Manovich, Lev. 2007. Cultural Analytics. Unpublished ms., http://www.manovich.net/cultural_analytics.pdf (accessed January 28, 2009).

Manovich, Lev. 2008. Software Takes Command. Unpublished ms., http://www.manovich.net/ (accessed April 10, 2009).

Manovich, Lev. 2009. How to Follow Global Digital Cultures: Cultural Analytics for Beginners. In *Deep Search: The Politics of Search beyond Google*, ed. Konrad Becker and Felix Stalder, 198–212. Edison, NJ: Transaction.

Marres, Noortje. 2000. Somewhere You've Got to Draw the Line: De politiek van selectie op het web. MSc thesis, University of Amsterdam.

Marres, Noortje. 2005. No Issue, No Public: Democratic Deficits after the Displacement of Politics. PhD dissertation, University of Amsterdam.

Marres, Noortje. 2006. Net-Work Is Format Work: Issue Networks and the Sites of Civil Society Politics. In *Reformatting Politics: Networked Communications and Global Civil Society*, ed. Jodi Dean, John Asherson, and Geert Lovink, 3–17. London: Routledge.

Marres, Noortje. 2009. Web-Based Tools for Environmental Social Science. Paper presented at MSCs, School of Geography and the environment, University of Oxford, November 23.

Marres, Noortje. 2011. Re-distributing Methods: Digital Social Research as Participatory Research. *Sociological Review: Goldsmiths Research Online*, http://eprints.gold.ac.uk/6086/ (accessed December 29, 2011).

Marres, Noortje, and Richard Rogers. 1999. To Trace or to Rub: Screening the Web Navigation Debate. *Mediamatic* 9/10:117–120.

Marres, Noortje, and Richard Rogers. 2000. Depluralising the Web, Repluralising Public Debate: The GM Food Debate on the Web. In *Preferred Placement*, ed. Richard Rogers, 113–135. Maastricht: Jan van Eyck Editions.

Marres, Noortje, and Richard Rogers. 2008. Subsuming the Ground: How Local Realities of the Ferghana Valley, Narmada Dams and BTC Pipeline Are Put to Use on the Web. *Economy and Society* 37 (2):251–281.

Marvin, Carolyn. 2004. Peaceable Kingdoms and New Information Technologies: Prospects for the Nation-State. In *Technological Visions: The Hopes and Fears That Shape New Technologies*, ed. Marita Sturken, Douglas Thomas, and Sandra J. Ball-Rokeach, 240–254. Philadelphia: Temple University Press.

Masanès, Julian. 2006. Web Archiving: Issues and Methods. In *Web Archiving*, ed. Julian Masanès, 1–53. Berlin: Springer.

Massa, Paolo, and Federico Scrinzi. 2011. Exploring linguistic points of view of Wikipedia. Proceedings of the 7th International Symposium on Wikis and Open Collaboration (WikiSym '11), ACM, New York.

McLuhan, Marshall. 1951. *The Mechanical Bride*. New York: Vanguard.

McLuhan, Marshall. 1964. *Understanding Media: The Extensions of Man*. New York: McGraw Hill.

McMillan, Sally J. 2000. The Microscope and the Moving Target: The Challenges of Applying Content Analysis to the World Wide Web. *Journalism and Mass Communication Quarterly* 77 (1):80–98.

Metahaven. 2008. *Multipolar Search—EXODVS*. Published on the occasion of Pancevo Republic! 13th Biennial of Art. Pancevo, Serbia.

Michel, Jean-Baptiste, Yuan Kui Shen, Aviva Presser Aiden, Adrian Veres, Matthew K. Gray, Google Books Team, Joseph P. Pickett, Dale Hoiberg, Dan Clancy, Peter Norvig, Jon Orwant, Steven Pinker, Martin A. Nowak, and Erez Lieberman Aiden. 2011. Quantitative Analysis of Culture Using Millions of Digitized Books. *Science* 331 (6014):176–182.

Miller, Claire C. 2011. Seeking to Weed Out Drivel, Google Adjusts Search Engine. *New York Times*, February 25, A1.

Miller, Daniel, and Don Slater. 2000. *The Internet: An Ethnographic Approach*. Oxford: Berg.

Mills, C. Wright. 1971. *The Sociological Imagination*. Harmondsworth: Penguin.

Moulier-Boutang, Yann. 2008. Worker Bee Economy. Paper presented at the Society of the Query Conference, Institute of Network Cultures, Amsterdam.

Mueller, Milton L. 2002. *Ruling the Root: Internet Governance and the Taming of Cyberspace*. Cambridge, MA: MIT Press.

Murdoch, Steven, and Ross Anderson. 2008. Tools and Technology of Internet Filtering. In *Access Denied: The Practice and Policy of Global Internet Filtering*, ed. Ron Deibert, John Palfrey, Rafal Rohozinski, and Jonathan Zittrain. Cambridge, MA: MIT Press.

MVF Global. 2010. Online Marketing in the Top 50 Internet Economies: Lead Generation and Internet Marketing in Iran. London, http://www.mvfglobal.com/iran (accessed October 20, 2011).

National Science Board. 2005. *Long-Lived Digital Data Collections: Enabling Research and Education in the 21st Century*. Washington, DC: National Science Foundation.

Nature. 2005. Supplementary Information to Accompany Nature News Article "Internet Encyclopaedias Go Head to Head." *Nature* 438: 900–901, http://www.nature.com/nature/journal/v438/n7070/extref/438900a-s1.doc (accessed February 27, 2012).

Neff, Jeff. 2011. Will Social Media Replace Surveys as a Research Tool? *Advertising Age* 21 (March), http://adage.com/article/news/p-g-surveys-fade-consumers-reach-brands-social-media/149509/ (accessed May 24, 2011).

Nelson, Theodor Holm. 1965. Complex Information Processing: A File Structure for the Complex, the Changing and the Indeterminate. *ACM/CSC-ER Proceedings of the 1965 20th National Conference*, 84–100. New York: ACM Press.

Nelson, Theodor Holm. 1999. Xanalogical Structure, Needed Now More than Ever: Parallel Documents, Deep Links to Content, Deep Versioning, and Deep Re-use. *ACM Computing Surveys* 31 (4).

Net Applications. 2011. Search Engine Market Share: Iran, Islamic Republic of. https://marketshare.hitslink.com/search-engine-market-share.aspx?qprid=4&qpaf=-000%09101%09IR%0D&qptimeframe=Y (accessed October 20, 2011).

NetBina. 2010. Online Marketing in Iran. Tehran, http://new.netbina.com/resources/2/docs/Online_marketing_in_Iran_2010.pdf (accessed October 20, 2011).

Nicholas, David, Paul Huntington, and Anthony Watkinson. 2005. Scholarly Journal Usage: The Results of Deep Log Analysis. *Journal of Documentation* 61 (2):248–280.

Niederer, Sabine, and José van Dijck. 2010. Wisdom of the Crowd or Technicity of Content? Wikipedia as Socio-technical System. *New Media and Society* 12 (8):1368–1387.

NIOD. 2002. *Srebrenica. Een veilig gebied. Reconstructie achtergronden en analyses van de val van een Safe Area*. Amsterdam: NIOD Instituut voor Oorlogs-, Holocaust- en Genocidestudies.

Noman, Helmi. 2008. Tunisian Journalist Sues Government Agency for Blocking Facebook, Claims Damage for the Use of 404 Error Message Instead of 403. Open Net Initiative, September 12, http://opennet.net/node/950 (accessed September 9, 2011).

Norman, Donald. 2004. The Truth about Google's So-called "Simplicity." Donald Norman's jnd website, http://www.jnd.org/dn.mss/the_truth_about.html (accessed December 22, 2008).

November, Valerie, Eduardo Camacho-Hubner, and Bruno Latour. 2010. Entering a Risky Territory: Space in the Age of Digital Navigation. *Environment and Planning D: Society and Space* 28 (4):581–599.

Nyirubugara, Olivier. 2011. "Everything about the Past": Wikipedia and History Education. Paper presented at MiT7, Cambridge, MA, May 13–15, http://web.mit.edu/comm-forum/mit7/papers/O_Nyirubugara_Wikipedia%20%20History%20Class.pdf (accessed October 12, 2012).

Open Net Initiative. 2005. Internet Filtering in Iran in 2004–2005: A Country Study. University of Toronto, http://opennet.net/studies/iran (accessed September 9, 2011).

Open Net Initiative. 2009. Internet Filtering in Iran, 2009. University of Toronto, http://opennet.net/sites/opennet.net/files/ONI_Iran_2009.pdf (accessed September 9, 2011).

PADI. N.d. Legal Deposit. Preserving Access to Digital Information initiative, National Library of Australia, https://www.nla.gov.au/padi/topics/67.html (accessed September 9, 2011).

Panciera, Katherine, Aaron Halfaker, and Loren Terveen. 2009. Wikipedians Are Born, Not Made: A Study of Power Editors on Wikipedia. Proceedings of the International Conference on Supporting Group Work (Group '09), ACM, New York.

Pariser, Eli. 2011. *The Filter Bubble*. New York: Penguin.

Park, Han Woo, and Mike Thelwall. 2003. Hyperlink Analyses of the World Wide Web: A Review. *Journal of Computer-Mediated Communication* 8 (4).

Park, Han Woo, and Mike Thelwall. 2005. The Network Approach to Web Hyperlink Research and Its Utility for Science Communication. In *Virtual Methods: Issues in Social Research on the Internet*, ed. Christine Hine, 171–181. Oxford: Berg.

Pasquinelli, Matteo. 2009. Google's PageRank Algorithm: A Diagram of Cognitive Capitalism and the Rentier of the Common Intellect. In *Deep Search: The Politics of Search Engines beyond Google*, ed. Konrad Becker and Felix Stalder, 152–162. Edison, NJ: Transaction.

Pass, Greg, Abdur Chowdhury, and Cayley Torgeson. 2006. A Picture of Search. In *InfoScale '06*. New York: ACM.

Pfeil, Ulrike, Panayiotis Zaphiris, and Chee Siang Ang. 2006. Cultural Differences in Collaborative Authoring of Wikipedia. *Journal of Computer-Mediated Communication* 12 (1): 88–113.

Pinsent, Ed, Richard Davis, Kevin Ashley, Brian Kelly, Marieke Guy, and Jordan Hatcher. 2008. *PoWR: The Preservation of Web Resources Handbook*. London: Joint Information Systems Committee (JISC).

Poblete, Barbara, Myra Spiliopoulou, and Ricardo Baeza-Yates. 2008. Website Privacy Preservation for Query Log Publishing. In *Privacy, Security and Trust in KDD*, ed. Francesco Bonchi, Elana Ferrari, Malin Bradley, and Yücel Saygin, 80–96. Lecture Notes in Computer Science. Springer.

Poster, Mark. 1991. *The Mode of Information*. Chicago: University of Chicago Press.

Powezek, Derek. 2006. What Would Google Do? *Vitamin*, May 14, http://web.archive.org/web/20080221164325/http://www.thinkvitamin.com/features/design/what-would-google-do (accessed October 19, 2012).

Prensky, Marc. 2001. Digital Natives, Digital Immigrants. *On the Horizon* 9 (5): 1–6.

Price, Derek J. de Solla. 1963. *Little Science, Big Science*. New York: Columbia University Press.

Quenqua, Douglas. 2009. Blogs Falling in an Empty Forest. *New York Times*, June 5.

Quick, Bill. 2002. I Propose a Name. *Daily Pundit*, January 1, http://www.dailypundit.com/backupcreateblogarchiveposts/backup000229.php (accessed October 12, 2012).

Read, Brock. 2006. Can Wikipedia Ever Make the Grade? *Chronicle of Higher Education* 53 (10):A31.

Reagle, Joseph M. Jr. 2010. *Good Faith Collaboration: The Culture of Wikipedia*. Cambridge, MA: MIT Press.

Rector, Lucy Holman. 2008. Comparison of Wikipedia and Other Encyclopedias for Accuracy, Breadth, and Depth in Historical Articles. *RSR. Reference Services Review* 36 (1):7–22.

Rennie, David. 2002. UN Weapons Inspector Is Leader of S&M Sex Ring. *Daily Telegraph*, November 30.

Rheingold, Howard. 1991. *Virtual Reality: Exploring the Brave New Technologies*. New York: Summit.

Rheingold, Howard. 1993. *The Virtual Community: Homesteading on the Electronic Frontier*. Reading, MA: Addison-Wesley.

Rheingold, Howard, ed. 1994. *The Millennium Whole Earth Catalog*. San Francisco: Harper.

Rheingold, Howard. 2002. *Smart Mobs*. Cambridge, MA: Perseus.

Rhoads, Christopher, and Farnaz Fassihi. 2011. Iran Vows to Unplug Internet. *Wall Street Journal*, May 28.

Rhodes, John S. 2002. In the Trenches with a Weblog Pioneer: An Interview with the Force behind Eatonweb, Brigitte F. Eaton. In *We've Got Blog: How Weblogs Are Changing Our Culture*, ed. John Rodzvilla, 99–103. Cambridge, MA: Perseus.

Riles, Annelise. 2001. *The Network Inside Out*. Ann Arbor: University of Michigan Press.

Roberts, Hal, Ethan Zuckerman, and John Palfrey. 2011. 2011 Circumvention Tool Evaluation. Berkman Center for Internet and Society, Research Publication no. 2011-08, Harvard University, August.

Rogers, David. 2007. Documents on the Internet as Prior Art. *Journal of Intellectual Property Law and Practice* 2 (6):354–355.

Rogers, Richard, ed. 2000. *Preferred Placement: Knowledge Politics on the Web*. Maastricht: Jan van Eyck Editions.

Rogers, Richard. 2002. Operating Issue Networks on the Web. *Science as Culture* 11 (2):191–214.

Rogers, Richard. 2003. The Viagra Files: The Web as Anticipatory Medium. *Prometheus* 21 (2):195–212.

Rogers, Richard. 2004. *Information Politics on the Web*. Cambridge, MA: MIT Press.

Rogers, Richard. 2007. Electronic Media Policy Field: Metrics for Actor Impact and Resonance. Report to the Ford Foundation, July 19.

Rogers, Richard. 2008. Consumer Technology after Surveillance Theory. In *Mind the Screen: Media Concepts According to Thomas Elsaesser*, ed. Jaap Kooijman, Patricia Pisters, and Wanda Strauven, 288–296. Amsterdam: Amsterdam University Press.

Rogers, Richard. 2009. The Internet Treats Censorship as a Malfunction and Routes around It? A New Media Approach to the Study of State Internet Censorship. In *The Spam Book: On Viruses, Porn, and Other Anomalies from the Dark Side of Digital Culture*, ed. Jussi Parikka and Tony Sampson, 229–247. Cresskill, NJ: Hampton Press.

Rogers, Richard, Fieke Jansen, Michael Stevenson, and Esther Weltevrede. 2009. Mapping Democracy. *Global Informaton Society Watch 2009*, 47–57. Association for Progressive Communications and Hivos.

Rogers, Richard, and Noortje Marres. 2002. French Scandals on the Web, and on the Streets: A Small Experiment in Stretching the Limits of Reported Reality. *Asian Journal of Social Science* 30 (2):339–353.

Ronfeldt, David, and John Arquilla. 2001. Networks, Netwars and the Fight for the Future. *First Monday* 6 (10).

Rosenzweig, Roy. 2006. Can History Be Open Source? Wikipedia and the Future of the Past. *Journal of American History* 93 (1):117–146.

Roth, Daniel. 2009. The Answer Factory: Demand Media and the Fast, Disposable, and Profitable as Hell Media Model. *Wired* 17 (11).

Royal, Cindy, and Deepina Kapila. 2008. What's on Wikipedia, and What's Not . . . ?: Assessing Completeness of Information. *Social Science Computer Review* 27:138–148.

Rucht, Dieter. 1999. The Transnationalization of Social Movements: Trends, Causes and Problems. In *Social Movements in a Globalizing World*, ed. Donatella della Porta, Hanspeter Kriesil, and Dieter Rucht, 206–222. New York: Macmillan.

Rumsey, Mary. 2002. Runaway Train: Problems of Permanence, Accessibility, and Stability in the Use of Web Sources in Law Review Citations. *Law Library Journal* 94 (1):27–39.

Ryan, Terry, Richard H. G. Field, and Lorne Olfman. 2003. The Evolution of U.S. State Government Home Pages from 1997 to 2002. *International Journal of Human-Computer Studies* 59 (4): 403–430.

Sack, Warren. 2002. What Does a Very Large-Scale Conversation Look Like? *Leonardo: Journal of Electronic Art and Culture* 35 (4):417–426.

Salkever, Alex. 2003. Google Here, There, and Everywhere. *BusinessWeek Online*, December 16, http://www.businessweek.com/technology/content/dec2003/tc20031216_9018_tc047.htm (accessed December 22, 2008).

Schmidt, Eric. 2009. Prosperity or Peril? The Next Phase of Globalization. Lecture at the Princeton Colloquium on Public and International Affairs, April 18, http://www.youtube.com/watch?v=9nXmDxf7D_g (accessed September 9, 2011).

Schneider, Steve, and Kirsten Foot. 2002. Online Structure for Political Action: Exploring Presidential Web Sites from the 2000 American Election. *Javnost (Ljubljana)* 9 (2):43–60.

Schneider, Steven M., Kirsten Foot, Michele Kimpton, and Gina Jones. 2003. Building Thematic Web Collections: Challenges and Experiences from the September 11 Web Archive and the Election 2002 Web Archive. 3rd ECDL Workshop on Web Archives, Trondheim, Norway, August 21, 2003.

Schneider, Steve, and Kirsten Foot. 2004. The Web as an Object of Study. *New Media and Society* 6 (1):114–122.

Schneider, Steve, and Kirsten Foot. 2005. Web Sphere Analysis: An Approach to Studying Online Action. In *Virtual Methods: Issues in Social Research on the Internet*, ed. Christine Hine, 157–170. Oxford: Berg Publishers.

Schneier, Bruce. 2007. Why "Anonymous" Data Sometimes Isn't. *Wired*, December 13, http://www.wired.com/politics/security/commentary/securitymatters/2007/12/securitymatters_1213.

Segal, David. 2011. The Dirty Little Secrets of Search. *New York Times*, February 12.

Seigenthaler, John. 2005. A False Wikipedia "Biography." *USA Today*, November 29.

Severson, Kim. 2009. Butterballs or Cheese Balls, an Online Barometer. *New York Times*, November 25.

Shaviro, Steven. 2008. Money for Nothing: Virtual Worlds and Virtual Economies. In *Virtual Worlds*, ed. Mary Ipe, 53–67. Hyderabad: Icfai University Press.

Sherman, Chris. 2004. Yahoo! Birth of a New Machine. *Search Engine Watch*, February 18, http://searchenginewatch.com/article/2066311/Yahoo-Birth-of-a-New-Machine (accessed October 18, 2012).

Shields, Rob. 2003. *The Virtual*. London: Routledge.

Shirky, Clay. 2003. People on Page: YASNS . . . Blog posting, *Corante's Many-to-Many*, http://many.corante.com/archives/2003/05/12/people_on_page_yasns.php (accessed October 18, 2012).

Shirky, Clay. 2005. Ontology Is Overrated: Categories, Links, and Tags. *The Writings of Clay Shirky*, http://www.shirky.com/writings/ontology_overrated.html (accessed January 28, 2009).

Shirky, Clay. 2008. *Here Comes Everybody*. New York: Penguin.

Silvestri, Fabrizio. 2010. Mining Query Logs: Turning Search Usage Data into Knowledge. *Foundations and Trends in Information Retrieval* 4 (1–2):1–174.

Slee, Mark. 2009. Opening More Control for Everyone. *The Facebook Blog*, March 16, https://blog.facebook.com/blog.php?post=60186587130 (accessed February 21, 2012).

Smith Magazine. 2006. User 711391. *Smith Magazine*, August 10, http://www.smithmag.net/2006/08/10/user-711391/ (accessed February 25, 2011).

Somboonviwat, Kulwadee, Takayuki Tamura, and Masaru Kitsuregawa. 2006. Finding Thai Web Pages in Foreign Web Spaces. 22nd International Conference on Data Engineering Workshops, Atlanta, GA.

Sørum, Hanne, Rony Medaglia, and Kim Normann Andersen. 2009. Assessment of Website Quality: Scandinavian Web Awards Right on Track? In *Electronic Government*. Heidelberg: Springer Berlin.

Spigel, Lynn. 1992. *Make Room for TV: Television and the Family Ideal in Post-war America*. Chicago: University of Chicago Press.

Spink, Amanda, and Bernard J. Jansen. 2004. *Web Search: Public Searching on the Web*. Dordrecht: Kluwer.

Spool, Jarod. 2006. Homepage Googlization. *User Interface Engineering*, April 5, http://www.uie.com/brainsparks/2006/04/05/home-page-googlization/ (accessed December 22, 2008).

Stabile, Carol. 1995. Resistance, Recuperation and Reflexivity: The Limits of a Paradigm. *Critical Studies in Mass Communication* 12:403–422.

Sterling, Bruce. 2010. Atemporality for the Creative Artist. *Wired*. February 25, http://www.wired.com/beyond_the_beyond/2010/02/atemporality-for-the-creative-artist/ (accessed April 27, 2011).

Stevenson, Michael. 2009. Archived Publics? On Methods for Reconstructing Context with the Internet Archive. Paper presented at Changing Cultures: Cultures of Change, Barcelona, December 10–12.

Stone, Allucquère Rosanne. 1995. *The War of Desire and Technology at the Close of the Mechanical Age*. Cambridge, MA: MIT Press.

Stvilia, Besiki, Abdullah Al-Faraj, and Yong Jeong Yi. 2009. Issues of Cross-Contextual Information Quality Evaluation: The Case of Arabic, English, and Korean Wikipedias. *Library and Information Science Research* 31 (4):232–239.

Stvilia, Besiki, Michael B. Twidale, Linda C. Smith, and Les Gasser. 2008. Information Quality Work Organization in Wikipedia. *Journal of the American Society for Information Science and Technology* 59 (6):983–1001.

Sullivan, Danny. 2007. Google Ramps Up Personal Search. *Search Engine Land*, February 2, http://searchengineland.com/google-ramps-up-personalized-search-10430 (accessed December 22, 2008).

Sullivan, Danny. 2008. Anonymizing Google's Server Log Data — How's It Going? *Search Engine Land*, October 10, http://searchengineland.com/anonymizing-googles-server-log-data-hows-it-going-15036 (accessed March 12, 2011).

sumoto.iki. 2007. web2DiZZaster: Screenshots of the Ten Emblematic Web2.0 Sites. http://www.lrntrlln.org/web2dizzaster/ (accessed March 12, 2011).

Sunden, Jenny. 2003. *Material Virtualities: Approaching Online Textual Embodiment*. New York: Peter Lang.

Sunstein, Cass. 2001. *Republic.com*. Princeton: Princeton University Press.

Sunstein, Cass. 2006. *Infotopia: How Many Minds Produce Knowledge*. New York: Oxford University Press.

Swartz, Aaron. 2006. Who Writes Wikipedia? Blog post, *Raw Thoughts*, September 4, http://www.aaronsw.com/weblog/whowriteswikipedia (accessed October 18, 2012).

Taksa, Isak, Amanda Spink, and Bernard J. Jansen. 2008. Web Log Analysis: Diversity of Research Methodologies. In *Handbook of Research on Web Log Analysis*, ed. Bernard J. Jansen, Amanda Spink, and Isak Taksa, 506–522. Hershey, Pennsylvania: IGI Global.

Tatum, Clifford. 2005. Deconstructing Google Bombs: A Breach of Symbolic Power or Just a Goofy Prank? *First Monday* 10 (3).

Technorati. 2011. Blog Quality Guidelines. *Technorati*, http://technorati.com/blog-quality-guidelines-faq (accessed September 9, 2011).

Thelwall, Mike. 2004. *Link Analysis: An Information Science Approach*. San Diego: Academic Press.

Thelwall, Mike, and Laura Hasler. 2007. Blog Search Engines. *Online Information Review* 31 (4):467–479.

Thelwall, Mike, Laura Vaughan, and Lennart Björneborn. 2005. Webometrics. In *Annual Review of Information Science and Technology. 39*, ed. Blaise Cronin, 81–135. Medford, NJ: Information Today.

Thelwall, Mike, and Liwen Vaughan. 2004. A Fair History of the Web? Examining Country Balance in the Internet Archive. *Library and Information Science Research* 26 (2):162–176.

Thompson, Clive. 2006. Google's China Problem (and China's Google Problem). *New York Times*, April 23.

Time. 1943. Who Listens to What. *Time* 41 (1):4.

Toma, Kevin. 2008. Elfriendo. *Mister Motley* 18:66–67.

Torrence, Samantha A. 2011. Freelance Writing Jobs in Decline after Google Algorithm Change. *Digital Journal*, May 6, http://www.digitaljournal.com/article/306410 (accessed October 17, 2012).

Tumasjan, Andranik, Timm O. Sprenger, Philipp G. Sandner, and Isabell M. Welpe. 2010. Predicting Elections with Twitter: What 140 Characters Reveal about Political Sentiment. *Proceedings of the International AAAI Conference on weblogs and Social Media*. North America, May, http://www.aaai.org/ocs/index.php/ICWSM/ICWSM10/paper/view/1441/1852 (accessed May 24, 2011).

Turkle, Sherry. 1995. *Life on the Screen: Identity in the Age of the Internet*. New York: Simon and Schuster.

Turner, Fred. 2006. *From Counterculture to Cyberculture*. Chicago: University of Chicago Press.

Turow, Joseph. 2006. *Niche Envy*. Cambridge, MA: MIT Press.

Ubois, Jeff. 2002. The Oakland Archive Policy: Recommendations for Managing Removal Requests and Preserving Archival Integrity. School of Information Management and Systems, U.C. Berkeley, December 13–14, http://www2.sims.berkeley.edu/research/conferences/aps/removal-policy.html (accessed February 10, 2012).

Udell, Jon. 2005a. Heavy Metal Umlaut. Movie, http://jonudell.net/udell/gems/umlaut/umlaut.html (accessed April 12, 2011).

Udell, Jon. 2005b. Heavy Metal Umlaut: The Making of the Movie. *O'Reilly*, http://www.oreillynet.com/pub/a/network/2005/02/07/primetime.html (accessed April 12, 2011).

U.S. Air Force. 2009. Our Mission. U.S. Air Force Website, http://www.af.mil/main/welcome.asp (accessed January 12, 2011).

Vaidhyanathan, Siva. 2007. Where Is This Book Going? *The Googlization of Everything Blog*, September 25, http://www.googlizationofeverything.com/2007/09/where_is_this_book_going.php (accessed December 22, 2008).

Vaidhyanathan, Siva. 2011. *The Googlization of Everything*. Berkeley: University of California Press.

Van Couvering, Elizabeth. 2004. New Media? The Political Economy of Internet Search Engines. Paper presented at the Annual Conference of the International Association of Media and Communications Researchers, Porto Alegre, Brazil, July 25–30.

Van Couvering, Elizabeth. 2007. Is Relevance Relevant? Market, Science, and War: Discourses of Search Engine Quality. *Journal of Computer-Mediated Communication*, 12 (3).

Van der Veen, Harm. 2006. *Het Drama van Srebrenica*. Hooghalen: Herinneringscentrum Kamp Westerbork.

Van der Velden, Daniel. 2004. *Meta Haven: Sealand Identity Project 2003–2004*. Maastricht: Jan van Eyck Academy.

Van der Vlies, Laura. 2008. Googlization: A New Form of Mass Media Critique. MA thesis, Media Studies, University of Amsterdam.

Van Dijck, José. 2009. Users Like You? Theorizing Agency in User-Generated Content. *Media Culture and Society* 31 (1):41–58.

Van Doorn, Niels. 2009. Digital Spaces, Material Traces. PhD disseration. University of Amsterdam.

Van Ess, Henk. 2005. Google Secret Lab, Prelude. *Henk van Ess's Search Engine Bistro*, June 1, http://www.searchbistro.com/index.php?/archives/19-Google-Secret-Lab,-Prelude.html (accessed December 22, 2008).

Van Oostrom, Frits. 2007. *A Key to Dutch History*. Amsterdam: Amsterdam University Press.

Venturini, Tommaso. 2010. Diving in Magma: How to Explore Controversies with Actor-Network Theory. *Public Understanding of Science* 19 (3):258–273.

Verkade, Thalia. 2007. Mabel en Friso pasten lemma aan. *NRC Handelsblad*, August 29.

Veronin, Michael A. 2002. Where Are They Now? A Case Study of Health-Related Web Site Attrition. *Journal of Medical Internet Research* 4 (2):e10.

Vikipedije. Slobodna enciklopedija. 2011a. Razgovor:Masakr u Srebrenici/Arhiva01. *Vikipedije. Slobodne enciklopedije*. Wikimedia Foundation, Inc., October 3, http://sr.wikipedia.org/sr-el/Разго вор:Масакр_у_Сребреници/Архива_1 (accessed January 12, 2012).

Vikipedije. Slobodna enciklopedija. 2011b. Razgovor: Masakr u Srebrenici/Arhiva02. *Vikipedije. Slobodne enciklopedije*. Wikimedia Foundation, Inc., July 19, http://sr.wikipedia.org/wiki/Разговор :Масакр_у_Сребреници/Архива_2 (accessed January 12, 2012).

Vikipedije. Slobodna enciklopedija. 2011c. Razgovor: Masakr u Srebrenici/Arhiva03. *Vikipedije. Slobodne enciklopedije*. Wikimedia Foundation, Inc., July 19, http://sr.wikipedia.org/wiki/Разговор :Масакр_у_Сребреници/Архива_3 (accessed January 12, 2012).

Villeneuve, Nart. 2006. Testing through Proxies in China. *Nart Villeneuve Blog*, April 10, http://www.nartv.org/2006/04/10/testing-through-proxies-in-china/ (accessed September 9, 2011).

Volčič, Zala. 2007. Yugo-Nostalgia: Cultural Memory and Media in the Former Yugoslavia. *Critical Studies in Media Communication* 24 (1):21–38.

Vuong, Ba-Quy, Ee-Peng Lim, Aixin Sun, Minh-Tam Le, and Hady Wirawan Lauw. 2008. On Ranking Controversies in Wikipedia: Models and Evaluation. Proceedings of the International Conference on Web Search and Web Data Mining (WSDM '08), New York: ACM.

Walker, Jill. 2005. Feral Hypertext: When Hypertext Literature Escapes Control. Proceedings of the Sixteenth ACM conference on Hypertext and Hypermedia, September 6–9, Salzburg, Austria, 46–53.

Watts, Duncan. 1999. *Small Worlds*. Princeton: Princeton University Press.

Webb, Eugene J., Donald T. Campbell, Richard D. Schwartz, and Lee Sechrest. 1966. *Unobtrusive Measures: Nonreactive Research in the Social Sciences*. Chicago: Rand McNally.

Weber, Ingmar, and Carlos Castillo. 2010. The Demographics of Web Search. Proceeding of the 33rd international ACM SIGIR conference on research and development in information retrieval (SIGIR '10), New York: ACM, 523–530.

Weber, Ingmar, Venkata Rama Kiran Garimella, and Erik Borra. 2012. Mining Web Query Logs to Analyze Political Issues. ACM International Conference on Web Search and Data Mining, 2012.

Weinberger, David. 2002. *Small Pieces Loosely Joined: A Unified Theory of the Web*. Cambridge, MA: Perseus.

Weltevrede, Esther. 2009. Thinking Nationally with the Web: A Medium-Specific Approach to the National Turn in Web Archiving. MA thesis, University of Amsterdam.

Weltevrede, Esther, and Anne Helmond. 2012. Where Do Bloggers Blog? Platform Transitions within the Dutch Blogosphere. *First Monday* 17 (2).

West, Kathy, and Janet Williamson. 2009. Wikipedia: Friend or Foe? *RSR. Reference Services Review* 37 (3):250–271.

Whetstone, Rachel. 2010. Controversial Content and Free Expression on the Web: a Refresher. *The Official Google Blog*, April 19, http://googleblog.blogspot.com/2010/04/controversial-content -and-free.html (accessed September 9, 2011).

Wiggins, Richard W. 2001. The Effects of September 11 on the Leading Search Engine. *First Monday* 6 (10).

Wikimedia. 2010. An Appeal from Wikipedia Founder Jimmy Wales. Wikimedia Foundation, Inc., http://wikimediafoundation.org/wiki/Appeal2/en?utm_source=2009_Jimmy_Appeal1 (accessed September 22, 2011).

Wikimedia. 2011a. List of Wikipedias. Wikimedia. Meta-Wiki. Wikepedia Foundation, Inc., September 24, 2011, http://meta.wikimedia.org/wiki/List_of_Wikipedias (accessed January 12, 2012).

Wikimedia. 2011b. Requests_for_new_languages/Wikipedia_Montenegrin_4. Wikimedia. Meta-Wiki. Wikimedia Foundation, Inc., July 19, 2011, January 4, 2012, http://meta.wikimedia.org/ wiki/Requests_for_new_languages/Wikipedia_Montenegrin_4 (accessed January 12, 2012).

Wikimedia. 2011c. Requests for New Languages/Wikipedia Serbo-Croatian. 2011. Wikimedia. Meta-Wiki. Wikimedia Foundation, Inc., July 8, http://meta.wikimedia.org/wiki/Requests_for _new_languages/Wikipedia_Serbo-Croatian (accessed January 12, 2012).

Wikipedia. 2006a. Talk: Srebrenica Massacre/Archive 1. *Wikipedia: The Free Encyclopedia*. Wikimedia Foundation, Inc., November 28, http://en.wikipedia.org/wiki/Talk:Srebrenica_massacre/ Archive_1 (accessed January 12, 2012).

Wikipedia. 2006b. Talk: Srebrenica Massacre/Archive 4. *Wikipedia: The Free Encyclopedia*. Wikimedia Foundation, Inc., November 28, http://en.wikipedia.org/wiki/Talk:Srebrenica_massacre/ Archive_4 (accessed January 12, 2012).

Wikipedia. 2009. Category:Wikipedia_sockpuppets_of_Historičar. *Wikipedia: The Free Encyclopedia*. Wikimedia Foundation, Inc., June 29, http://en.wikipedia.org/wiki/Category:Wikipedia_sockpuppets_of_Historičar (accessed January 12, 2012).

Wikipedia. 2010a. Talk: Srebrenica Massacre/Archive 11. *Wikipedia: The Free Encyclopedia*. Wikimedia Foundation, Inc., May 30, http://en.wikipedia.org/wiki/Talk:Srebrenica_massacre/Archive_11 (accessed January 12, 2012).

Wikipedia. 2010b. Talk: Srebrenica Massacre/Archive 16. *Wikipedia: The Free Encyclopedia*. Wikimedia Foundation, Inc., January 28, http://en.wikipedia.org/wiki/Talk:Srebrenica_massacre/Archive_16 (accessed January 12, 2012).

Wikipedia. 2010c. Talk: Srebrenica Massacre/Archive 17. *Wikipedia: The Free Encyclopedia*. Wikimedia Foundation, Inc., December 9, http://en.wikipedia.org/wiki/Talk:Srebrenica_massacre/Archive_17 (accessed January 12, 2012).

Wikipedia. 2011a. Category:Wikipedia_sockpuppets_of_Emir_Arven. *Wikipedia: The Free Encyclopedia*. Wikimedia Foundation, Inc., August 4, http://en.wikipedia.org/wiki/Category:Wikipedia_sockpuppets_of_Emir_Arven (accessed January 12, 2012).

Wikipedia. 2011b. Talk: Srebrenica_massacre/Archive_18. *Wikipedia: The Free Encyclopedia*. Wikimedia Foundation, Inc., July 7, http://en.wikipedia.org/wiki/Talk:Srebrenica_massacre/Archive_18 (accessed January 12, 2012).

Wikipedia. 2011c. Wikipedia: About. *Wikipedia: The Free Encyclopedia*. Wikimedia Foundation, Inc., December 26, http://en.wikipedia.org/wiki/Wikipedia:About (accessed January 12, 2012).

Wikipedia. 2011d. Wikipedia: Neutral Point of View. *Wikipedia: The Free Encyclopedia*. Wikimedia Foundation, Inc., December 30, http://en.wikipedia.org/wiki/NPOV (accessed January 12, 2012).

Wikipedia. 2011e. Wikipedia: Policies and Guidelines. *Wikipedia: The Free Encyclopedia*. Wikimedia Foundation, Inc., December 30, http://en.wikipedia.org/wiki/Wikipedia:Policies_and_guidelines (accessed January 12, 2012).

Wikipedia. 2011f. Wikipedia: WikiProject Countering Systemic Bias/Geography. *Wikipedia: The Free Encyclopedia*. Wikimedia Foundation, Inc., December 28, http://en.wikipedia.org/wiki/Wikipedia:WikiProject_Countering_systemic_bias/Geography (accessed January 12, 2012).

Wikipedia. 2012a. Wikipedia: Consensus. *Wikipedia: The Free Encyclopedia*. Wikimedia Foundation, Inc., January 12, http://en.wikipedia.org/wiki/Wikipedia:Consensus (accessed January 12, 2012).

Wikipedia. 2012b. Wikipedia: No Original Research. *Wikipedia: The Free Encyclopedia*. Wikimedia Foundation, Inc., January 11, http://en.wikipedia.org/wiki/Wikipedia:No_original_research (accessed January 12, 2012).

Wikipedia. 2012c. Wikipedia: Systemic Bias. *Wikipedia: The Free Encyclopedia*. Wikimedia Foundation, Inc., January 11, http://en.wikipedia.org/wiki/Wikipedia:Systemic_bias#Interwiki_language_issue (accessed January 12, 2012).

Wikipedia. 2012d. Wikipedia: Verifiability. *Wikipedia: The Free Encyclopedia*. Wikimedia Foundation, Inc., January 7, http://en.wikipedia.org/wiki/Wikipedia:Verifiability (accessed January 12, 2012).

Wikipedia: De vrije encyclopedie. 2011. Overleg: Val van Srebrenica. *Wikipedia: De vrije encyclopedie*. Wikimedia Foundation, Inc., December 23, 2011, http://nl.wikipedia.org/wiki/Overleg:Val_van_Srebrenica (accessed January 12, 2012).

Wikipedia. Slobodna enciklopedija. 2009. Razgovor: Genocid u Srebrenici/Arhiva 1 Genocid u Srebrenici. *Wikipedia. Slobodna enciklopedija*. Wikimedia Foundation, Inc., September 23, http://bs.wikipedia.org/wiki/Razgovor:Genocid_u_Srebrenici/Arhiva_1_Genocid_u_Srebrenici (accessed January 12, 2012).

Wikipedija. Slobodna enciklopedija. 2006. Razgovor: Dešavanja u Srebrenici jula 2005. *Wikipedija. Slobodna enciklopedija*. Wikimedia Foundation, Inc., July 19, http://sh.wikipedia.org/wiki/Razgovor:Genocid_u_Srebrenici (accessed January 12, 2012).

Wikipedija. Slobodna enciklopedija. 2010. Razgovor: Masakr u Srebrenici. *Wikipedija. Slobodna enciklopedija*. Wikimedia Foundation, Inc., May 4, http://sh.wikipedia.org/wiki/Razgovor:Masakr_u_Srebrenici (accessed January 12, 2012).

Wikipedija. Slobodna enciklopedija. 2011a. Korisnik: OC Ripper. *Wikipedija. Slobodna enciklopedija*. Wikimedia Foundation, Inc., August 3, http://sh.wikipedia.org/wiki/Korisnik:OC_Ripper (accessed January 18, 2012).

Wikipedija. Slobodna enciklopedija. 2011b. Razgovor: Genocid u Srebrenici. *Wikipedija. Slobodna enciklopedija*. Wikimedia Foundation, Inc., September 22, http://hr.wikipedia.org/wiki/Razgovor:Genocid_u_Srebrenici (accessed January 12, 2012).

Wilkinson, Dennis, and Bernardo Huberman. 2007. Cooperation and Quality in Wikipedia. Proceedings of the international symposium on Wikis (WikiSym '07), New York: ACM.

Williams, Raymond. 1974. *Television: Technology and Cultural Form*. London: Fontana.

Woolgar, Steve. 2002. Five Rules of Virtuality. In *Virtual Society? Technology, Cyberbole, Reality*, ed. Steve Woolgar, 1–22. Oxford: Oxford University Press.

Wouters, Paul, Iina Hellsten, and Loet Leydesdorff. 2004. Internet Time and the Reliability of Search Engines. *First Monday* 9 (10).

Wright, Joss, Tulio de Souza, and Ian Brown. 2011. Fine-Grained Censorship Mapping: Information Sources, Legality and Ethics. FOCI'11 (USENIX Security Symposium), August 8, San Francisco, http://static.usenix.org/events/foci11/tech/final_files/Wright.pdf (accessed September 9, 2011).

Wu, Paul H. J., and Adrian K. H. Heok. 2006. Is Web Archives a Misnomer? How Web Archives Can Become Digital Archives. Proceedings of the Asia-Pacific Conference on Library and Information Education and Practice 2006 (A-LIEP 2006), Singapore, April 3–6, pp. 298–305. Singapore: School of Communication and Information, Nanyang Technological University.

Yahoo! 2008. What Is the "By Popularity | Alphabetical" Feature Shown above Site Listings? Directory Basics FAQ, http://help.yahoo.com/l/us/yahoo/directory/basics/basics-21.html (accessed December 22, 2008).

Zarrinbakhsh, Niaz. 2011. Living as a Criminal: An Ethnographic Study of the Iranian National Web and Internet Censorship. MA thesis, University of Amsterdam.

Zimmer, Michael. 2010a. "But the Data Is Already Public": On the Ethics of Research in Facebook. *Ethics and Information Technology* 12 (4):313–325.

Zimmer, Michael. 2010b. Web Search Studies: Multidisciplinary Perspectives on Web Search Engines. In *International Handbook of Internet Research*, ed. Jeremy Hunsinger, Lisbeth Klastrup, and Lisbeth Allen, 507–521. Dordrecht: Springer.

Zinman, Aaron, and Judith Donath. 2007. Is Britney Spears Spam? Paper presented at the Fourth Conference on Email and Anti-Spam, Mountain View, CA, August 2–3.

Index